The Heydays

of embassies, foreign adventures, and a dog

Jeanne JieAhn

Studio Publishing & Design, LLC

Copyright 2006
All rights reserved. No part of this work may be reproduced or transmitted in any form by any means, electronic or mechanical, including photocopying and recording, or by any information storage or retrieval system, except as may be expressly permitted by the 1976 Copyright Act or in writing by the publisher.

Requests for such permission should be addressed to:
Studio Publishing & Design, LLC
P. O. Box 27272
Scottsdale, AZ 85255

JieAhn, Jeanne
   The Heydays
      of embassies, foreign adventures and a dog

Cover Design: Manjari Graphics
Layout: J. L. Saloff
Fonts used: Century Schoolbook, Bradley Hand
Photographs are provided by the author.
Several names in the text have been changed.

10-Digit ISBN: 0-9779113-0-6
13-Digit ISBN: 978-0-9779113-0-1
Library of Congress Control Number: 2006903234
Copyright Tu1-267-169

First Edition

Printed on acid free paper in The United States of America

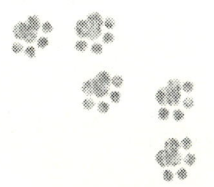

Acknowledgments

To Jamie Saloff for her professionalism, guidance and great patience—thank you.

To Manjari Henderson, thank you very much for your professional assistance with the cover design.

My sincere gratitude goes to Ralph Tanner who volunteered his personal time and substantial publishing experience that it might benefit me, and it did.

For DeAnna Lee, I offer a special hug for her ear. I am grateful for her many positive suggestions, and for often having been a substitute Mom to Nipper and Amy during our transitory years. We love you.

To Pat Elias, Sherrill Littlefawn, Elizabeth Williams, Ron Chase, Betty Nelson and John Robertson, thank you for your thoughtful and candid comments.

For the Porkers,

Sincerely,

Deanne Judah

Introduction

Sudan, Africa
Autumn, 1985

    The giant jetliner moved smoothly through a million stars over the dark African continent that night sooooooo long ago.
    All was quiet in the cabin, with an occasional snore from a sleeping passenger. I was sleeping also, but fitfully, curled up like a pretzel by the window seat. Restlessly shifting positions to get more comfortable, I squirmed one way and then another, stretching my long legs across the aisle. My hair was messy and sticking out, my clothes wrinkled.
    Suddenly, the loudspeaker broke the quiet of the cabin. I opened my eyes with a start!
    "Ladies and gentlemen, this is your captain speaking. We have just crossed the Libyan border. We are flying at an altitude of approximately 35,000 feet over Sudan's El 'Atun Oasis and expect to arrive in Khartoum by midnight, right on schedule. The weather in Sudan is a pleasant 125 degrees Fahrenheit."
    There were only a handful of travelers in the cabin, mostly Sudanese in their traditional white galabiyahs and taigas. One man wore earphones, listening to music with closed eyes. Another was clicking on his lap computer, perhaps a business man returning from a trip abroad.
    The flight attendant began serving refreshments, and as I sipped my hot coffee my emotions fluctuated between excitement and trepidation. Anticipation and dread. It was the unknown which lingered behind my anxiety that night. The unknown, and Khartoum itself, which was getting closer as the clock ticked.

I was on the brink of realizing a long held dream, and so I admonished myself for my fears. It is just that, well, Khartoum is not what I originally had in mind. Known to be a veritable pressure cooker of African countries, Khartoum is not likely to be an easy first Foreign Service assignment. I was not sure I could handle it.

"Oh, drink your coffee and stop worrying," I told myself. "Khartoum will be a stepping stone. Think positively. It will be just fine." I reached over and scratched Nipper's ears as he slept on the seat next to me.

While I always knew that one day, somehow, I would make my dream come true, I had not known when or how, or that it would be shared with a very special dog! And this is where the pot sweetens. Meet Nipper!

Nipper was a young miniature Schnauzer, and it was a rare privilege, to be sure, for a dog to travel inside the plane's cabin—with his own seat yet—but unusual circumstances had made it possible.

He came into my life when he was three months old, already possessed with an air of quiet dignity and wisdom beyond his age. He had the fine lines and features of a champ—indeed, he descended from two generations of champion show dogs. But it was not a champion I wanted—just a little pal.

Despite his impressive credentials, Nipper had actually been a summer clearance sale! At the time, I was a real estate broker in Phoenix and, having just closed a house sale, I promised to reward myself with a pup. It would be my first dog, and I had no clue just how quickly I would get hooked.

The ad in the paper had said, "Price reduced—two pups left." I made an appointment. As I walked into the owner's kitchen, the two pups scrambled for my attention. I was immediately captivated by this canine charm, but was especially drawn to Nipper's easygoing good nature.

We stopped at the supermarket on our way home. As I carried the bag of groceries, Nipper sat inside on top of a head of lettuce. I laughed at him. He licked my nose. We had bonded.

A few months later, the State Department contacted me with an offer for a career in the Foreign Service. The offer came after a lengthy 22 months of evaluation and investigation, and within weeks I was on my way to Washington, D.C. for Orientation classes.

The timing was good. My daughter had recently spread her little wings and joined the Army. She was quite suddenly—Gone!—Kapoot!

For awhile I suffered with Empty Nest Syndrome, and yet I was itchy to sow my own wild oats.

You could say I was also very naïve. Certainly, I knew nothing about international travel, but my passion to wander overshadowed any glaring lack of worldly savoir-faire.

For the following 16 years, foreign countries would be our home. It was a feast—a colorful rollercoaster. But the piper must also be paid—and was—with hard work, terrorism, tedious bureaucracy.

Nipper died in Paris at the age of fifteen. He was one special guy. But hey, Nipper, didn't we have fun!

In memory of Nipper,
and for DeAnna Lee

Somewhere

Beyond

A strange foreign land

A distant sea

Somewhere

Far, far away

Secrets beckon

They whisper and call

Their secrets are calling

Me

1
The First Three Months

Washington, D.C.
June 5, 1985

    I was all eyes in the backseat of the taxi as we drove from National Airport to the hotel in Roslyn. It was already dark outside—a lovely early summer evening—and the air was soft and fragrant.
    The city felt quietly exciting with its lights, wide boulevards, and famous government buildings. In the distance, the brightly lit monument of Abraham Lincoln gazed outward like an immense grandfather.
    Located on the fringes of Washington, the small Virginia city of Roslyn was the site of the Foreign Service orientation classes. A new campus—to be known as the Foreign Service Institute—was in the planning stages and would be located in Arlington, but in 1985 we were roughing it at scattered class locations throughout Roslyn and D.C.
    My taxi passed through Roslyn's small business center and entered certain ethnic neighborhoods. Street lamps cast a friendly glow over the wooden houses with their old fashioned swings and American flags hanging from the porches.
    I had been forewarned that D.C. is not pet-oriented, and so I arrived without Nipper. He remained in Phoenix, and will join me later when orientation classes are completed.
    For a few days, I stayed in the hotel and then found a lovely studio apartment in Roslyn for my 3-month stay. The studio was completely furnished, down to dishes, linens and telephone. It was quite comfortable. Because Roslyn becomes quiet and deserted in the evenings, its location is well suited for studying. Studying?

During the day, the streets are alive with walkers. Roslyn's terrain is hilly with steep walking paths and everybody seemed to be wearing white tennis shoes! It is a city of government workers, military personnel, foreigners, and American transients, and all those white tennis shoes.

We were a group of about fifteen adult students, mostly women, from all over the United States. Future Foreign Service Secretaries were we—with the additional title of "diplomat."

Our first day of orientation was a long, tedious one for us in the Class of '85. Jam packed with information, most of it was forgotten by the end of the day! But one thing I recall from one of the many lecturers was, "The Foreign Service—you'll love it and you'll hate it." Oh, baby! Was she right!

The same lecturer spoke about pets. "By all means, bring your pet with you overseas. Traveling with your pet will have some headaches, but you'll be richly rewarded with a very special kind of bonding." Again she was right.

A guide led us students on a general tour of the massive State Department, possibly the largest building I have ever been in. The many long corridors are color coded and have wall maps for reference. There are conference rooms and auditoriums, flag and ceremonial rooms, and the various Bureaus of Africa, Europe, South America, Asia, comprising staid offices cluttered with bulky mahogany furniture and the imposing "computer."

The computer was replacing the familiar typewriter, and it could be seen on the desks throughout the State Department. As Foreign Service Secretaries, we were expected to learn how to use it. I was secretly terrified of this cold grey machine with its big eye.

By mid-morning of our first day we were escorted to the elegant Jefferson Room for a swearing-in ceremony, a large room with red carpets and chandeliers hanging from high ceilings. Dozens of chairs surrounded the podium near a large American flag.

As we arrived, each student received a sealed envelope containing a notice of our individual security clearances, the result of our lengthy background investigations. My own clearance—a "1" for Top Secret—authorized me to work worldwide and to handle classified material up to Top Secret. Anything less than a "1" has restrictions.

A welcome speech was given by a State Department official, beginning with the proverbial opening joke, and then we were asked to stand as our names were called and take an oath of allegiance into the Foreign Service. That done, a photographer roamed among us taking pictures and waiters dressed in black appeared with silver trays of refreshments as we all enjoyed a brief social break.

The first question everyone seemed to ask each other was, "Where is your first tour?" or "Where are you going?" The mixed assignments included Jerusalem, Geneva, Paris, Korea, Athens, and Khartoum. Our various tours of duty were for periods of two to four years each, to be followed by a new assignment in a different country. An air of gaiety and camaraderie filled the room and bonded us as students. We were Trailblazers that morning, one and all!

"What qualifies a post—that is, embassy or consulate—to make the list of most difficult, the hardest of hardship posts to be assigned to?" I asked this of a seasoned officer that morning who was mingling with us during the break.

"The degree of poor economic and living conditions of a country, the level of its terrorism and crime, and/or civil war all make up a hardship post," he said.

Lima, Peru in 1985 headed the hardship list because of all the above. But also, the air in Lima was unhealthy, heavy with the foul odor of garbage in the streets, strong enough to make one nauseated.

Khartoum ranked third among hardship posts from nearly 260 U.S. posts worldwide. I began hearing little war stories about Khartoum that day, but my fortitude remained intact. "It can't be all that bad," I told myself. (It was.)

Classes began the following day. They were interesting and challenging, focusing on the peculiar nature of foreign affaires. We attended various lectures, a three-day terrorist seminar, and delightful excursions around town to broaden our education.

Those of us going to Moslem countries visited an Islamic mosque in D.C. We took our shoes off at the door before entering, as was the traditional practice. A guide gave us a tour of the mosque and a short lecture on the Islamic faith.

The computer classes began immediately and were intense. Most of us had not grown up with this mysterious machine and had to learn from scratch—literally how to turn it on! There were a few in the group who knew what they were doing and seemed to enjoy showing off, and the rest of us hated them for it.

In the years to follow, of course, even kindergarten students will be taught to use the computer. But everything has a beginning, and I recalled the old black telephone and the introduction of television in the 1940's. As a very young girl, I just knew little people lived inside the television.

Adjusting to the beat of a strange city can cause one to be disoriented and accident prone. Take the D.C. metro train system, for example, designed after the one in Paris. Clean and efficient, to be sure, but for a newcomer to the city it was daunting. More than once I was swept into the wrong train by rush hour mobs, or sat in a train heading north when I wanted south, or yet got off at the wrong station.

The platforms and escalators alone could confuse a newcomer. In the Roslyn station, a certain escalator is so long it could make me dizzy when I dared to look downward.

But what I call my 'skirt incident' was the worst.

I was wearing a new white cotton skirt—rather flattering on me, I thought—as I stepped onto that long escalator at the Roslyn Station. It was a hot, humid afternoon. I was tired after attending classes all day, and not fully alert.

A large woman stepped onto the escalator behind me. Almost immediately, she lost her footing and fell forward against me, and I—daydreaming—promptly lost my own balance and was knocked forward from the impact. Like a game of dominoes, everyone in front of us began to fall.

We all struggled, but could not stand up. People began screaming. Chaos took over. The station manager came running to shut off the moving escalator as we all tried to regain our composure.

By now I was caught almost upside down with my underpants showing! The teeth of the escalator had me locked fast in its grip, and my skirt had to be torn to release me! I was bruised and embarrassed, and my new skirt was twisted and gnarled with black grease.

A few hours later, soaking my sore muscles in a tub of hot sudsy water, the whole incident struck me as comical and I began to laugh. The look on the face of that station manager as he came running to rescue us was priceless! I laughed harder, and gave the faucet a twist with my big toe to let in more hot water.

Yes, in retrospect, it was funny. But I sure felt bad about my new white skirt, which was ruined beyond repair and now in the waste bin.

An Independence Day ceremony was being held on a hot sunny morning at Arlington National Cemetery. People filled the hilly terrain, sitting on the grass or standing among the orderly rows of white tombstones.

The President stood near the flame of the Tomb of the Unknown Soldier, and spoke about the significance of the day. The Marines and other military officials attending the ceremony looked impressive in impeccable dress uniforms. The bright morning sunshine glistened off their shiny brass buttons.

As the haunting echo of 'taps' was played out by the Marines, the crowd was hushed and solemn. Heavy emotions hung in the air and were written on the faces of the people. For many, loved ones had been lost to foreign wars.

The spirit of dead soldiers was felt among us as the mournful taps faded into the hot morning.

Washington has many such ceremonies and patriotic events. It is a city rich in history with fascinating places to visit. On weekends, my fellow students and I toured the area—the White House, the Capitol Building, perhaps the Library of Congress. Roaming around quaint, historic Georgetown or Alexandria on a leisure Saturday was immensely entertaining.

The Smithsonian Institute, a collection of individual museums, is a treasure trove of American culture. Yet, it was founded by a European whose name was Smithson. There is no entrance fee to these wonderful buildings, and I spent many of my Sundays in them.

My most special outing took place on a sunny Saturday in July. I rode an early bus from Roslyn to the Boardwalk in Atlantic City to meet my brother. Tom was the youngest of my four brothers, and he lived in Manhattan, New York. I did not know him since our family broke up when we were small children. We grew up in separate foster homes and a large Children's Home. But this day would be ours.

Inside the appointed restaurant on the Boardwalk facing the ocean, I ordered some iced tea and contemplated my brother as I waited for him to arrive. Would I recognize him? What is he like today?

But I recognized him immediately when he walked in. Tall and good-looking, he was a young Marlon Brando in his late thirties. After a few awkward moments, conversation became easier. We spent the day visiting, eating, and strolling along the shore of the water. When the sun went down, Tom walked with me to the bus stop and kissed me goodbye. I never saw him again, but will always cherish our day together.

The Kennedy Center held a new discovery for me, a love for the music and drama of the live stage. The richness of the experience feeds my soul, runs away with my imagination, and leaves me somehow transformed.

Occasionally Laura joined me for an evening's concert. She was the oldest of my fellow students. At sixty, she barely made the cutoff age for acceptance into the Foreign Service.

Laura and I exchanged letters for awhile after we moved on to our individual foreign assignments. She had served at the embassy in Kathmandu, Nepal, and I was sad to learn that Laura died during her first year at Kathmandu from the bite of a poisonous bug.

I had a certain conversation with Laura once as we sat on a park bench in D.C. tossing popcorn to the pigeons. We talked about the role of the modern day secretary. I had deserted the profession years ago, I told her, because I had found that secretaries are treated not quite like a piece of furniture, but almost.

"Oh, come on, don't be so selfish," said Laura. "Why would you want to deprive the office bully of that fun? Tell me, why are you re-entering the secretarial field?" she asked.

"I have background experience in secretarial work," I told her. "I can fill a need of the Foreign Service and at the same time see the world by working my way through it. But I have a little concern that I may be unable to adjust to the role of a secretary."

"Well, dear, I'm sure conditions have improved," said Laura, her eyebrows twisted in doubt.

"Look at it this way," she continued. "This is almost the 21st century. Today's secretary has responsibilities unknown twenty, or even ten, years ago. And the embassy is dedicated to serving the American people—surely it is also committed to strict fairness and respect for the human rights of everyone who works there. Don't worry, it will be fine. You'll see."

Orientation classes were over. In another few days, I would be leaving the United States for Khartoum, but all I could think of that particular morning was Nipper's arrival in D.C.

I was on my way to National Airport to meet his plane coming in from Phoenix, and I was happy at the thought of seeing him again. I had missed my friend. Along the way, I stopped to purchase special treats and little toys as welcome gifts for Nipper, soon to be a Foreign Service Brat.

Inside the air terminal, I waited patiently as his plane landed. Soon passengers began to exit. As I watched, the plane's conveyor began carrying suitcases and one lone dog kennel to the terminal. I dashed around the corner to the location for arriving dogs, and I again waited.

Finally, the special lone kennel was brought to me and I quickly knelt to unlatch the hook. Out he bounded, knocking me over, slobbering my face with kisses, and wetting on my tee shirt. I didn't mind Nipper wetting my tee shirt—it had been a long flight for him. After all, he's only human!

It was a joyous reunion. I picked up my little pal, and together we left the terminal.

Yes, orientation had been fun. There is no place quite like the patriotic flavor of Washington, D.C., and in the years to come I would spend many fun filled visits there—all under the guise of "attending classes" or other "official business."

A common sight around Roslyn and D.C.—the State Department's small shuttle buses—somehow sums up my impressions of those 3 months of orientation:

The shuttles can be seen going uphill, coming around a corner, or pulling up in front of the State Department on "C" Street. One could hop on and off between classes, and I often did.

Conversations inside the shuttles hint at the mixture of lifestyles, and were often entertaining. Listen: "What do you think of the NATO update today on the crisis in Abubabubah?...My Russian classes are brutal, they're almost worst than Arabic!...The Berlin assignment was fun, but now they're sending me to Ouagaduga!...Do you remember Joanie from the embassy in Croatia? Well! I heard she was kicked out of the Foreign Service!"

The deafening roar of the engines . . . the sudden escalation of rapid speed . . . the gradual lifting up of the giant jetliner into the air. From the window seat inside the plane, I watched as Washington's monuments and famous buildings grew smaller, and then disappeared altogether.

When our plane left American soil behind, the fun of flying eluded me completely. Intense homesickness for my family had settled in, and I turned my face to the window to hide my tears.

But the hours slipped away and before long we had entered Europe and were moving smoothly through sunny skies toward France. A small sense of adventure returned as I thought of Paris, where Nipper and I will have a 3-day stopover before continuing on to our destination of Khartoum.

The soft, lovely voice of a French singer filled the plane to put passengers "in the French mood." And then, finally, the captain's voice came over the loudspeaker in English, then French, and then German: "Ladies and gentlemen, we are preparing to land in Paris. Please fasten your seatbelts." I fastened my seatbelt, and let my anticipation take over. Ahhh, oui.. Paris . . .

Hello, Paris!!
Yahoo!

I had the window seat. A skinny man with a mustache who did not speak English sat next to me, breathing over my shoulder as he stretched his neck to look out my window. We were flying low now over the rooftops of Paris, the bourgeois lady of France. Moscow, London and Madrid are the Men of Europe. Paris is a Lady.

"Ahhhhh, Vive la Fraaaance," he said in his French accent, his voice soft and sensuous. I felt compelled to turn my head for a closer look at him. Our noses touched briefly, and I quickly looked away.

Several marvelous days in this famous city! I was wild with excitement! While I knew nothing at all of foreign travel, I exited the plane that day at Orly International Airport a seasoned woman of the world! A modern day Emelia Ehrhardt! The world was my oyster—bring it on!

But the airport terminal felt "different" and confusing. Uncertainty plucked at my enthusiasm as I moved among the bustling travelers and listened to the various languages around me. A French voice was making announcements over the loudspeaker, and from somewhere a baby was screaming at the top of its lungs!

I followed the other passengers, and stood in a long line for tourists with blue passports. After twenty minutes or so, I noticed the shorter, faster line for black diplomatic passport holders like myself. It was a tiny discovery too late, but would be useful in the future. I was learning.

Some of the terminal signs made little sense. "Sortie" with an arrow must indicate the baggage claim area where people sort their luggage. I referred to my small translation book, and smiled at my ignorance. "Sortie" was French for "exit." "Chariot" is the airport cart used to carry luggage. Stick with the little pictures, not the words, I told myself.

Luggage was just rolling down the ramp in the baggage claim area under the sign "Air France 123." Traveling light was not yet something I had learned and I retrieved not just a few pieces of luggage, but eight suitcases from the moving ramp. I loaded them all onto a "chariot" and then went in search of Nipper.

Nipper was in his kennel in the doggie arrival area, looking frazzled and anxious. I unlatched the door, and lifted him out for a warm hug to myself. Then, propping him in one arm, I added his kennel to the load of suitcases and pushed the loaded chariot with my other hand. I followed the little "sortie" signs to the exit, and located the outside taxi queue. I was in control.

The taxi driver took my slip of paper with the name and address of the hotel where I had reservations. He did not seem to understand English, but grunted in recognition of the address and then quickly loaded my luggage and Nipper into the cab. We were off.

Sitting in the back seat of the taxi, confidence returned in full measure. I was pleased with myself for having found a hotel in Paris for only fifteen dollars a night! It was listed in a very (very) old tourist book. Who said Paris is so expensive?! If anyone can stretch the old dollar, I can. I smiled to myself, and settled back to enjoy the ride.

Everything I'd heard about Paris taxi drivers was true. The driver sped deftly through quaint and narrow streets at amazing speed. Nobody seemed to observe any rules of the road. To my horror, I watched as a small automobile jumped the curb onto a sidewalk. Pedestrians seemed oblivious to the chaos around them.

Screeching around a corner, my taxi driver barely missed colliding with a motorcycle. The cyclist wore a sleeveless leather vest, exposing muscles and tattoos. He had pink and purple hair, worn in a rooster style. My driver was unimpressed. Windows rolled down and loud angry words were exchanged between them, and then we roared off.

Tearing down the street, we bumped a corner fruit stand. Oranges and bananas went flying, but my driver never looked back. I did, and saw an angry shopkeeper running after us, shaking his fist.

We zipped through the historical and beautiful Place de la Concorde, its magnificent fountains alive with splashing water, and then turned onto yet another narrow street. Amidst a blur of small blue and white street signs attached to the corner buildings—Rue this, Rue that—old fashioned shops and picturesque street scenes fell behind us.

Abruptly, we came to a stop. We had arrived. I stared at the hotel for a moment with a sinking feeling in the pit of my stomach. So this is what $15.00 a night in Paris will buy!

I couldn't possibly stay here, I thought. But I'd better at least go inside and speak with the proprietor a moment, and cancel my reservations. It would be the polite thing to do.

The taxi driver understood that I'd like him to wait for me. I went inside the hotel to a small reception area, dark and dismal. A woman was smoking a cigarette at the desk, and looked up when I entered. I gave her my name, gestured to her that I had reservations. She flipped through her little reservation book. "Ah, oui," she said.

She led me up six flights of stairs to a tiny, dirty room with a mattress on the floor. A mattress on the floor! Nothing else, just a mattress on the floor!

I've seen enough, I thought. I gestured to Madame to cancel my reservation. This seemed to agitate her, and she spoke excitedly to me in French. Unwavering, I hurried down the stairs but Madam was close at my heels, loudly yelling something about "obligatoire."

Exiting the hotel, I quickly climbed into the taxi. "Please, Monsieur, help me find another hotel." He understood and off we sped, leaving a puff of smoke and Madame behind.

For the next few hours, we drove up and down the streets inquiring at one completely booked hotel after another. There were several large conventions being held in Paris, we were told, and the hotels were full. But we persevered, without luck.

By now I was on the verge of tears. The driver seemed kindly, despite all, and had pity on me. But he was clearly growing frustrated.

Then I thought of the U.S. Embassy—they speak English at the embassy and would help me! Why didn't I think of it sooner?! The driver understood, and lost no time in driving me there. We pulled up at the front entrance, and I climbed out. The familiar U.S. flag waved gently in the morning breeze, and a Marine stood on guard at the gate.

I turned to the driver to ask if he would mind waiting for me—just in case—but saw that he was already unloading the eight suitcases and dog kennel to the sidewalk. He quickly helped himself to the French franc from my outstretched hand and—before I could remember how to say "Merci beau coup, Monsieur"—he had disappeared. I watched him disappear around the corner, and suddenly I felt alone. Really alone.

My tears were at the breaking point. I was exhausted from my long flight, the turmoil of the morning, and my unsuccessful search for lodging. Slowly I walked over to the young Marine who stood on duty.

The Marine said "Good morning" in plain English. The friendliness in his voice broke my last thread of courage, and the tears gushed out and ran down my cheeks. Sobbing and babbling, I explained my entire dilemma to him. He listened politely, and then suggested I inquire at Hotel E'tat, just around the corner.

The hotel was clean and pleasant, and yes, they did have an opening. Pushing all eight pieces of luggage and my dog kennel into the tiny hotel "lift," I squeezed in on top of the luggage and pushed a button. The door clanged shut and the antiquated lift hesitated, jerked, and then slowly began ascending.

As we crawled upward floor by floor, I felt so very far from home. What in the world am I doing here? I don't mean here in this elevator, I mean here, in this country. Homesickness and self pity took over as we passed floor three. By floor five, I was sobbing out loud and blowing my nose, and I had made a decision. I would not stay in Paris. I did not like Paris. Paris is noisy and unfriendly. I will get on the telephone, and reserve the next plane out.

But the French phone in my room was totally perplexing. Everything I had always taken for granted—such as using a telephone—now seemed to present a challenge. I decided to take a nap and figure out the French telephone later.

Exhausted, I blew my nose one more time, flopped down on the bed with Nipper, and soon fell asleep.

When I awoke, afternoon shadows had already begun to dim the room. Nipper was still sleeping on a pillow. For a moment, I stared at the imposing black French telephone sitting on top of the table. I was afraid of it.

My brief nap had refreshed me and given me a small measure of renewed curiosity. I really should see a little of the nearby streets as long as I'm here, just so I can say I've "seen Paris." Then—tomorrow—I will make my plans to depart.

Nipper slept undisturbed, and I could leave him for a short while. But first, I need to use the bathroom.

"Le bain" had a tub, a sink, and an odd looking toilet with no handle to flush it, just a faucet which sprayed water. I had never seen a French bidet before and naturally assumed it was the toilet.

It was not until the following day that I discovered the "real toilet" in an obscure so-called Wash Closet—all but hidden behind the front door. A toilet in a closet, all by itself?

Outside my room, the long hall was quiet with the exception of the creaky floor as I walked on it. The worn red carpets and dimly lit chandeliers suggested Old Money, I thought. I pressed a button for the lift, and waited.

I could hear the sudden lurch of the old narrow cage of fancy wrought iron, and I listened as it slowly and noisily crawled upward to my floor. It stopped, and I climbed in. As we descended, I could gaze through the wrought iron of the lift onto each open floor.

A menu was posted on the inside wall of the lift, and I turned my attention to it. "The food here is lousy. I don't recommend it." The voice belonged to a young American man who was in the elevator with me. I had thought I was alone! How good it felt to hear an American voice—we smiled and exchanged a few pleasantries.

As the lift moved slowly down past floor two, I explained my morning's entire dilemma to the American. Approaching floor one, he told me the maid was cleaning his room and he had some spare time. Would I care to have coffee with him? At the ground floor, my new friend and I stepped out of the elevator and left the hotel together in search of a coffee house.

In a crowded smoke filled Tabac, we sat at a table and ordered café au lait. I told him of my decision to depart Paris as soon as I can figure out the French telephone.

"But that would be a shame. You must stay and not be discouraged," he said. We sipped our coffee, and on the small table he spread out a collection of French franc. He explained the value of each coin by equating it to the American coin. At that moment, I fell in love with the romance of foreign currency, and would regret the boring Euro of later years.

We left the Tabac and walked for awhile as the American continued to give me useful information and helpful advice. He pointed out landmarks that I should be aware of so that I could find my way back to the hotel and not get lost.

We strolled past the Louvre and the Tuilleries, along Rue Rivoli and then back toward the U.S. Embassy. Behind the embassy and just around the corner from my hotel was Faubourg St-Honore, the famous street of designer shops. Here we gazed into the elegant windows of Christian Dior, Nina Ricci, Yves St-Laurent, Chanel, and others.

Finally, he took my hand in his and wished me a happy visit in Paris. I never saw him again, but knew with certainty that he was an angel sent to help me. I always knew when I was in the presence of an angel.

I decided to remain in Paris.

The little blue perfume bottle of Evening in Paris displayed in the window of Chanel's had caught my eye. I had to have a small sampler bottle to honor our first evening in Paris.

I placed a small drop of perfume behind each ear and a drop behind Nipper's ears, and then we left our hotel room in search of a restaurant. In Paris, dogs are welcome inside the restaurants.

An authentic French dinner was what I had in mind—a treat after the absolutely harrowing day we had been through. A charming place caught my eye, and we walked over to the menu mounted on a small post by the entrance. As I stood trying to read the French selections, a tall woman walked up and stood behind me.

The woman was English and she, too, was in Paris for only a few days. She was on a buying trip for Burberrys of London, the establishment she was employed by. Our mutual English bonded us slightly as we chatted about the menu, and we decided to share a table inside for dinner.

And so on our first evening in Paris we shared a French dinner with a new acquaintance from London. Meredith, the English lady, did most of the talking. In her crisp British accent, she told me about the famous London Fog raincoats of Burberrys, and of her life in London.

The following evening we again met Meredith for dinner. I enjoyed her company, her bright wit and friendly conversation. We sat outside at a side street café and ordered a delicious crepe dish of spinach and cheeses. It was prepared as only the French can do.

I had been very curious about the French cuisine, and wanted to learn their secrets. So far I observed that the food was very fresh, exquisitely seasoned, served attractively in small portions. A good wine. Cheese followed the main course.

We placed our order and sat visiting. Minutes later, an American man sat down at a nearby table. We listened with amusement as he made awkward attempts to place his order. Meredith stepped in to rescue him, and invited him to join us at our table. His name was John, a tall Texan with a good sense of humor, who loved French wine.

For hours we sat together at the small outside table eating and talking. We were strangers, yet not strangers any longer. This leisurely European way of lingering over dinner is completely enjoyable, and I embraced it immediately. The waiter never hurries us away, and the camaraderie left each of us feeling good.

Discothèques do not appeal to me. I prefer a book in the later evening, and so Nipper and I left our companions and returned to the hotel. Along the way, I purchased some fresh pink roses at one of the street flower vendors and placed them in a drinking glass in my room. The beauty and fragrance of the flowers add cheer to a strange hotel room, and was a ritual I would practice for years to come.

Once back in our room, I unfolded a napkin with a steak bone which I had brought from the restaurant. Nipper enjoys a little chew before retiring.

As for me—an evening soak in the tub is special. Le bain smelled of lavender oil, and I placed a candle on the sideboard as the hot water filled the tub with sudsy bubbles. As the soft candlelight sent shadows dancing across the ceiling, I let my daydreams drift.

Twenty minutes later, I turned the faucet with my big toe to let in more hot water and thought of how the simple pleasures in life really are the best. Even in Paris.

Paris is a city for walkers and Nipper and I walked all day long. We saw a few major sights—the Eifel Tower and Montmartre—explored the Latin Quarter, and ferried down the Seine. Frantic sightseeing was not for me. I liked to roam and follow whatever caught my eye.

Getting lost happens a lot, but it is a wonderful way to discover things not found in a tourist book. Off the beaten paths are enticing. If I became seriously lost, genuinely lost, I simply flagged down a taxi and handed the driver my hotel address written on paper.

It was Saturday morning, our third day in Paris, when Nipper and I strolled down the narrow streets of St. Germaine filled with the unique French architecture, the sooty stove pipe chimneys jutting up into the sky. Chestnut trees were in full bloom and the sun threw lacy patterns over the streets as it filtered through the branches.

The local women were busy with their weekly cleaning. Passing beneath a window, a maid suddenly shook her dust mop vigorously over our heads! But, unlike my first morning in Paris, I love this city by now. The maid could have dropped her entire mop on my head, and I would not mind.

We could hear neighbor ladies gossip with each other over their balconies, the soft French laughter musical in the early morning. A boy whizzed by on his skateboard, and an old man strolled with his dog. Parked cars were closely lined along the street, on the sidewalks, in front of shops, or by a doorway. Since honking is against the law except in dire necessity, the streets were fairly quiet.

Apartment buildings often house little shops on the street level, their outside bins full of fresh vegetables and fruit. The delicious aroma of plump chickens roasting on outside skewers enticed me to stop and purchase a new bone for Nipper. Within the butcher shop, I watched as the butcher discretely weighed a slab of ham with a heavy thumb while a small line of housewives waited their turn.

One of those small wrinkled dogs—the Chinese Shar-Pei?—was stretched out in the middle of the butcher shop entrance, but shoppers simply stepped over him as they went in and out. The French seem to be that way—preferring to inconvenience themselves rather than a dog. This endeared me to them.

Delicious aromas seemed to be coming from the boulangerie, a popular shop on a Saturday morning. Inside, rows of fresh bread sat on shelves behind the display cases filled with petite candied fruit tarts, whipped creams and custards. I pointed to this and that, not knowing enough French to be coherent.

Stepping out of the boulangerie, I barely missed being run over by a man on his bike. He was clutching a bundle of baguettes with his free arm, and yelled loudly at me in French to get out of his way! The nerve! I am almost mowed down by the man's bike and he has the gall to say I was in His way! Brute . . .

Although he was already gone, I impulsively sent several thumps to my bent arm in his direction. This, I was told, is the French equivalent of giving him the finger. But I think I did it wrong.

Nipper and I liked to stop for a snack or drink every few hours when we are out. All of this junk food cannot be good for the figure! But, oh well, we are on holiday. Nipper sat on my lap as we watched the people and activities around us at an outside café and shared a platter of French fries and mayonnaise—one for you, one for me, another for me.

Just as I opened my mouth for a bite, a gust of exhaust fumes from a passing motorist filled the air. I gasped. I coughed. I choked. The French fry became stuck in my throat. People sitting at adjoining tables began to turn their heads and look at me with mild interest as I fought to regain my breath, but nobody came to my aid!

My composure regained, I picked up my purse and Nipper to leave when I noticed that the man at the next table was still staring. "What?!" I asked, annoyed at his stare, and then embarrassed myself further by tripping over his foot.

Those famous outside café scenes used in advertisements to romance the tourist do not warn of the ghastly traffic fumes! False advertisement, I call it, as I tossed a cough drop into my mouth.

The lovely Bois de Bologne is a large woodsy park filled with walking paths, a famous horse track, lakes with geese and little boats. It will be near our Paris home one day ten years later, but I had no idea of that on this particular Saturday morning.

In the Bois de Bologne, we sat on a bench and watched a small group of local men play the popular French game called petanque. This ball game resembles the American sport of pitching horseshoes.

Returning to Rue Rivoli, mimics were entertaining the tourists near the Louvre. They were fascinating. How can they stand so perfectly still for so long? I tried to divert their attention a little—just a tease—to see if they will at least blink an eye. But they did not move. I tried again, this time telling a really funny joke, but still with no reaction. I decided they were not mimics at all, but real statues. Still, I was not really sure. . .

Rue Rivoli is lined with gaudy French antique shops from the Louis XV era, lovely display windows of Hermes scarves, jewelry, crafts, crystal and porcelain. I lingered for awhile to purchase mementos to send back home. It goes for a good cause—to support the French economy!

Do tourists spend more money in souvenir shops than on plane tickets and hotel bills? I think so, yes.

Angelina's is a favorite tea salon dating from the turn of the 20th century. Inside, polished wooden display cases are filled with French chocolate candies and petite cakes. Chandeliers hang from high ceilings, and an old wooden staircase winding upward to the second floor gives Angelina's an early 1900's charm.

High tea, four o'clock in the afternoon, at Angelina's is always crowded. Tourists and shoppers sit at the small tables drinking hot creamy chocolate with mounds of whipped cream, visiting or simply relaxing. A small dish of delectable French pastries can be seen at each table. I wonder—if "high tea" includes scones and petite sandwiches, would tea without fare be called "low tea?"

A waitress brought hot chocolate for me and a small bowl of fresh cold water for Nipper. The water was served on a silver platter with paper lace doily, and two small dog cookies free gratis. Gently, Nipper lifted a cookie from the platter. As he looked up at the waitress—who lingered to watch him eat his cookie—they seemed to exchange smiles with each other.

We were tired. It had been a full day, so we returned to the hotel where Nipper immediately fell asleep on a pillow and I began to run a hot scented bath.

I had managed to extend our stay in Paris by an extra day, but tomorrow would be our last.

When I walk down a Paris street alone, little notice is taken of me. But when Nipper is with me—especially when he wears his red turtleneck which says "I hate cats"—people smile and often stop me to ask questions about him, to pet him, and talk to him. It is a pleasant neighborly interaction, and a chance for me to practice my French.

Nipper takes this attention in stride, but always politely acknowledges the stranger with a lick on their nose or cheek. This brings on a gush of even greater smiles or outright laughter, and lots of doggie talk.

Parisians love their dogs, and allow them to run playfully loose in the parks. Watch where you step! Dogs are welcome just about everywhere. My picture albums are filled with snaps of Nipper in the gardens around the Eifel Tower, playing with Poodles, Irish Blood Hounds, Dachshunds, St. Bernards, Greyhounds, and the wrinkled Shar-Pei. There were no squabbles seen among "les chien".

We stood in front of the Louvre and watched an amateur artist propped on a stool sketching caricatures of people. The artist had a hat on the ground for donations of change in return for a sketch. "Bonjour, Monsieur. Por favor, will you do a sketch of my dog?" "Oui, oui," he said. We sat down on a step, Nipper on my lap, and the artist began to sketch.

Passersby gradually stopped to watch. Soon a small crowd had gathered. Smiling faces were admiring the sketch, making favorable little comments.

Voila! The artist was finished! The sketch was complete! I stood up, stretched my legs and placed some coins in the hat. The crowd surrounded us and broke out with applause, laughing and attempting closer inspection of Nipper and his sketch.

The best way to make friends with the French, I decided, is to have a dog with you!

Fontainebleau Castle was built around 1520 on the site of the original castle from the 12th century. It is a short bus ride from Paris. Surrounded by a forest of the same name, and adjacent to a small and delightful town, Fontainebleau was a beloved home to generations of French kings. As with many famous castles, it seems Antoinette also slept here!

Within the walls of that immense majestic castle, historic events took place in days gone by. Napoleon gave his resignation there in 1814. It became headquarters for the Nazis during their occupation of France in World War II.

Along with a dozen other people, I followed the tourist guide through the elegant rooms, and wiggled my way to the front of the group so I would not have to look over people's heads. A tourist guide can impart great pieces of historical and interesting facts, and I don't like to miss a thing.

After a few hours inside the castle, I disappeared to the small neighboring village. The air was sweet with the fragrance of hot crepes baking on a grill from a nearby vendor, and I was hungry. Moments later, I happily roamed the old cobble stoned streets eating a crepe piled high with fresh whipped cream and strawberries. Life doesn't get any better than this.

But later that day I was overcome with homesickness yet again. Walking along the promenade of the Seine with Nipper, I felt a deep sadness and longing for my home in the U.S. and the familiar faces of those I love the most in the world.

The piper must also be paid, I thought. Adventures have a price, including homesickness and loneliness.

I turned off on a side street and ordered a café au lait at an outside café. By now I was deep in the throes of self pity. Pensively observing my surroundings, I wondered what my daughter was doing right now. Wouldn't it be fun if she were here? She would have a joke to crack, and we would laugh.

Nipper sat quietly on my lap, and I hugged him a little closer to me. Sipping my coffee, I began to watch the people. A slender man with a thin moustache and a black beret pulled over his eyes was sleeping at the next table, his long legs stretched halfway across the sidewalk. People simply walked around him.

Over there, an older man—does he resemble, just a little, Lawrence Olivier? He was meticulously dressed, and delicately nibbled on a croissant as he read the newspaper. Older people in this city are always well dressed when they go out in public, even if only to have a coffee.

Then my attention was drawn to a very large woman and her small dog. They were walking toward us on the sidewalk. She, too, was all dressed up—red heels, feathers in her hat, strands of pearls around her neck. Suddenly, little Emile decided to squat on the sidewalk. The woman became excited and scolded him—Non, Emile, non! She was dragging him by his leash off the sidewalk. But it was too late. Emile left a little pooh on the sidewalk.

My eyes were firmly fixed on Emile. Nipper, too, was fascinated.

Then—sure enough—out came the waiter. He was wearing a long white apron and balancing a tray over his head filled with wine glasses. Not seeing the pooh on the sidewalk, he stepped right into it and slid. Wine glasses went flying. Angry heated words from the waiter mingled with profuse apologies from the lady as she quickly picked up Emile and hurried off.

I ordered another café au lait—the idle activity around me was becoming interesting, and I was forgetting my self.

By and by, a young man laid his hat on the ground just across the narrow street and began playing his violin. The strains of his music were soothing and I became absorbed and lost in this unexpected one man concert. Mozart's Magic Flute sweetly filled my ears and softly crept into my soul. I began to relax.

The violinist was exceptionally good. I wondered about the millions of talented people in the world, such as this young man, who may never be discovered and know well deserved recognition.

Finally, I crossed the street and placed some coins in the man's hat. The late afternoon sun felt warm on my face as we continued walking, my heart just a little lighter than it had been earlier.

Our last evening in Paris had arrived. Nipper and I visited the lovely park and gardens near the Petit Palais where there were many scents for him to investigate. I simply sat on a bench to watch the people and enjoy the atmosphere. Across the elegant street was the American Embassy. In the opposite direction—at the end of Champs-Elysees—the Arc de Triumph stood grand and majestic.

Sitting next to me on the bench was a short roundish old lady. She sat alone and, like me, was enjoying the evening.

The old lady asked me a question. Although she spoke in English, she had an accent. German? We exchanged pleasant chitchat. Yes, she was from Germany, spending a holiday weekend here alone, and she would be returning by train to Frankfurt later that evening, she told me.

We were two strangers, two lone women travelers who became brief friends in the park. She invited me to join her for a bite to eat.

On nearby Champs-Elysees, we sat at an outside table and ordered a sandwich and salad. I was mystified with the hubbub of this famous street lined with theaters, restaurants and pricey boutiques. People filled the sidewalks, literally swarming in the streets. We sat quietly eating—it was almost too noisy to talk.

But over there, can you see it—the ghost of General Charles DeGaulle leading his vast army troops, ghost soldiers one and all? They marched, weary but triumphant, under the Arch de Triumph and down the Champs-Elysees in 1945 amidst happy cheers of the people of France who were celebrating the end of World War II. The Germans had been given the boot, and France was liberated.

It was not something my German lady friend and I talked about. We just quietly ate our sandwiches, and watched the people.

It was time to leave Paris and continue on to Khartoum. I piled my luggage and dog kennel into a taxi and off we sped at breakneck speed for Charles de Gaulle Airport.

The driver quickly unloaded my suitcases onto the sidewalk at the airport terminal. As he plunked the dog kennel on the pavement, a loose screw fell off and rolled out of sight, weakening the top of the kennel.

At the baggage counter, the young French clerk would not accept the kennel. She snippily told me in French—though I clearly understood—that the kennel was broken and not secure. It could not go on the plane. Impossible, she said, stand aside.

I attempted to converse with her in gestures along with my pathetic grasp of French.

"Madame, I have no tools. Is there a maintenance man in the airport with a screw and a screwdriver?" No. "Can I buy a new kennel at the airport?" No, impossible. "Could I take my dog with me into the cabin?" No, impossible. "Is there a supervisor who speaks English that I could discuss the problem with?" No, impossible. "Do you understand what I am trying to say?" No, impossible.

I was becoming desperate. Only one who has experienced the difficulties of communicating with another in an unfamiliar language can appreciate how draining this is.

Time was running out and I might miss my plane. Khartoum is not a popular destination. Planes to Khartoum are infrequent.

Reasoning with the desk agent clearly was not working. When she stubbornly insisted that I take my broken kennel and step aside, I lost it. I threw a full blown temper tantrum, demanding some assistance, or else!

Suddenly, like magic, a supervisor appeared, a woman speaking limited English. She politely—if coldly—listened to my problem and then told me I could buy a paper bag for Nipper and she would authorize his acceptance into the cabin of the plane. I bought the paper bag and ran to the boarding desk.

Just moments later I stepped into the plane, holding Nipper in my arms. He was tucked into the paper bag with only his eyes visible. The hostess greeted me with a large smile, but her smile faded when she saw Nipper in the paper bag. She opened her mouth and began to say, "I'm sorry, but. . ."

The hostess and I stood staring at each other for one chilling moment. The doors to the plane were closing. Suddenly, all civil politeness left me, and my temper tantrum returned with fury. "...I have permission! . . . I will not get off! . . . What's wrong with you people!? . . . Are you all crazy!? . . . It was only a screw! . . ."

The big engines began to roar for take-off. With me in my seat and Nipper in his bag, we were soon in the sky and on our way to Khartoum.

There were to be many airport struggles over the following years—lost luggage, language confusions, airport bomb scares, and sticky security interrogations. In one incident, someone placed Nipper on the wrong plane.

It was in Atlanta, and the airport was very crowded and busy. I stood in line at a TWA counter and asked the agent to verify that Nipper was on the plane I was to shortly board. The agent argued that it was not necessary. "TWA does not lose dogs, Madam. Please step aside."

I asked if he would verify anyway. "No. Stand aside," he said. But I persisted, even though he was becoming visibly annoyed with me.

Finally, to be rid of me, the agent picked up the phone to make the inquiry, irritably and impatiently tapping his fingers on the counter.

"Not on TWA 112!? Where, then?" The agent looked slightly embarrassed as he hung up the phone and told me that my dog seems to be misplaced. Airport Security began a search of the vast airport, but could not locate him. I was frantic with worry.

Finally, half an hour later, Nipper and three other dogs were found—they had mistakenly been placed on a plane about to depart for Beijing! In China, they eat dogs!

In another incident—this time at O'Hare Airport in Chicago, an immense airport—I gathered my luggage and dog together and searched for a cart. We had just been on a long international flight, and were exhausted.

I could not find a cart, and the trek through the terminal to the taxi curb was long. Oh God, how do I handle all this baggage? It was only a thought.

Voila. A quiet spoken man appeared out of the crowd and took the luggage from me. He smiled and asked me to follow him. I carried Nipper and followed the man as he led me straight through the airport and directly to a taxi.

The kind man placed my luggage into the trunk of the taxi, and as I turned to thank him, he was gone! He was an angel sent to help me—I always recognize angels. But I could not thank him. He was gone.

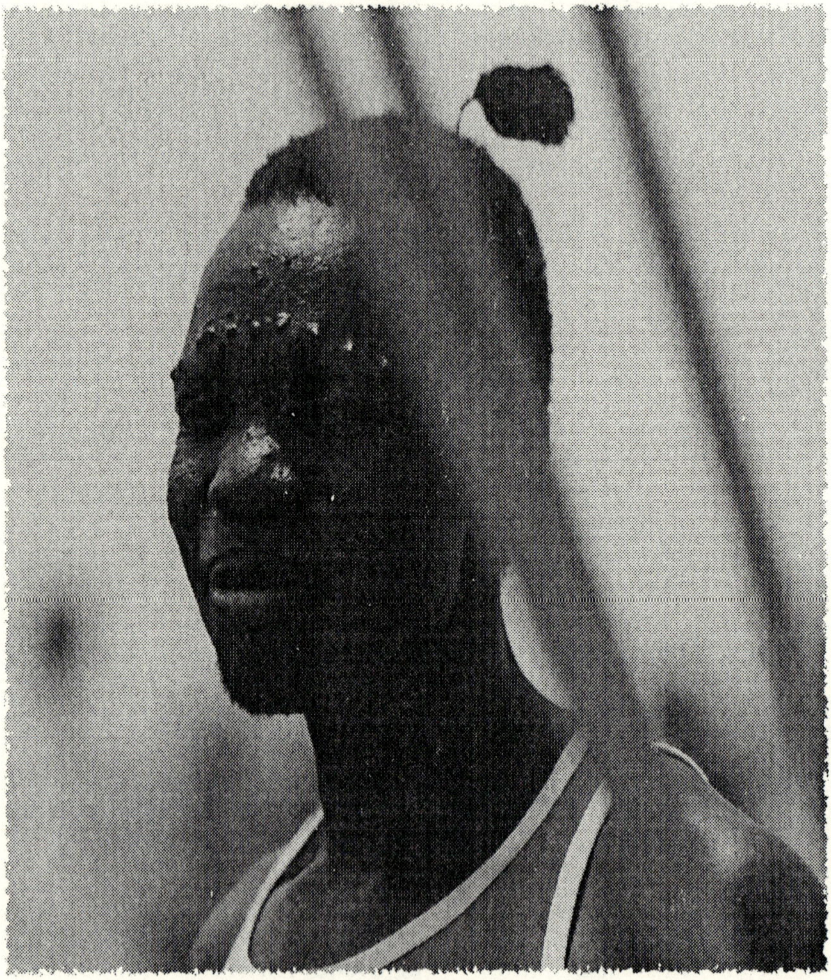

2

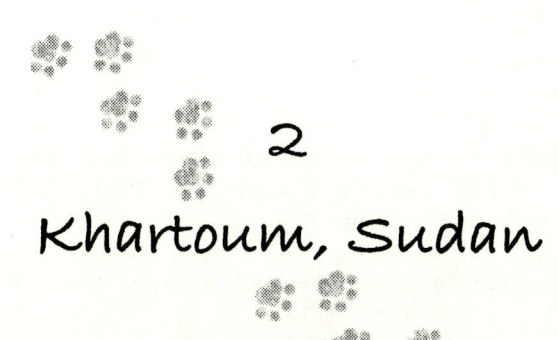

Khartoum, Sudan

At Khartoum International Airport, our plane landed, bumped a few times, and then came to a stop. We were here, we were really here. We had arrived, a million miles from home.

Inside the plane cabin, passengers began to stand up and collect their hand luggage. I stood also, feeling stiff and tired. Nipper had managed this long flight without having to go, but I knew he could not hold it much longer! Just as I picked him up from his seat, he began to wet. Worse, I had no way of stopping him. I grabbed a blanket and wrapped it snuggly around his bottom, but there was no stopping him now. He peed, and peed and peed.

I propped Nipper in one arm and my hand luggage in the other, and stepped off the plane unconcerned about how I must look and smell after the long flight. My thoughts instead were focused on what I would find outside this plane. Someone from the embassy is to meet me, but what if there was a mishap somehow? Would they find me?

The air was warm and the hour past midnight when we disembarked. Surrounding the foot of the plane were three truckloads of dark Sudanese soldiers, watching us, rifles held firmly in their hands. Something resembling vague fear lightly touched at the pit of my stomach, but then was gone. The soldiers did not seem hostile, really. Probably their presence was a precaution only.

Following the others, I walked past the soldiers and toward the terminal where a small group of people were waiting to greet us. Nipper was clutched tightly in my arm. As I passed the soldiers, they stared at him. Smiles broke out on their faces as they pointed at him and made comments in Arabic.

Nipper was unlike the wild street dogs of Khartoum. His beard was neatly trimmed and he wore a grey tee shirt. The soldiers had probably never seen a dog wearing a shirt before, but I felt the plane might be chilly. Now they were laughing out loud and making noisy remarks. I hurried by.

The airport terminal resembled a long garage with tin roof. It was crude and basic. An American couple stood by the entrance smiling, and said they were my sponsors. As I followed them into the terminal, I could still hear the soldiers. They were howling now with laughter as they continued to enjoy their unexpected amusement over Nipper.

For the next half hour, I waited as my sponsors cleared the way for me with airport officials and answered their questions. Then I was told that my suitcases were lost. Actually, my suitcases were not lost but had not been removed from the plane which was now back in the air and on its way to Cairo.

To make matters worse, tomorrow will be the first day of Ramadan, the ten-day Islamic holiday. During Ramadan, the entire city of Khartoum comes to a halt. No services are in effect, and I could not expect to receive my suitcases until after Ramadan.

My suitcases contained important items like medicine and reading glasses in addition to my clothing and toiletries. As I became a more seasoned traveler, I carried such important items with me. But I was inexperienced the night I arrived in Khartoum. I was also tired, and said nothing.

We left the airport and drove half an hour through the city to my new residence located in the New Extension on 9th Street.

Khartoum had few or no street lamps and the city was dark. In the moonlight, I could glimpse bleak and barren streets with large potholes, and an occasional animal. We entered a somewhat pleasant residential area, and pulled up in front of a wrought iron gate.

Inside the yard, a small brick walkway led to the wooden steps of a wide veranda. The veranda fronted a two-storied house, and a friendly glow from the veranda's nightlight spread over the yard.

The lower portion of the house was leased by our embassy and was to be mine. The upper level was occupied by the son of the Sudanese owner. He was seldom there, and in fact I was never to meet him.

A Sudanese guard was sleeping on the front steps. He awoke

with a start when he heard our voices and seemed flustered at being caught asleep, but smiled and said "Saalam Alaik," and disappeared to the front gate.

The U.S. government hires Sudanese guards to provide 24-hour coverage at the homes of the Americans. It is a common problem for guards to sleep on duty, and new people to the embassy—like me—are assigned the oldest and least able of the guards available. They were paid the current rate, about fifty dollars a month in Sudanese pounds, for twelve hour days, seven days a week.

As we stepped inside the house, I was impressed and delighted. The living room was bright, elegant, and spacious. It was beautifully furnished with new Ethan Allen chairs, tables, and a couch. High ceilings and large shuttered French windows gave the room an open pleasant feeling.

An alarm system was wired to the windows. It would sound off if a door or window was opened and although I had been shown where the alarm was and how to control it, by morning I had forgotten.

Telephones in Khartoum were scarce and antiquated. Most Americans had a walkie-talkie called a radio, operated by a battery. Mine was filled with static and frequently unreliable. Only one conversation could take place at a time, and everyone with a radio could listen in.

Since the hour was late, Jim and Lilian gave me a quick briefing, and then departed. The night felt strange and surreal. I washed my face and curled up in the big bed, finding comfort in being close to Nipper. We fell asleep.

A mosquito from the swamp cooler above my bed buzzed around my face and woke me on that first morning in Khartoum. I opened my eyes with a lot of effort. Bright sunshine filled the room through the cracks of the shuttered window.

Where was I? Reality quickly returned—we were here, finally, after months of planning and training. A sense of adventure returned, and I got out of bed to explore my new surroundings.

The marble floors felt cool on my bare feet as I walked through the hallway into the large, beautiful living room. All was quiet. The living room was bright with filtered sunshine. The new upholstered chairs and couch were white—very pretty, but not too practical. Still,

I mused at the thought of the fun I would have decorating with plants and a few accessories.

I began to unlatch the shutters, forgetting about the alarm system. A loud siren went off and shattered the quiet of the early morning. For a moment, I was stunned.

Where is the alarm?! I could not remember! Running through the unfamiliar house, I looked everywhere. Frantic, I ran outside to the guard for help. He followed me back into the house, located the alarm in a remote closet, and turned it off. Quiet returned, and I was wide awake now.

The kitchen, a big room with pipes exposed along the high ceilings, was stark white and totally lacking in charm. It had several large appliances and a water tank mounted to the ceiling which had been installed by the embassy for emergency.

On the floor by the kitchen window, I noticed an immense chest—a "welcome kit" from the embassy—containing basics on temporary loan to me. There were towels, an iron, dishes, a coffee pot.

Just then, shivers ran down my spine as a roach—or beetle—the size of a mouse ran across the floor! It was the first, but not the last, to be seen in the house.

When I threw back the kitchen shutters I was startled to find myself looking into the smiling brown eyes of an Arab woman who was looking out of her own kitchen window near mine. She had a beautiful face with a colorful veil over her black hair, and she waved and greeted me in Arabic. I smiled and waved back.

I continued exploring the house. In the bathroom, modern by Khartoum standards, there was a makeshift shower, a tub, and a toilet which promised to have constant plumbing problems.

But it was the old swamp cooler over my bed which posed some concern. Malaria was a big problem here, and I saw the swamp cooler as a potential breeding place for mosquitoes. Still, the cooler will be useful in the hot weather—which could soar above 130 degrees Fahrenheit. Air conditioning was unavailable in this country, although the very thick walls of my house will provide good insulation.

Having acquainted myself with my new home, I sat for awhile and thought about the next ten days of Ramadan. Without my suitcases, I was at a loss. The medication was not available locally and without it I will become sick within a week. Without reading glasses, I cannot fill my time with reading. Clothing and toiletries were also essential. But I was not yet feeling the full effects of these important missing items. I will not worry about it until tomorrow.

Jim and Lilian returned that first morning to take me shopping for food. The sun was very bright and the heat already intense as we climbed into their car. With the exception of an occasional voice or call of a camel or wild dog, the streets were quiet.

Slightly lush trees and bougainvillea plants gave the immediate area a colorful, almost tropical appearance. The potholes in the dirt road appeared more severe by daylight, and garbage strewn along the roadside smelled in the heat.

"Most of your neighbors are Sudanese and do not speak English," Jim said. Their houses were large with flat roofs, built to accommodate big families of children, grandparents, aunts, uncles, and cousins. Many houses were fenced with brick walls facing the road.

We drove to a local market with a fair selection of food, and then stopped briefly at the small American PX where products like coffee and peanut butter were imported from the U.S.

Along the side of a road near the PX, a family with about six small children lived in a cardboard hut on a dirt floor. Their only water came from a faucet jutting up from the ground nearby. The degree of their poverty was astonishing. How do they manage to live like this, I wondered, particularly in weather so hot?

Shopping finished, we went for a short drive around Khartoum. Everywhere, I saw utter poverty unlike any I had before seen.

A large open dirt field was filled with hundreds of cardboard huts, homes to whole families. Again, there was no water.

Small naked children played in the dirt. There were flies on their cheeks and bodies. Garbage, a few dead animals, and even a dead person lay in the dirt fields or along the road! Goats and camels roamed freely, and wild dogs ran in packs.

This is surely the poorest of the poor.

Over the first few days, several Americans came to the house to welcome me. A kind woman from the embassy had brought clothes and toiletries and a small tape recorder with music, mostly tapes of Mozart. I played those tapes over and over again. In later years, Mozart's music would always bring back memories of early days in Khartoum.

My new American colleagues reminded me of the rules: "Boil drinking water in a solution, and soak vegetables and fruit in a solution. Do not let the water tank get low. Keep your "radio" charged.

Avoid going in public alone. Always cover your arms and legs in public—shorts and skimpy clothing is offensive in this culture. Taking photographs of public buildings is prohibited.

Some Sudanese people are afraid of the camera. They believe the camera will rob them of their spirit, so do not take pictures of them."

Much of this I had been briefed on in Orientation, but reminders were helpful.

By about the third day, the flurry of visitors dwindled to a stop. They had kindly paid their respects, and I was alone now, alone to wait out the ten days of Ramadan.

I sat in a lounge chair on the veranda as the day came to an end. Although the August weather was hot, there was a nice breeze after the sun went down.

Without glasses to read with, I had much time to sit and think. What I thought of that evening was Sudan, this country which, until only a few short months ago, I knew little about.

Khartoum is the capital city of Sudan, the largest country in Africa and one of the poorest countries in the world. Sudan has a population of over 22,000,000. The land is largely flat and infertile with vast bleak deserts and a hot, arid climate. Sugar cane, sesame seed, and cotton are the country's main farming products, and nomadic herding (cattle, sheep and over 14 million goats) is Sudan's principal activity.

The cultivated land is irrigated by the White and Blue Niles, which are also an invaluable source of hydroelectric power. The rivers are disease ridden, and not safe for either swimming or drinking.

Khartoum's public transportation is primitive. After WWII, old buses were purchased from Germany. They are not plentiful and people cram them to over-capacity, clinging to the footboards, the doors, and even the roof!

The strong haboobs—dust storms—blow often through the city and fill the air and homes with layers of sticky dirt. The sticky dust is also breathed in by the people.

Power failures and water shortages are routine. Plumbing is antiquated, made worse during water shortages, and the dirty water can make one very sick.

I had been given countless inoculations before my arrival in the Sudan, and I continued to take preventive medicine for malaria. But some diseases were still a threat, particularly malaria.

The few hospitals of Khartoum have scarce supplies, and the number of available doctors and nurses is insufficient to take care of the sick. The shortage of beds often results in patients having to lie on the dirt floors.

Begging is widespread, and children are actively involved in begging in the streets or markets. Mothers beg with a sleeping baby in their arms as they sit in front of shops or on street corners. It is said they drug their babies to keep them quiet, and further hope the sight of a sleeping baby will bring them sympathy and an extra coin in their cup.

I had been warned to avoid beggars because often they spend the coins on drugs, but I made a personal decision to give whatever I could and trust that it will be well spent.

Sudan is a male dominated society. Women are submissive and considered inferior to men. A man is permitted up to four wives, unless he is wealthy enough to support more than four, but a woman cannot have more than one husband.

Arranged marriages are still practiced in Sudan. If a Sudanese man sees a girl he would like as his wife, he visits the girl's father and tries to convince the father that he has the means to support the daughter. The girl in question has little or nothing to say in the matter.

Women as well as men are circumcised. For women, circumcision is practiced in order to increase the pleasure of intimacy for men. That is its one objective.

If a man is wealthy, his wives often are well endowed with gold. They wear a lot of it at one time—bracelets, necklaces and earrings. A handful of jewelry shops are filled with the very shiny African gold, and the Americans and other foreigners find it to be "very good buys."

Women rarely live alone in Khartoum, and as an American

woman living alone I would be viewed with suspicion. I was also a light skinned woman with blond hair in a predominantly dark country, and was destined to receive plenty of unwanted stares in public. I would never grow comfortable with it.

The striking henna designs which Sudanese women paint on their hands and nails for beautification were especially traditional for weddings and, unlike other tattoos, the designs wear off.

The women also wear a certain strong musk scented perfume, which I would come to distinguish always and exclusively with the Sudanese women.

While Moslem men dress in white taigas and galabiyahs, the traditional wear for Moslem women is a colorful dress—or wrap—called a toab. The toab is a long narrow strip of material which is wrapped around the woman—difficult to do, but very distinctive in its design.

Islam and Christianity are the predominant faiths in Khartoum, but Christianity is more prevalent to the south of Sudan. Islam, the Moslem religion, holds that there is only one god, Allah. Its Koran teaches Sharia Law, a practice which sometimes has political undertones.

Sharia Law forbids consumption of alcohol, but bootlegging in the home is common. The homemade alcohol is crude and potent—puts hair on your chest, I was told.

Also under Sharia Law, a woman caught in adultery is punished by being placed in an open pit, her head covered with a bag, and then stoned to death! She must first be proven guilty, but sometimes the accusation alone is enough to stone her.

Hacking off a hand is the fate of one caught stealing. The right hand is hacked first, a particular humiliation for the victim since the left—used for wiping after urinating—is considered unclean. And anyone caught running from the law may expect to have his or her left foot hacked.

The rationale behind the hand and foot practice is that, with only a right foot and a left hand it is exceedingly difficult for a person to walk with a cane if the good foot is injured.

A victim of Sharia Law can occasionally be seen crawling along the busy streets without feet and sometimes without both feet and hands, but this is more likely to be a birth defect from intermarriages among family members.

Finally, there is the high threat of terrorism. Abu Nudal was an example of a ruthless and elusive leader who had established his headquarters in underground Khartoum, but there were others.

I had never experienced jet lag or culture shock until now. Culture shock left me mildly bewildered and disoriented, and jet lag caused short attention spans and frequent bouts of severe fatigue. For me, both hung on for weeks.

It was surprising to learn, at a later time, that one could experience culture shock in our own country after a long absence. The very idea, culture shock in our own country!

Still sitting on my veranda that evening, I thought of the many ex-patriots who live and work in Khartoum. The diplomatic community of foreigners comes from around the world.

For all of us, there was little to do except work, work, work. But I had just arrived, and knew little yet of these things.

After the first few days following our arrival in Khartoum, Nipper and I were alone most of the time. American visitors were scarce. I began to look forward to the end of Ramadan when the embassy resumed its schedule and I could begin working.

An early attempt to take Nipper for a walk and see the neighborhood ended abruptly. We walked to the front gate and stepped out onto the dirt road, but immediately pulled back inside. About five hundred yards away I saw a pack of a dozen or so wild dogs, squabbling and fighting among themselves for a piece of meat they had found.

Instinctively, I felt the danger of the wild dogs and never attempted another walk with Nipper. The fenced yard became his domain.

But I did walk alone, and my first walk was a memorable one. Despite the intense heat, the fresh air would do me good and I was curious about the area. Smiling and nodding to the guard sitting at my gate, I set off down the road. I carried a stick for protection—from what, I was not sure.

As I strolled down the dirt road, my thoughts were of the guards at my gate. Christian guards wore tan shirts and pants and Moslems wore white galabiyahs and taigas. Despite dirt in the city, the white galabiyahs always looked clean and bright.

The streets were deserted. I wandered slowly, admiring the bougainvillea and other flowering plants spilling out over the walls and windows, giving touches of color and beauty to the otherwise austere surroundings. The roads were unpaved, dusty and in poor condition with large potholes. An Arab riding a donkey passed me by.

Garbage strewn alongside the roads was eaten by the goats who roamed the streets. The goats also ate tin cans, rubber, and anything they found. There is no garbage pickup service, per se. The goats are the "Waste Management" of Khartoum.

Embassy people had their goat jokes. When our ambassador departed post a number of months later, our unique farewell gift to him would be a beautifully framed photograph of goats busily eating in a pile of garbage. He loved it.

A camel sat in the shade of a building, out of the sun. Along with the wild dogs and goats, camels and donkeys can be seen roaming freely in the city. I stopped for a closer look—I had not seen many camels in my life.

The hump of the camel's back stores water. I thought this fact interesting—how nature provides for the camel—since they are desert animals where water is scarce. In Khartoum, many Sudanese ride the camel or load heavy baggage on its back. The gentle looking animal is a beast of burden.

Animals are not respected in Khartoum. They are poorly treated, and often brutally abused. I would witness this disturbing abuse first hand during my stay in Khartoum.

To my horror, I suddenly realized I was lost! The streets and houses all looked alike, and there were few or no street signs! An occasional stranger walked by but did not understand my English, and kept walking.

I sat down by the side of the road, lost in close to 130F degree heat.

For a very long time I sat there on the curb, frightened and nauseated and even throwing up. Eventually a young dark woman approached me in the street. She understood, and kindly helped me to locate my house.

The haunting call to prayer breaks the silence of the early morning just before dawn. From a distant loudspeaker, the beautiful

Arabic voice calls out over the city each morning at 5:30 as I sit on my veranda and sip hot coffee.

Five times daily, Moslems stop what they are doing, face east to Mecca and on bended knees with their heads touching the ground, they offer up their prayers.

My Moslem guards also answer the call to prayer, observing this ritual within my yard. I am intrigued as I watch. The culture is simply doing what it has done for thousands of years, and it added a quiet reverence to my own morning.

I had been curled up in a living room chair one evening when the house was suddenly in utter, complete blackness. A power failure. Slowly I groped my way along the walls, from room to room, trying to locate my flashlight. The "radio" was on a table and I tried to reach the embassy Marine, but the static was too heavy.

With the flashlight, I made my way into the bedroom and sat on the edge of the bed, waiting. The city itself was completely black and silent except for some voices heard in the distance. There seemed to be nothing I could do but wait for the return of the power. And so I waited.

A few hours went by, and the power was not yet restored. Without power, the swamp cooler was not operable and the room was soon stifling hot. I opened the window for air, ignoring the mosquitoes which began to drift in. A small amount of breeze came into the room and after awhile I fell asleep on the bed.

By morning the power had been restored, but my body was covered with red, itching bites from the mosquitoes which had come in through the open windows.

The days slowly slipped away, and my stiff upper lip began to droop. Isolation and the harshness of my new surroundings were having their way with me. I could no longer talk myself out of feeling alone and cut off from the world.

I knew nobody. I had no telephone, television or radio, no

eyeglasses to read by. I was homesick, and without my medicine I had begun to feel physically ill.

There was simply too much time to myself with too little to do, and the weather was very, very hot. Very hot. What can of worms had I opened, I asked myself, by coming here to this strange country? Despair began to consume me like a nightmare where you try to scream but no sound comes out.

I began to cry, and once I started I could not stop. I cried, and cried, and cried. I cried every day, for weeks and months.

3
Alcoholics Anonymous Abroad

"My name is Jeanne, and I am an alcoholic." Similar words are said thousands of times every day at AA meetings throughout the world.

Paul and I held our first meeting together in my living room within the first few weeks of my arrival. He was the only other AA member living in Khartoum at the time, but it only takes two to hold a meeting. I was extremely grateful that he was there.

Alcoholics Anonymous was almost unheard of in Sudan, in part because Sharia Law forbids drinking. If nobody drinks, who needs AA? While there were other Americans in Khartoum suspected of having a drinking problem, nobody wanted to admit to it and face the stigma attached to alcoholism. Word gets around in those small embassies and diplomatic communities.

At the State Department, one individual within the huge Medical Division is responsible for Foreign Service AA members worldwide. "George" was this individual at the time I was hired. All applications of aspiring F.S. diplomats who are AA members must be reviewed and approved by George. He had the final say on a) whether the applicant had a strong enough sobriety to allow being hired; and b) which country the applicant could be assigned to.

Such an applicant is not normally given a number "1" security clearance, but rather a "2" clearance. This is a protection for the AA member. Since many countries do not have the fellowship of Alcoholics Anonymous, such an assignment could jeopardize the sobriety of the recovering alcoholic.

George was a gruff, older man with a very soft heart. He himself was a recovering alcoholic, with many years of high quality sobriety, and he had held his position at the State Department for a long time.

When I first met George during my 3 months of Orientation classes in Washington, he ushered me into his cozy cluttered office and closed his door so we could have a private conversation.

He apologized to me for my assignment to Khartoum, a country with no AA, a first tour assignment in a very difficult hardship post. He also apologized for the error of a number "1" as opposed to a number "2" security clearance. Because of unusual circumstances, he told me, these things had happened without his knowledge.

George wanted to make changes for me—but since he felt responsible for the mistakes, he preferred to ask my permission first. I told him to leave the decisions as they stood, that perhaps "providence" had a hand in those mistakes for a good reason. Of course, it was an easy thing for me to say while in the comfort of that big old leather chair in George's cozy office. I knew that if I should change my mind at any time, George would be there for me.

In hindsight, I could see that his willingness to allow my decision was a tribute to his faith in the quality of my sobriety. George was not one to be shy about speaking his mind or being hard nosed if he had to be. He had the sharp eye to spot a con artist—alcoholics possess that con artist tendency—and he would have none of it!

In the years to come, I always went to visit George during my interludes in Washington. I often witnessed his harsh reprimands with an AA member who was in need of a swift kick in the behind. More often than not, I saw that soft, kind, caring side of George. He was our friend, and we all knew it.

The Medical Division of the State Department required AA member applicants to have a minimum of one year's sobriety and a clearance report from a psychiatrist chosen by the State Department. In my case, I had two years of sobriety at the time my application was in the long 22-month processing stage.

Two years earlier, I had entered AA of my own cognizance. I knew immediately that this "program of living" would save my own life.

I spent five weeks in rehabilitation at the Casa de Amigos, a big older house converted into a women's rehab in downtown Phoenix.

There, I learned a great deal about the debilitating, unprejudiced disease. It can claim anyone—regardless of culture, rank, age, sex, financial status.

During those first two sober years, I attended many, many meetings. While I initially hated going to them (went only because I "had to"), hated the stigma, hated admitting I had the disease, I eventually grew to love it all—the fellowship, the AA way of life, the people in it. Most of all, I loved sobriety.

There is a danger in becoming too comfortable in AA. I believe we honor our gift of sobriety—at the appropriate time and under the appropriate conditions, of course—by letting go little by little—not of the program, but of any possible cocoon-like dependence on it to the exclusion of living in the real world. Accepting a career overseas meant that I had to let go.

Paul and I held our meetings in my living room or his, one evening each week. The coffee pot was always on—an AA meeting without coffee is unthinkable! We talked and listened to each other. We studied the Big Book of AA. Between those bare bone meetings and my Big Book, there was never a threat to my sobriety.

Most important, I never missed a day of thanking my Higher Power for the gift He gave me.

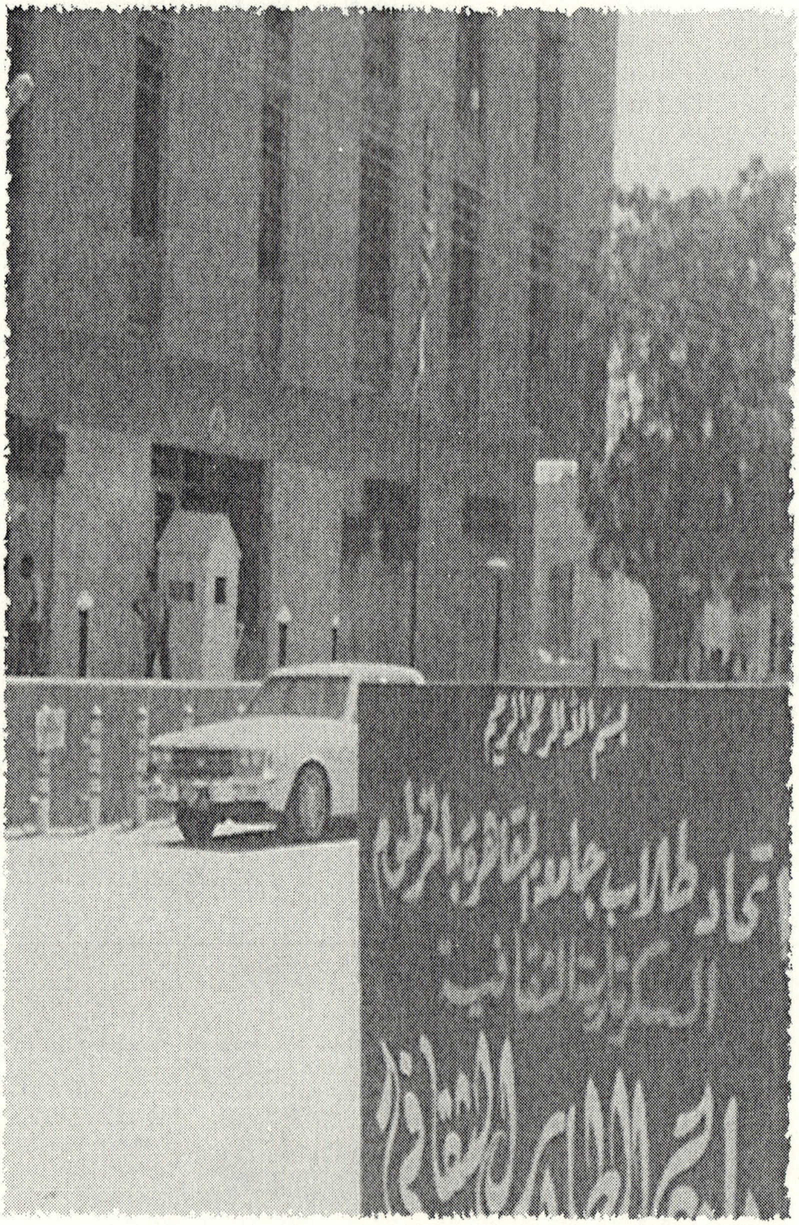
بسم الله الرحمن الرحيم
طلاب جامعة القاهرة بالخرطوم

4
American Embassy Khartoum and Daily Life

With the passing of Ramadan, my suitcases appeared at my doorstep like magic. They had been searched and robbed, but the medicine was there.

The embassy resumed its normal schedule, and this brought some semblance of relief to me. Filling my days with work would be good medicine.

An embassy is a group of people headed by an ambassador working in a foreign land with a mission to accomplish. While the mission is far reaching, it essentially strives to promote good relations with other nations, to protect Americans abroad, and to exchange information within diplomatic communities.

In 1985, the United States had about 260 embassies and consulates throughout the world. Some were no bigger than an outpost, and others were large and sophisticated.

The so-called "diplomatic community" is the combined presence of many embassies and consulates residing in the host country. These include the embassies of the U.K., Japan, Saudi Arabia, Australia, the Soviet Union, to name a few. The diplomatic community exchanges information and interacts through meetings or official receptions and dinners.

44 / Jeanne JieAhn

    The American eagle emblem identified the building—Embassy of the United States of America. It was an ordinary standalone structure in downtown Khartoum. Plain brick. About five stories high. A double steel guard rail ran along the front to protect the building from suicide bombers in automobiles or trucks.

    Dusty, noisy downtown was a conglomeration of small shops not unlike tin sheds. There was the usual honking traffic, all the more chaotic because there were no road rules. Beggars sat on street corners with their can. Strange odors and sounds filled the air.

    It was a sun drenched morning when I arrived for my first day of work. The American flag hung near the entrance of the embassy, and a Marine stood on guard. Just inside, two large portraits of President Ronald Reagan and his Vice President smiled down on me, the same portraits which hang at every U.S. embassy and consulate around the world.

    Inside, I passed through security scanners and presented my paperwork to a Marine on duty. A colleague waited to welcome me and give me a tour of the facilities. The halls were almost deserted, dim and shadowy. Office doors were closed, and many were locked with combinations. With a click, click, click of her finger, my colleague had the locks open and we entered the offices.

I was introduced to the people inside the offices, and then we moved on. The Ambassador was a friendly and unpretentious man, a gentleman, and I liked him immediately. With his Deputy Chief of Mission, second in command, and their assistants, they comprise the Front Office. Much of my work will come to this office for approvals and revisions.

The Administrative Officer, ADM Officer for short, greeted me with "Welcome to the Hell Hole." Odd man, he was. Here in this office I filled out paperwork, and we again moved on.

As we continued our tour, my colleague explained the positions of the people we were meeting:

Foreign Service Nationals (FSN's) are local hires, citizens of the host country. Third Country Nationals are also local hires, citizens of a third country.

Hafees, a tall Sudanese man who always dressed in his white galabiyah, was in charge of the Budget & Fiscal Office (B&F). These were primarily Foreign Service Nationals. Here I met Rita, who was also my neighbor though I had not known that. We were to become good friends in the future.

The Spooks are Central Intelligence Agents. They work incognito within many offices—pretending to be one of us when they are not. "Of course," my colleague said, "we often know they are spooks, and they know we know, but we all pretend not to know."

The best loved may be the young Marines, who remind others of a son or a brother. Their mission is to protect the embassy and Americans, and they all live together in the Marine House.

"Every November," my colleague told me, "the Marines sponsor a ball, a birthday party for the U.S. Marine Corps. In Khartoum, the ball takes place outside by the Nile River. It is the highlight of the Americans' social season, with a special dinner and live dancing."

We passed the Bubble Room, a heavily padded room where the most delicate of secret meetings take place.

A small American clinic with one nurse on duty, a cafeteria, and offices housing other U.S. agencies, such as USIS and USAID, finished up my tour of the embassy.

Finally, I was shown to my own office in the Political Section. Unremarkable but private, it had a window overlooking the rooftops of the downtown sheds and cheery sunlight streaked across the room. My desk was loaded with work waiting for my arrival—an omen of my entire future Foreign Service career.

I settled in to a routine, and there in my small office I spent most of my time. While the work was interesting, I found being behind locked doors for long hours to be claustrophobic and confining. I was terribly homesick, had much to learn, and no friends. I managed to keep a tight reign on my tears until I was home in the evenings—then I could let it all out to Nipper.

Got to toughen up, I told myself. Got to get a tough hide. Yes—that's it. A tough hide.

Combination locks controlled our lives. I was regularly locking and unlocking Something. They were found on office doors, safes, mailboxes, and cable boxes.

I was told to memorize the combinations immediately. Easy for them to say. Just try it—memorize those numbers for six or seven combinations when you still have jet lag!

The numbers swam in my head. Three swirls of the lock to the right, stop on 8, two swirls to the left, stop on 35, and two swirls back to the right to 18. No, that's not right. One swirl back to the right and stop on 18? Why isn't the lock opening? Maybe its only two swirls and stop on 8, then . . .

Finally, I considered doing what every woman in the embassy must surely have considered—writing the various combinations on a small piece of paper, and tucking the paper in my bra for easy reference!

With a stretch of the imagination, one could say that I held a key to U.S. national security inside my bra!

Shhhhhhhh. If you tell, I'll deny it!

All this security awareness and pink slips for violations of security if you're caught! Really, it was tiresome. Yet, simple practices soon became second nature:

The Heydays / 47

Never leave classified material unattended. Never discuss it with non-cleared personnel. Monitor conversations in public. Be aware of your surroundings. Vary your daily routes. Do not be predictable, as you may be watched.

Relationships with foreigners must be reported to the Regional Security Office (RSO). An intimate relationship with a foreigner could be detrimental to a career. It happens. A young officer was in a serious romance with a foreign girl and wanted to marry her. When the RSO ran a security check on the girl, it was found that—although not a spy herself—she was related to a spy for a country hostile to the U.S.

The officer did marry the girl, but he was returned to headquarters in Washington and demoted to a mundane position with no access to classified material.

There is the matter of foreign diplomacy and protocol. A whole Foreign Affaires Manual is written on the proper do's and don'ts. Understanding ranks and titles in the embassy is one thing—but the ever changing lists of the diplomatic community makes it all very challenging. Ranks, titles, cultural differences, language peculiarities, proper seating at dinners, and preparation of official papers such as diplomatic notes to the Foreign Minister—the list goes on.

Perfection is essential on any papers requiring the ambassador's signature. The slightest error sends the rejected paper back to the typist.

An ambassador is addressed as Mr. Ambassador or Ambassador Jones, a title he retains for life. When he enters a room, everyone in the room stands until the ambassador sits down.

Since there is a 4-year probation period in the Foreign Service before tenure, I focused my efforts on learning quickly and doing well.

It did not take long to receive that first formal invitation in a white quality envelope with embossed engraving. "Ambassador H. and Mrs. H. request the pleasure of your company at a reception in honor of . . ."

Attendance at a diplomatic reception or dinner hosted by the ambassador is mandatory for the Americans. The event may be very formal or informal. Sometimes the guests are quite noteworthy—a prince from Saudi Arabia, a dignitary from the host country, an esteemed missionary.

The event is typically held at the Ambassador's Residence. These are by and large the finest homes available in the host country, with the utmost good taste in décor, each room meticulously furnished. Since the Ambassador holds the highest embassy position and entertains frequently, such a mansion is expected.

At 5:30 p.m. an embassy driver drove me to the front door of the Ambassador's Residence. After passing through a security check, I stood in a line with other guests to be greeted by the Ambassador and his wife.

Soft music, a vase of fresh flowers atop a highly polished grand piano, the atmosphere was elegant. I could see others quietly chatting with each other in the exquisite living room, cocktails in their hands. Many were from the diplomatic community, and their various accents mingled together to form an interesting mix of gibberish.

The guest of honor that day was the Ambassador to the United Kingdom. He was departing Khartoum, and the gathering was to bid him farewell.

My task was to mingle, to seek out the foreign guests and help them feel welcome. I was nervous. This is not something I have had much experience with. Putting on a pleasant smile, I approached one little group, then another, but was ignored by both. Someone in the group was always talking, and nobody gave me so much as a nod!

I moved to yet another group, and again I was ignored. For awhile I simply stood there, glass in hand, awkward. Smile fading.

Finally I moved to the sideline to watch the activity and eat peanuts. The waiters, I notice, are very well trained. They glide through the room like ghosts—quick to notice anyone in need of a drink or bite to eat.

Ah, a colleague entered the room, spotted me, and came to my rescue. With her by my side, I was less uncomfortable. She explained things to me about official functions.

"Understanding protocol," she said, "is important. It will serve you well and suggest that you are polished in social graces. Take titles, for example. If a German doctor has more than one degree, he may be addressed as Doctor Doctor Schmidt. For every degree, another doctor is added to his title. It is much like stuttering! Guten Tag, Doctor Doctor Doctor Schmidt!"

"Some guests will only mingle with others who can benefit them somehow. To whom they address their idle friendly chitchat is often well chosen," she added.

At that moment, my colleague and I were suddenly approached by a German visitor with his cocktail in his hand. We all smiled largely at each other, holding out our hands in greeting.

His first question to us was, "Und vaht do you young ladies DO at the embassy?" When we explained that we are secretaries, he said "Ah so." But he was already moving on to another group.

I do not care much for official functions. Given a choice, I will always decline.

An informal invite, on the other hand, to the ambassador's home or that of any American was more to my liking. Ambassador H. was easygoing and liked to laugh. We felt free to stretch out on his living room floor for, perhaps, pizza prepared by the cook.

A sense of humor helped during those days in Khartoum. Little everyday happenings were humorous, if not overlooked:

The fish truck coming into the city from Port Sudan which hit a curb, turned over, and spilled fish all over the streets.

The Marine who made an announcement over the loudspeaker, and then forgot to turn it off. Everyone in the building listened with great interest as the Marine and his colleague chatted about the details of last night's date.

A group of young Sudanese men trying hilariously to maneuver a large bulky desk down the narrow stairwell from floor five to floor one.

I especially loved the one about the arrogant ADM officer—the one who greeted newcomers by welcoming them to the hell hole. It seems he enjoyed his drink, which must have been a problem for him in this city prohibiting alcohol. He had a special interest in U.S. shipments coming into Khartoum. The crates had to be cleared through Customs, and he insisted on being there personally.

At the airfield one day, the Customs official asked his usual question—"Was there any alcohol in the shipment?"—and the officer responded with the usual answer—"No." But just at that precise moment, a single can of beer fell lose from a crate and rolled between the two men! What timing!

We took our laughs where we could, because the serious side was always present. Anti-American demonstrations, for example, hate mail, telephone bomb threats.

Periodic drills were practiced much like a school drill—the sounds of three distinct sirens told us whether there was a bomb threat, a fire, or a terrorist invasion.

The procedure was to lock classified material in the safes and exit the building quickly. In an authentic emergency, the classified material must be fully shredded before leaving the building so that it will not fall into the hands of an enemy.

Just being American seemed to be enough reason to be hated by radicals. It was never known when violence would strike.

A few years earlier, the then U.S. Ambassador and Deputy Chief of Mission were attending a social gathering in a private home. Without warning, a small group of terrorists managed to break into the home. They opened fire on the Ambassador and DCM, killing them both.

I was asked to sponsor an American visitor from the U.S. Embassy in Tel Aviv during his brief business visit in Khartoum, to welcome him and show him around. The visitor, Robert, had been one of the 49 Americans taken hostage in Iran a few years earlier. They had been taken, he said, at gunpoint by terrorists who overtook the Marines and stormed the embassy.

He told me how their hands were tied and a dark hood kept over their heads. Their captivity lasted many long months, and they never knew from day to day whether they would be released or shot.

Hate mail came onto my desk daily. As I plowed through the stacks of incoming cables and paperwork, the threats seemed to leap off the pages: "We will drink the blood of the Americans. We will drag their bodies through the streets of Khartoum. Their bloody heads will hang from the highest post."

The people who write this stuff do not seem to like us, I thought. What did we ever do to them?

Departing the office after a long workday and returning home was seldom the end of the day's strife. Home repairs frequently awaited my attention. Something was always breaking down. A toilet plugged up with mud, a power failure and spoiled refrigerated food, a broken washing machine, electrical problems. Bugs. Lazy guards.

The guards—some were extremely old—who were to sit at the front gate and protect the property were often stretched out in the yard sleeping. The more audacious ones slept in my chaise lounge on the veranda. Sometimes I would catch them peering into the windows of the house!

The old guards did not speak English. Politely, I tried to gesture that "sleeping in yard no good. Must sit at gate, protect house!" With a pleasant smile, I watched them slowly move back to the gate. But invariably the next day I would return home to find them once again sleeping in my yard.

My efforts to daily deal with the elements at work and at home were gradually wearing thin.

A crew of Sudanese maintenance men—headed by Costa, the chief—were sitting in their truck outside my front gate. They were waiting for me to return home in the embassy shuttle bus so they could attend to yet another maintenance problem inside the house.

The weather was very hot, and it had been a difficult day at work. I looked at Costa and his crew with a blurry eye. Costa was a huge man, a Third Country National from Columbia working at the embassy. He was a pretty decent sort, if a bit macho. He seemed to view me as a marshmallow, one who cried a lot.

I noticed the gate was again unguarded. With Costa and his crew following at my heel, we entered the yard. The very old guard was sleeping peacefully in the shade of a tree. His bare feet—sticking out from under his white galabyia—were propped up on a pillow fetched from my chaise lounge. Sandals lay nearby. A half eaten apple was on his lap.

I stopped short within the yard, Costa stopped abruptly behind me, his crew behind him. We were a silent little group, and for one moment we all stared at the sleeping guard. The guard—possibly sensing our presence—stirred for a moment, slowly waived a fly from his nose, and continued sleeping.

Hell hath no fury like a woman scorned.

Timid politeness and patience flew out the window, or the yard. Infuriated anger replaced my usual helpless, defeatist demeanor—a good sign, I think. With great authority, I lifted an arm and pointed a long finger to the gate. "Out! Out! Get out!" I yelled at him in a very loud voice. "And don't come back!" I could hardly believe my own ears. Even Costa looked at me with a trace of alarm in his eyes!

The old guard awoke with a jolt, looked at me in terror, grabbed his sandals, and ran barefoot out of the yard.

I threw the half eaten apple after him, but missed!

The daily struggles were tedious, wearing me down little by little. I still cried easily, waiting until I was safely at home with Nipper. Like an old soul, Nipper takes over with his concern and caring, trying to protect me from whatever the trouble may be.

It seemed that life in Khartoum had taken over my psyche. It eroded me and swallowed me up. There was no life away from this life—no civilized world out there, and no America. Nipper and I had each other, but often we felt so alone.

This little spot on the globe was all there was.

Friends make all the difference. My new day guard became such a friend. His name was Musa, and life became easier when Musa was assigned to me. He was a young Sudanese Christian with dark smiling eyes and a thick black Afro, and he dressed in tan shirt and pants. Pleasant, dependable and trustworthy, Musa never slept on the job. I liked him.

Musa spoke good English, with an accent. As I came to know him better, I sometimes invited him onto my veranda for some mangos or popcorn, and we would visit.

He told me a little about his family who lived in a small settlement in Southern Sudan. His father was a farmer and his mother a housewife, and he had several brothers and sisters. But job opportunities were scarce and he migrated to Khartoum seeking work.

One Saturday morning I sat with my coffee on the veranda as

Musa came on duty. He had brought his breakfast with him and gave me a sample. It was a tasty Sudanese dish, much like American chile. Not bad.

Musa told me about the strong home-brewed alcohol and offered to bring me a sample, but I declined. Even if I did drink—which I do not—the crude stuff puts hair on the chest, according to some Americans. Of course I knew this was not literally true—I am not that naive—but why take the chance?

Musa did not work nights, and substitute guards were assigned. I did not know them. One evening, without mentioning it, the night guard slipped away for a bite to eat in town, leaving the house unguarded, and an intruder gained entrance to my yard.

I had been sitting in a living room chair reading a book when Nipper began that low growl which tells me someone is approaching. Through a panel of heavy clouded glass on my front door, I observed the shadow of a giant man with a bushy beard, dressed in a long black robe and taiga.

How did this man get through the gate? An icy finger touched the pit of my stomach.

The stranger knocked loudly and began twisting the doorknob. My knees began to shake, but I moved toward the door and asked who he was. He responded, though I could not understand his heavy Arabic.

I reached for my radio and tried to dial the embassy Marine, but static kept me from getting through. Moving back from the door, I retreated to the hallway with Nipper held tightly.

Where is the guard?! My heart was pounding as I waited, hoping the man would leave.

Now he was peering through the cracks of my living room window shutters! From my hiding spot in the hallway, I could see him. He began banging on the window with the butt of a gun, calling to me in angry words.

With that, Nipper broke away from my grip, ran into the living room and literally flung himself against the front door with a loud thump. He was barking in his most ferocious tone. The intruder could not see that Nipper was small and harmless.

Silence followed on the other end of the door. A moment passed. Then, the shadow disappeared. The stranger was gone.

I waited in my hiding place. Nipper had stopped barking and returned to lick my hand.

"Nipper, Nipper, you are my hero," I told him. "If I had to choose between you and Harrison Ford, I would choose you. Who can hold a candle to such fearless loyalty and friendship?"

With that, we went into the kitchen for ice cream and dog biscuits.

It had been a case of mistaken identity, as I later learned. The intruder was looking for the previous occupant of the house, not for me.

Maria was part of my small "staff." She was a young Ethiopian woman who spoke no English, and she came to my house each week to clean. The marble floors throughout the house were a challenge, easily covered with grime from the regular haboobs, but Maria kept them spotless.

The gardener was an old man with a worn, friendly face and no teeth, and he came to tend my yard on Saturday mornings. He and Nipper had quickly bonded, and Nipper followed him around the yard as he worked. I sometimes sat on my veranda with a bowl of fruit and watched.

These Sudanese people—Musa, Maria and the gardener Samir—were my friends. And then, Rita entered my life, as well.

Rita lived just across the road with her parents and housekeeper. She came to my house to visit one day many months after my arrival.

Foreigners are sometimes slow to friendship, never rushing into anything.

She was somewhat Americanized after sixteen years of working at the American Embassy. She had strawberry blond hair and large expressive eyes, and her sense of humor was appealing.

Rita liked color. Bright splashy dresses—especially red—and very high heeled colored shoes. She always had a wrist full of shiny gold bracelets. When I say gold, I mean the good stuff gold. The 24k gold. Rita was a working woman of 36, and had never been married. She spent much of her money on gold.

I thought of how, by contrast, in fashion-minded Paris the French women wear a lot of black—black shoes, black stockings, black dress, black coat—and very little jewelry.

Women are naturally curious about the lifestyles of other women, especially when our cultures are so different from each other. I was to learn much from Rita about the ways of women in the Sudan and neighboring countries such as Ethiopia.

Across the road, I often saw her mother sitting on the veranda as she crocheted, or the housekeeper shaking out rugs or sweeping the walkway. Neither parent spoke English, nor did the housekeeper. But as I began visiting their house, we found our own ways of communicating.

Their house had large rooms with high ceilings, and in the immense kitchen—a real cook's delight—the housekeeper could often be found preparing exotic dishes. Rita and I liked to sit and help—peeling potatoes or cutting up strawberries—while we talked and snacked.

Traditionally, in Sudan, the role of an unmarried daughter is to take care of her aging parents, forgetting about marriage and children of her own. It is her duty, it is expected, and not to be questioned or resented.

But Rita did resent this expectation, although she loved her parents. Her sister was married and lived in Italy; her brother lived in his own home in Khartoum. As the youngest, the responsibility fell to her.

It was her dream to use her green card and relocate to the United States, and it seemed an impossible dream. Her parents had a strong hold on her. It would take a lot of courage for a woman in her situation to pull off such a major move.

Rita's father died unexpectedly one night in his sleep. Since embalming is not practiced in Khartoum, burial must take place quickly, within twenty four hours. His body was placed in a traditional bag and buried in a simple gravesite.

On the evening of his death, a memorial gathering took place in their home. I walked across the road to pay my respects and condolences. In their living room, a dozen or so chairs were arranged in a circle around the widow, who was dressed entirely in black and sat quietly twisting a handkerchief.

The room was still. I walked over to Rita's mother and took her hand, expressing my sympathy to her. Suddenly, she burst out crying, howling and wailing loudly! I was alarmed, and quickly held her for a moment trying to comfort her. Then, I let her go and took a chair with the others. At once, she became quiet again.

Family and friends slowly arrived. With each arrival, I noticed that the widow again went through the same loud howling expressions of grief. It seemed to be a ritual expected of her.

Finally, the chairs were all filled, and the doorbell rang no longer. We all sat quietly with the widow for about two hours. Nobody spoke.

This was the traditional observance of a widow grieving.

Christmas season in Khartoum came and went and was unremarkable. Since Moslems do not acknowledge Christmas, the shops held almost nothing in the way of décor. The city was devoid of Christmas cheer.

A small scrawny floor plant in my living room would serve as a Christmas tree, I decided. I placed it on an end table, tied ribbons on it, and called it my Charlie Brown Christmas tree.

At the American PX, shelves were almost bare. I spoke with the clerk who told me they were waiting for a late shipment from the U.S. She said their small supply of canned pumpkin mix was so old that a few cans had actually exploded!

When the Christmas shipment arrived a few days before Christmas, each American family was rationed a one pound bag of flour and small assortment of ingredients.

As for incoming Christmas presents from the U.S., all of my gifts were stolen. Thieves were thick at the port of entry. Scoundrels!

Christmas Day itself arrived, my first Christmas away from

home in the U.S. I was invited to a Christmas buffet at the home of an American. It was pleasant enough, but it was not home.

Omdurman, North Khartoum

One would never know—in visiting a souk—that there was a shortage of food in Sudan.

These open markets took place on big stretches of dusty fields, under the hot African sun, the largest of which was held in nearby Omdurman. For me, the souks held an element of exotic festivity.

A conglomeration of tents and sheds serving as shops, the souk is a dirty, bustling, noisy place with camels bellowing, chickens squawking in their cages, vendors calling out to come see their wares. The air is thick with the scent of incense, manure, and Turkish coffee brewing from a stall.

As I meandered through the stalls, little children, dirty and ragged, tugged at my shirt. They wanted to act as my guide for a small piece of change. Shoppers dressed variously in western wear or traditional galabiyahs and strolled around the open dirt fields and stalls, bargaining with vendors. I began to bargain, also; the vendors expect it, said my American colleagues.

A small group of exotic women were often seen at the souk. They followed a few steps behind their shared husband. Culturally, they are subservient to him and not allowed to walk by his side. Expensive gold bracelets adorned their wrists, and they dressed in black robes from head to toe. Dark veils covered their faces, all but their eyes, as they moved among the sheds of the souk.

Tropical fruits and vegetables were plentiful and could be purchased cheaply. Burlap bags filled with beans, rice, dates and nuts were stacked on the dirt floors inside and outside the shops. Eggs, cheeses, unleavened bread—all are available and plentiful.

The unleavened bread is very tasty, but quickly becomes stale. Three times daily these breads are taken from ovens. Warm and crusty, I spread them with cheeses or butter. Not bad!

Slabs of meat hung from hooks in the butcher shed, buzzing with flies. The steaks are tender and delicious, and quite safe if they're carefully processed.

It is always fun to visit the African craft shops. The goods are generally stashed on shelves or the floor in no order, but this intrigued me much like a scavenger hunt. I enjoyed browsing among the dusty piles of brass incense burners or opium pipes, African busts of black ebony, oriental rugs, gold and ivory. Large colorful straw handbags and other decorative basketry from Eritrea could be bought for a pittance.

In 1985, ivory was available and cheap. It had not yet been banned, following the outrage over poaching of elephants. The ivory was carved into jewelry and miniature animals, or purchased as a large tusk.

Some shopkeepers—those selling rugs or incense burners—offer freshly brewed Turkish coffee to shoppers. The thick black syrupy stuff is served in a tiny cup with a handle so small it is impossible to get my finger through it.

This social coffee interlude with the Sudanese shopkeeper was pleasant. Our conversations might be in broken English on their part or pathetic Arabic on my part, or body language gestures.

Typically, we simply sat together—the shopkeeper and I—sipping our coffee and smiling at each other. I always made a small purchase, and was remembered when I returned.

There were few pleasure excursions in Khartoum, but a boat trip down the Nile was one I enjoyed. The water of the Nile is unsafe to drink or swim in, but still on the distant shore we see children bathing. When our boat reaches the point where the Blue Nile meets the White Nile, I expect to see a change in color. But of course all is grey.

As the boat moves along the Nile River, the primitive way of life is going about its business on the distant water's edge. Women in their long toabs are scrubbing clothing on the stones in the water. Long canoes moor along the shore.

I see a few small shack houses, and a donkey or mule in the distance carrying a bundle of goods on its back. An occasional naked child is seen at play. But otherwise, the shores are deserted.

Then, in the far distance of the Nile, immense, lavish mansions of the very rich suddenly appear, an indication of the split social class of rich and poor in the Sudan.

A few public restaurants are worth mentioning. I like the Chinese restaurant, and on rare occasions would have dinner there. A real treat. The Chinese restaurant was bombed early one morning just before I awoke. That was the end of my favorite restaurant.

It was a terrifying explosion to wake up to—certainly unlike your soothing wakeup call—and occurred just minutes before the morning call to prayer.

The Grand Hotel was a favorite of many and had an exotic flair, a foreign feeling about it. The tall arched entryways, enormous clay pots with bougainvillea climbing up the walls, stone steps leading to an open pavilion—yes, I would give it a four star.

On the pavilion of the Grand hotel, friends and I occasionally sat at small outside tables to sip a delicious "citrus" and watch the hustle and bustle. Arab businessmen scurry in and out of the hotel, up and down the pavilion steps, their white or colorful robes flowing behind them. They may carry a briefcase. They may be followed by a cluster of wives.

Mara was a young Sudanese doctor whom I met, quite by accident. She worked at an orphanage for Moslem babies, and invited me to join her one evening on her rounds.

The orphanage was small, a long building on the outskirts of Khartoum, sparsely equipped and understaffed. Inside were a few rows of makeshift cribs with dozens of orphan babies. They had runny noses, skin diseases, diaper rash, and malnutrition. Many were crying, or I should say whimpering. Not the spunky cry of a healthy baby.

I began donating time to the orphanage. My responsibilities included holding the bottles for the babies and snuggling them in my arms. Had any ever known the love of a mother? I changed their diapers, rubbed cream into their little bodies, or just held them on my lap to talk and play.

Most of the babies were malnourished or on the brink of starvation. One evening as I sat on a bench with a sleeping baby on my lap, a boy of three months old was brought into the orphanage by a nurse. He had been abandoned and was severely malnourished.

As I looked at his little skeleton face with sunken eyes, I was shocked. What I saw was not a baby's face, but that of a very old man, too weak to even cry. Within three days, he was dead. It was sad news to me, but a fairly common outcome for many of the babies.

Mara brought a sick little boy home one day to nurse him back to health. He was skinny and whining, but in Mara's care he began to blossom into a plump, beautiful, happy child with large brown eyes. She wanted to adopt him, but she was unmarried and a Christian and the boy was Moslem.

While it took three years of effort, Mara won. Sami became her little Moslem son.

I had little interest at the time in a bible study group, per se. Still, a study group—a chance to mingle socially with other women who spoke English—presented itself, and I decided to join for the social benefits.

The group was small, only about five other women, and each week we met at someone's house. I began to look forward to these weekly gatherings. Both the studies and the fellowship with the other women helped me to deal with the harsh living conditions of Khartoum.

Two women from a Mission led the small group. Sadie had been a missionary with her husband in Khartoum for thirty years and Marianne was a volunteer from the Church of Scotland. She worked in the kitchen of the Mission.

Marianne became especially endearing to me, a large friendly Scottish woman whose husband had died at sea in a fishing accident in northern Scotland. Her hugely giving nature was fulfilled by her volunteer work.

I was invited to the Mission, and began to go when I could. There, the gardens were lovely with wild flowers and small benches to sit on and meditate. Wind chimes hung from a tree branch, tinkling in the breeze. Occasionally, I saw an old man working in the garden or a maid sweeping the walkway, and they were always friendly.

The main house resembled a Spanish hacienda. Thick walls kept the large old rooms cool. A gigantic living room was filled with comfortable furniture, and a baby grand piano at the walled bookcases often filled the room with music.

In the evenings, missionaries, workers, and guests often gathered around the piano to sing or listen to a concert. Small groups of people played games in a corner of the room, or simply sat and visited.

Marianne was usually found in the kitchen, I would guess the next most popular room after the living room. The kitchen always smelled good and the kitchen workers were a jolly and busy bunch, peeling potatoes, stirring large kettles over the stoves, baking homemade pies, talking and laughing among themselves as they worked.

On the second floor, Marianne's room was modest and sparse with only a bed, one small wooden table and straight chair, and a single ornament—a wooden cross—hanging over the bed. I was impressed by this simplicity, as I compared it to my own home with its artwork and accessories.

When I departed Khartoum a few years later, Marianne and I exchanged letters for awhile. She invited me to visit her in Scotland, and I looked forward to the day when I could do that. I thought of the fun of walking along the sea with her while we reminisced about the piano gatherings of that great old Mission.

The idea of a foreign dentist did not appeal to me. I had visions of pliers and crude drills. But dental work needed to be done, and I had no choice.

A Sudanese dentist is simply wired together different from any dentist I had previously known. That's all there is to it. Of course, I base this observation entirely on Dr. Kaboob.

Dr. Kaboob was recommended to me as one of the few well trained dentists available, so I arranged for a series of evening appointments. He only worked evenings, when he worked, that is.

Kaboob was a tall man with straggly hair, and seemed eccentric. Highly unpredictable. His dental clinic was small, just a room and a half located on the second floor of a dark and dilapidated building in downtown Khartoum.

An embassy driver routinely drove me to the clinic twice each week, left me, and returned two hours later to drive me home. Often the two hours were wasted because Dr. Kaboob did not show up. But even though his presence was never certain, I had to take my chances.

It was always the same. In the dark evening I climbed up the rickety wooden stairs to the second floor. The door to his clinic was always unlocked. There was no receptionist. I let myself in, and frequently sat alone in the waiting room. Sometimes another patient arrived.

Within the dismal room, a few chairs from the 1950's were placed here and there, and a lone picture hung crookedly on a wall. The blurred television was always turned on, and the same young veiled woman stared out from the tube as she reported—in a no-nonsense fashion—the evening news in Arabic. There was none of the horseplay and chitchat found with U.S. news reporters. The Sudanese woman stared stiffly out at the viewing public and reported the news. Period.

In a typical dental appointment, the minutes ticked slowly by— half an hour, an hour, then two hours—with neither hide nor straggly hair of Dr. Kaboob. I read. I stared unseeingly at the blurred TV screen. I snoozed. I stood and stretched my legs. Finally I walked out, and hoped for better luck next time.

When Kaboob did show up, he would burst noisily into the waiting room, letting the door bang shut behind him. With his long legs, it took only three strides for him to cross the room as he waived me into the dental chair.

He spoke broken English, but Dr. Kaboob seldom actually talked to me. He did talk often to himself or whistle softly under his breath. Once in full swing, Kaboob took his work very seriously. He proved to be a skilled dentist, and my teeth were eventually fixed.

I really never doubted you, Dr. Kaboob. Did I?

Khartoum was experiencing one of its worst water shortages. There was simply no water, and bottled water did not exist. Plenty of Coka Cola, but no water.

The Americans each had an emergency water tank, as I did. During this most severe drought, I used water from my tank sparingly to brush my teeth and hand bathe, but soon had to abandon those luxuries and preserve the water strictly for drinking.

The weather was exceedingly hot, and the dry spell continued for well over a week. Toilets could not be flushed, posing a sanitation threat. Bathing was all but abolished. Worry began to mount among us that our emergency tanks would soon be depleted for even drinking. I wondered how the Sudanese were managing, since most did not have a supply of emergency water.

On the momentous day when water was expected to be restored

throughout the city, my emergency tank had only one gallon of water left!

The important announcement was made to us at the embassy on Friday morning with great aplomb by an embassy official. The end of the water shortage was truly a VIA (Very Important Announcement).

All day long, embassy people looked forward to going home and having a long, refreshing bath or shower. Some of us let our imagination go wild as we dreamed about the upcoming evening, soaking in a hot bath with bath salts perhaps, and candles. It would be a very special celebration in the tub. Everyone was in a good mood, cracking jokes.

As the shuttle bus pulled up in front of my house at the end of that day, I hurried inside. Nipper and I had our usual homecoming, and then I headed straight for the bathroom. As I ran through the hallway, I made a mental note of where my bubble bath was stored. Oh dear God, what a delightful thought.

Sitting on the edge of the tub, I turned on the faucet. Nothing happened, but I held my breath and waited. Then, slowly, a gurgling coughing noise came from within the faucet, followed by a trickle of brown water.

I checked everything once again. The plug was in place. The faucet was turned fully open. I continued to wait patiently. Half an hour later, the tub had only half a foot of water. It was muddy water and unfit to bathe in. It would be yet another day before the water cleared up. My disappointment was great.

The next day I returned to the tub. On bended knees and holding my breath again, I reached for the faucet and turned it on. Water began to trickle into the tub, and slowly became a mild flow. Within ten minutes, the tub was filled with clear hot water.

Beside myself with joy, I poured in scented bubble bath and lit some candles. Off came my clothes. I flung them quickly into a heap, picked up Nipper and climbed into the wonderful sweet smelling water. We soaked in the lovely bath for well over an hour.

Water. Liquid gold. I'll never take water for granted again. I promise.

5
Terrorism and Mob Madness

Bomb threats to the embassy were frequent and almost always made by anonymous telephone callers. Americans each had a list of questions to ask should we receive such a call. I kept mine tucked beneath the phone on my desk.

Personally, I did not expect such a caller to politely answer my questions. "What is your name, sir? Abu who? Your address? Do you have a telephone number? And the nature of your call? Could you repeat? I see. Exactly where did you plant the bomb? When may we expect it to go off?"

I did receive a threat call once. The voice was thick with accent, and I could barely understand him. He made his announcement and hung up before I could ask his name.

Threats are immediately reported to the embassy's Regional Security Office. Then, safes are locked and everybody exits the embassy quickly while a bomb squad searches the building. Usually a bomb is not found.

Something was going on. Why else would that special terrorist task force from the States be here? Did it have anything to do with the ongoing conflicts with Qadhafi, or the impending U.S. attack on Tripoli? We all knew that terrorists lived in the vicinity, such as Abu Nudal who had set up his underground headquarters in Khartoum.

It was April of 1986, my eighth month in Khartoum. The task force was flown in from the Defense Department in Washington to give embassy people intensive training. The training focused on how to protect ourselves if we're attacked or taken as hostages, and the three days of training were held outside on the banks of the Nile River.

Groups of us sat in the grass and listened to the instructors. We practiced what we were being taught, playing out hypothetical terrorist scenarios. We were shown how to use various guns and rifles, how to disentangle ourselves from a terrorist's hold, how to make split second escapes.

While the training was serious, we saw it as a reprieve from embassy work. We enjoyed our little tommy gun jokes and laughed at some of the Mafia-like strategies. We really did not realize the danger just days ahead.

John Garang, a black rebel leader fighting in South Africa with the Sudanese People's Liberation Army (SPLA), was blocking U.S. planes from delivering food packages to the starving people there. The planes were being detained by Garang and his guerrillas. It was a problem, and a story.

A lone independent female journalist from the U.S. came to Khartoum to seek an interview with Garang for a story. The journalist spent many days at the embassy while she waited for permission from Garang for the interview. I came to know her briefly, and on the evening when Garang's telegram was finally expected I was having dinner with her at her hotel.

We ate in the small restaurant of the hotel, a dilapidated musty smelling place in downtown Khartoum. After dinner, we sat together in the shabby lobby waiting for that very important telegram.

The telegram came, and she was off—a dangerous venture, to be sure, for an American woman alone. She climbed aboard the small aircraft—excited as I suppose only a journalist can be who is about to attain a good story. But she was not heard from again by any of us.

One of the instructors from the special task force had stayed behind in Khartoum for a few extra days after the training ended. His name was Mike, and he asked me out one evening before he left. Who was I to say No? Dates and social outings were rare.

We went to the Chinese restaurant, still intact, the nicest of the few restaurants available. It felt good to be with Mike for a few hours, and I found myself relaxing and laughing with him. He was enjoyable company.

When we left the restaurant a few hours later, it was dark outside. The scarcity of streetlights made Khartoum a dark city at night. Mike was driving, and as he turned off a main road he realized he'd made a wrong turn.

Too late, we found ourselves in a large open field in the midst of a crowd of Sudanese men. They seemed to be holding a public meeting of some kind, their white galabiyahs glowing in the moonlight.

Mike shifted gears and tried to turn the car around, but it was stuck in a deep pothole of mud. The wheels were skidding and taking us nowhere.

Diplomatic license plates on our car identified us as Americans, and gradually the crowd began to notice us. We locked our doors and windows, and Mike's attempts to get out of the pothole became more frantic.

The people were moving in our direction. They were becoming aggressive and boisterous. Mob madness began to take over as they approached our car, shouting and pressing their faces against the windows. I was terrified.

The clutch was jammed, and Mike could not get us out of the pothole. By now, the mob was pounding on the doors and windows, jumping on the roof, and trying to overturn the car.

A claustrophobic anxiety arose within me as I sat inside the locked car and felt the mobs press around us. This became a phobia, and has remained with me over the years.

Inadvertently, the banging of the car wiggled it out of the pothole enough for Mike to regain control. He spun the car around and stepped on the gas, driving at breakneck speed toward the main road. I looked out the rear window and saw a man actually clinging—momentarily—to the rear fender, and a few from the mob were running after us.

For about five minutes, we rode in relieved silence as Mike made his way through the main streets of the city. But then, almost simultaneously, we turned and looked at each other and burst out laughing. But it was a kind of nervous, relieved, unfunny laughter.

U.S. diplomatic license plates—identifying us as Americans—were removed from American cars after this and other incidents.

The pounding on my front door woke me, and as I looked at my clock I saw it was only five fifteen. I got up and hurried to answer the door.

An embassy van was parked at the gate, and a Marine stood at my door. "There was a terrorist attack last night," he said. "Stay in your house. Do not plan to go to work today. Keep your windows and doors locked. The ambassador will be calling us on our radio at a certain hour to give us a briefing. Be there at your radio."

When the appointed hour arrived, I had my radio turned on and heard the voice of our ambassador. He explained to all of us that one of our communicators working the evening shift last night had been shot in the head by terrorists as he made his way home.

The communicator had left the embassy around 9:30, got in his car, and began to slowly drive home, unaware of a car following him. As he drove through the poorly lit and almost deserted streets, the car following him suddenly sped forward and pulled up alongside him.

There were three men in the other car. Hanging out of a window, one man had a gun aimed at the communicator and shot five bullets at his head, causing his car to swerve and hit a tree. The terrorists fled.

A witness to the incident called the police. The communicator was in critical condition but still alive. He was taken to a local hospital, then airlifted by U.S. military plane to our medical facilities in Wiesbaden, Germany.

A similar attack, said our ambassador, had been carried out simultaneously on a communicator at the U.S. Embassy in Jeddah, but that incident caused less serious damage.

It would be many months before we received word on the communicator's condition. Most of the bullets, we later learned, lodged between his skull and the skin of the skull, but one bullet went deeper and caused paralysis. For a few years he was disabled, but eventually recovered and returned to work.

I turned off my radio the morning after the attack, and sat dumbfounded. The communicator was a friend, and his life hung by a thread. I myself felt in danger, and longed to cross the street and stay with Rita. But I could not, and for over two days Nipper and I stayed alone in the locked house.

An emergency evacuation plan was being drawn up by the State Department. Too many dangers were surfacing, and lives were on the line. The evacuation would initially involve over 300 nonessential people and take place on two separate nights.

In the meantime, we continued to stay in our homes and wait for the next call from our ambassador. He updated us on the evacuation plans and, before hanging up, told us when to expect his next call.

Humor is good medicine, relieving tension and fear. Each time the ambassador called, invariably there would be one American who missed the first part of the call, obliging the ambassador to repeat. Finally, the ambassador ended his calls by saying, "Be there next time, so I don't have to repeat."

With the next call, the ambassador barely finished giving us a lengthy update when—I couldn't believe my ears—a voice came over the radio from an American saying, "Ambassador, I didn't hear the first part of your message. Will you repeat it?" Silence followed on the radio.

The exasperated ambassador lost his temper and began to give the American a very good tongue lashing. But before he could finish, the American blurted out, "Just kidding, Ambassador! Just kidding! I heard every word!"

Someone on the radio began to giggle, then another. Soon we were all laughing, even the ambassador. Tension from the last few days was broken as we all had a good laugh.

The evening of the first evacuation of Americans had arrived. A thousand stars filled the desert sky in the dead of the night as an embassy colleague and I quietly made our way to the carefully selected location—an isolated 'safehouse'—outside of the city.

We pulled up in front of the safehouse. I could see several Marines, barely discernable as they surrounded the house and sat on the roof. They held their rifles in an alert position as they quietly watched and waited.

Tables were set up inside and we laid out the necessary paperwork—passports, Visa's, health certificates—which the evacuees would need. The house smelled of coffee brewing in large urns, and a handful of my colleagues were quietly working and speaking together in low voices. The atmosphere was thick with tension and stress.

As we worked, an embassy "caravan" of about ten cars was making its rounds in the city, picking up the American evacuees at their homes. They were almost entirely women, children, and USAID employees.

The caravan was expected at the safehouse by midnight, but the hour came and passed without their arrival.

We could hear the hum of the military plane circling overhead, waiting for the appointed moment. For security reasons, it could not land until the evacuees were ready to depart.

One o'clock, and no caravan. What was the holdup? None of us inside the safehouse were speaking now. The lights were dimmed, and all was quiet as we waited.

By one thirty, we finally saw the tiny caravan in the distance slowly snake its way toward us. I stood near a window and watched, fascinated, as the tiny line of dark cars without headlights moved cautiously through the desert.

Moments later, the caravan stopped just outside the front door. Motors were turned off, and for a split second the night was deadly silent.

Then, suddenly, the Marines surrounded the cars, opened doors, and rushed the tired, tense women and children into the house. Some children were crying, sensing the unease of their parents. Nobody spoke.

We greeted the people, offered them coffee, and quickly gave them a few instructions along with their paperwork. The entire process took less than fifteen minutes.

The pilot in the plane above us was signaled and immediately landed at the front door—much like a helicopter. Its doors were pushed open, and the Marines quickly escorted each evacuee to the plane, protectively covering them with their arms.

The doors closed, the plane lifted up into the sky, and it was over.

I lingered by the window and watched the plane disappear into the night. For awhile, I simply stood there with my thoughts and allowed the aftermath of stillness to wash through me.

Interrupting my thoughts, someone asked if I would like to sleep over at the safehouse or be given a ride home? I preferred to go home. Once in the car, the driver told me sharply to get down and away from the window! We were being watched, he said.

And so, we drove in silence as I crouched under the window, my arms folded over my head and my stomach churning.

The second evacuation two nights later took place in much the same manner. By now, over 300 Americans had departed Khartoum.

But the State Department wanted more Americans out. We were on a high danger alert, and the embassy was to be reduced temporarily to a skeleton crew. Along with a number of other Americans, my name now was on the list for yet a third evacuation.

The first two groups of evacuees had little notice and departed quickly in a military plane. They were not expected to return. But those of us in the third evacuation had a few days to prepare, and most of us were expected to return as soon as conditions were reasonably safe.

The military planes have restrictions—a limit of one small suitcase, for example, and no pets. No pets. This I seriously worried about. I could not possibly leave Nipper behind. It was out of the question.

I was expressing my concern about Nipper to a colleague. Far from being reassuring, she told me a disturbing story.

The story concerned an embassy terrorist evacuation where a woman evacuee—I'll call her Mary—arrived at the military plane with her small dog. Mary was told she could not take the dog, but she refused to leave without him. Finally, because of the urgency of the situation, the dog was pulled away from her and shot! Mary was forced into the plane for departure and, once inside, she became hysterical.

Oh, that sounds too brutal to be true. Still, the story stayed in my mind.

By a stroke of luck, I was evacuated on a commercial airline, with Nipper. Whoever had drawn up my Orders at the embassy made a second lovely mistake on my behalf. Rather than sending us to

Kenya—the site of most evacuees—we were being sent temporarily home to Arizona.

The long journey from Khartoum to the U.S. and then across the States to Arizona involves over 24 hours of travel. But again the journey was broken by a stopover in Paris.

It was April, the chestnut trees were almost in full bloom, the air was fresh, and the sun was shining. But delayed trauma had surfaced within me much as it may with a soldier returning from the battlefield. I found I wanted only to sleep, and for a few days did little else.

Gradually, fortitude returned and we began to venture out. It felt good to be in Paris again. I ate escargots en pots de chamber, snails baked in small earthenware crocks, took naps, and spent evenings in my room at the Hotel du Quai Voltaire, reading books by Virginia Wolf.

Back on the plane several days later, we flew over the great dark mass of the Atlantic Ocean. Little white caps sparkled from the bright sunshine on the ocean below and I could see an occasional ship, tiny as a speck of dust.

When we landed at Kennedy Airport, bouncing to a stop on American soil, my patriotic love surfaced. Ah, oui . . . America. Just the idea of being home felt good.

In New York, we changed planes to a small domestic flight to cross the States. The small plane is noticeably less comfortable, the air pockets and turbulence more easily felt than the large smooth international jet.

Arizona's infinite stretch of rugged desert and mountains marked the beginning of the end of the journey, and an hour later the distant lights of Phoenix could be seen like a blanket of glittering jewels in the night. Tiny cars became visible on the roads below.

The brightly lit Sun Devil Stadium was alive with the activity of a ball game in progress. We were now flying just over the bleachers filled with baseball fans. Vendors were selling hot dogs. The crowd was shouting!

I could almost hear John Denver singing—"Hey, its good to be back home again!"

Our visit in Arizona was short, but soooooo sweet.

I returned to Washington and for two months worked temporarily in the State Department. Then, I was asked if I would be willing to return to Khartoum. "The skeleton crew there was badly in need of help," they told me. "I was not obligated. There would be other—more favorable—options for me," they added. "I was needed in Khartoum, but feel free to say no."

I certainly was not a martyr, but I said yes. Was I crazy?

Despite all, it had seemed important to me that I return to Khartoum and complete my original 2-year assignment. I wanted to prove to myself that I could do this. Yes, I did say yes.

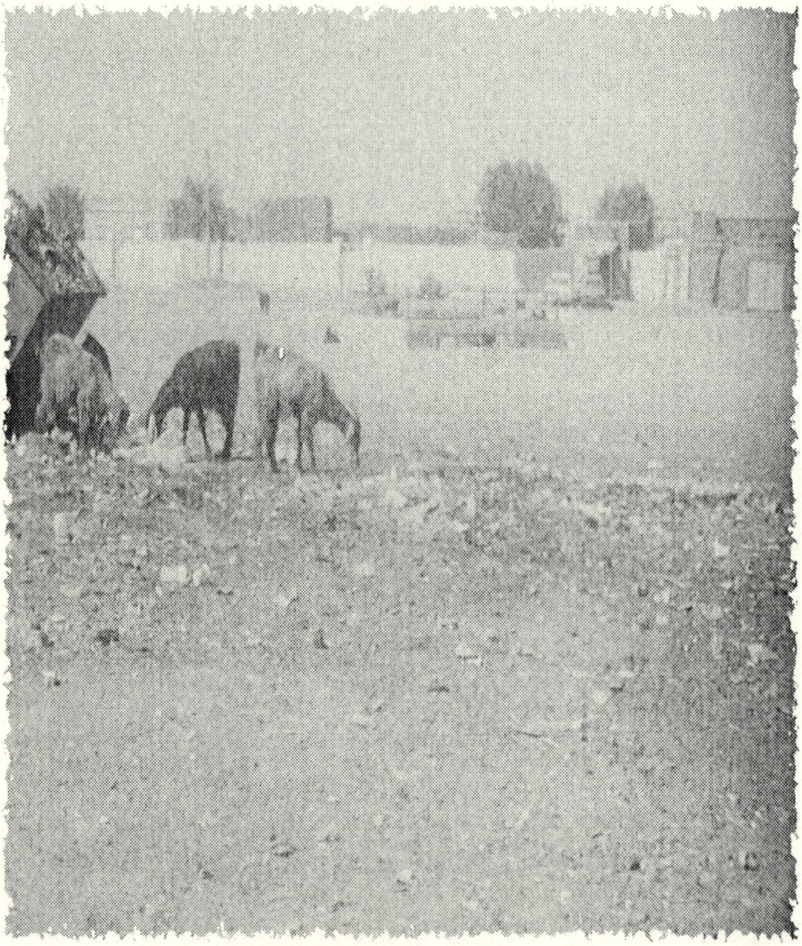

6
A Tougher Hide and a Softer Heart

From somewhere, I could hear the soft haunting music from the soundtrack of "Brigadoon" as I struggled to open my eyes.

Nipper and I had returned to Khartoum the previous night, and friends met us at the airport. Janet was a favorite colleague, and had brought us to her home to spend the night before returning us to our own house. We stayed up until dawn on her veranda, talking. She brought me up to date on the news.

It felt surprisingly good to be back in my own house later, with my own familiar belongings and privacy. Maria had been in to clean, and the floors were sparkling. Fresh flowers had been placed in a jar—wherever did she find them?

I was happy to see Rita and Musa again. The separation and the circumstances under which I left made me realize how much their friendship meant.

Living conditions were as harsh as ever, but I had acquired a tougher hide. My coping skills had improved, and I knew now what to expect and not to expect in Khartoum. With a greater sense of my own fortitude, I was less inclined to overlook any adventure or pleasure a day may bring.

At the embassy, the skeleton crew made for an especially quiet atmosphere. There was only one other secretary, and together we shared the workload normally handled by six. For months, I did little but work, work, work.

I was also making money, money, money. Fifty percent danger pay, twenty-five percent hardship post differential, ten percent Sunday differential (Moslem countries work on Sundays, and, as such, the embassy did as well) and all that overtime. I stashed my money like a little scrooge, and eventually I was debt free.

Within six months of my return, security conditions had improved and it was determined to be safe enough for the return of other Americans. The workload eased, and the embassy gradually returned to normal.

(This embassy would close altogether several years later, along with a number of other small U.S. posts across the globe.)

In my sleep, I vaguely heard it throughout the night, but now I was wide awake and heard it clearly. An animal was crying from the street.

It was Sunday morning. I went outside to where the night guard was sitting. Musa had not yet arrived. There in the dirt road, a large dog lay with a broken leg, and he was crying. "He had been run over by a car," said the guard. "But why have you let the poor dog lay there and suffer all night?" He only looked at me, and could not answer.

There was no point discussing the dog. The guard could not understand the empathy I felt for the animal. Maybe it was a cultural thing. I got in touch with the veterinarian who came and gave the dog a shot to put him to sleep. There was no way to save him, the vet told me.

A different, yet similar, experience occurred one morning as I sat in an embassy van with some Americans. We were on our way to a shopping excursion in the city. I sat gazing out from my window when a completely naked man ran alongside the van screaming at us. Nobody in the street paid any attention to him. Apparently mentally ill, he did not evoke the slightest interest from others.

I had developed a soft spot in my heart for the Sudanese people, a fondness of their simple ways and smiling faces. But could I ever really relate to a life such as what I am seeing in Khartoum? Is it possible to stretch the limits of my perceptibility and grasp their position, feel their hunger, know the bleak and harsh conditions they live with every day? Maybe if I were born into it, I thought.

If it is the only way of life one knows, maybe it is not as harsh as it appears. I considered this. Someone had said, "I didn't know I was poor because we were all poor."

Harsh reality came close one day when my colleague fell sick. He went to the embassy clinic, and the nurse mistakenly treated him for flu. In fact, John had both malaria and hepatitis! Malaria in the early stages can resemble the flu. Its progress is swift, and by evening he was in a coma.

John was flown by military plane to the American Hospital in Weisbaden where he remained in a coma for months. A priest who had accompanied him gave John his last rites, as he was not expected to live. His parents also flew to Weisbaden to be with him.

With a long year of treatment, John did recover and returned to work on a new assignment.

Dr. Ahmed was a veterinarian who had received his training in East Germany and he had a good reputation. He was a dark attractive Sudanese man who dressed in a tan uniform. His English was heavily accented. He was polite, and quite dependable.

Poisonous ticks are widespread in Khartoum and when Nipper fell seriously ill with the deadly tick fever, it was Dr. Ahmed I turned to.

Because of the scarcity of telephones, it was customary to contact Dr. Ahmed by delivering a written message to a small office location. Rita delivered the message while I waited at home and hoped for a quick response.

Within an hour, Dr. Ahmed was at my house and quickly gave Nipper a sedative. With Nipper lying between us—his head on Dr. Ahmed's lap and his rear end on mine—we sat quietly together trying not to bump each other's knees as we pulled out dozens of ticks with our tweezers. The ticks were placed in a bowl of water which is one of the few ways to kill them.

Finally, the doctor soaked Nipper in a solution, dried him, and gave him medicine. He told me that all we can do now is wait and watch. The next fourteen days would tell if Nipper survives, he told me.

Nipper slept a lot, and the days slowly passed. He began to show signs of improvement, and then made a full recovery. But Dr. Ahmed warned me that since he had tick fever once, he is susceptible to getting it again.

After Nipper's recovery, I made arrangements to have my house and yard fumigated. The fumigation used is so strong that all living things must be removed for about 10 hours during the process.

I made my arrangements. Nipper and my plants would stay at Rita's house during the fumigation while we were at work.

But Rita's mother apparently did not really understand the situation and left Nipper to play in her yard all day. Her yard was filled with ticks.

That evening I returned home from work. Nipper was waiting at the gate for our shuttle bus, happily wagging his tail when he saw me. I took one look at him, and was horrified! His little body was covered with ticks, from his eyelids and ears to his tail.

Rita apologized profusely for her mother's mistake. She got in her car and drove off to leave another message for Dr. Ahmed to come immediately.

I sat on my veranda with a lump in my throat as I waited for the vet's visit. Nipper lay on my lap and I again pulled the ticks off with tweezers and placed them in a bowl of water.

How can he possibly survive this and not get the tick fever again? We were lucky once, but again? Tears rolled down my cheeks and fell into the water bowl.

It was getting dark out when the front gate to my yard finally opened and Dr. Ahmed walked in carrying his medical bag. I was so relieved to see him that I hurried to greet him and unthinkingly gave him a hug. This was not something a woman should do to an Arab man, I later learned. I had innocently sent the wrong signal to Dr. Ahmed.

After Nipper became drowsy from the sedative, we laid him again between us on our laps and began pulling the ticks off with the tweezers. Why do I always get the tail end, I wondered?

A few hours later the ticks were removed, a solution applied, and Nipper was tucked lovingly into a soft bed. My heart was really, really heavy that evening. There would be the usual waiting period before I would know whether he was out of danger.

Before departing for the evening, Dr. Ahmed decided to collect from me what he thought I was earlier offering him! His sudden aggressive pass took me off guard. For an awkward few moments I tried to politely turn him away without offending him. But this only seemed to excite him more. Surely my resistance was only part of the game, part of the fun, he must have thought.

Polite was not working, so I became firm and rude. With that, Dr. Ahmed recovered his composure and left my house, with nothing but his medical bag.

Nipper did survive once again, and the tick fever did not return. I had learned some important lessons from this experience with poisonous insects. I became more aware, as well, and reticent in the presence of foreign men.

Then, too, as my grandmother used to say, "always carry a hat pin."

Sudanese social gatherings, as with most countries, centered around food and drink.

On a pleasant autumn evening, I had joined Rita and her Arabic friends around a very long crude table outside in the immense gardens of a friend's home. The table was filled with food. There were platters of meat and Arabic specialties, home baked breads stuffed with minced lamb, large olives, odd flavored vegetable dishes.

As in Europe, people lingered for hours around the feast table. They visited, they laughed, they casually snacked on this and that. Always, there was that home brewed fire water and conversations become louder as the evening wore on.

Since many Sudanese do not speak English, such social gatherings are awkward for me. I do not know what the others are saying or laughing about. Still, once in awhile I would go—just out of curiosity.

Rita's dream to relocate to the U.S. was eventually to come true, just months after I departed Khartoum. She wrote to me about it.

In her letter, Rita told me that Sami was an Egyptian hairdresser friend who had been working in Cairo and had returned to Khartoum. Together, they made a plan. They would utilize each other's assets and get married—for convenience only—and then go together to the United States. Rita had the green card and Sami had friends living in Chicago who were hairdressers. They had offered him a position in their shop.

Following their wedding and small celebration at home in Khartoum, Sami and Rita departed for the airport for "a honeymoon" in the U.S. They had told nobody about their plans to remain there, and not return to Khartoum. If they had, her family would have prevented it. It was very hard to leave her family in such a manner.

Sami and Rita settled in Chicago where he began working with his friends as a hairdresser. He spoke no English, but began to study the language.

Although staying together after they were settled in the U.S. was not part of the original plan, Sami and Rita—and their three cats—became a family. They had, she told me, fallen in love!

Years later, I was in Illinois visiting my mother who lived just outside of Chicago. Rita and I decided to meet in front of Marshall Fields Department Store in Chicago's downtown Loop.

I was full of anticipation as I took an "L" downtown, and wondered how this friend of mine from that backward life in Africa was faring in the big city of Chicago, USA.

She stood there waiting for me on the corner—not yet seeing me—and as I walked toward her I noticed how she had become a plump, happy faced woman. Her smile and large friendly eyes were the same as ever. We walked—arm in arm—into Marshall Fields' coffee shop for a happy reunion.

Serving at a hardship post usually entitles one to an R&R—a rest and relaxation getaway. Serving at the American Embassy in Khartoum entitled us to not just one, but two R&R's. If you don't use it, you lose it, they tell me.

There were only six months left to my assignment in Khartoum when I began to consider my R&R. I decided to visit England and Jerusalem, and I carefully began my plans.

Out came the suitcase. Ironed outfits were folded and packed. Nipper will stay with friends in Khartoum. Even if London did not have a 6-month quarantine—which it did—there are times when it is best to travel alone.

But Nipper always knew when he was not coming with. How do

dogs know these things? Little feelings of guilt tugged at me as he moped around, and quietly and sadly watched me pack.

For days my thoughts were filled with my upcoming trip and the two countries I would visit. I read about the cultures. I thought of their histories, and their "ways."

Take the English interior décor, for example. An English room can be so filled with knick knacks, pillows, books, lazy fat cats on the hearth—and still not look cluttered! The Brits know how to give a room comfortable pizzazz, and they may be among the few who can get away with holding a broken table up with a pile of books—and make it look charming.

Then there is the charisma of their dry wit, which must be largely in the telling. A bad boy Irish friend I knew years later in Paris found his own story so amusing as he told it to me that he could barely finish for laughing so hard:

Throughout his life, he said, he had a bad relationship with his mother. When she died a few months earlier, he decided against attending the memorial service to be held in a small funeral parlor in her hometown in Ireland, but three brothers and a sister attended. The sister was very drunk.

The parlor was quiet, with soft background organ music. Fresh flowers were on the altar, and a few friends and family members sat in the pews. Tall floor candelabras stood near the casket, the flames soft and glowing, symbolic of the flame of life. The three brothers and the sister stood quietly around the satin-lined casket saying their goodbyes.

But the drunken sister had trouble standing. Suddenly, she lost her balance and fell, knocking several candles over. The carpets caught on fire and soon the flames had spread to the satin-lined casket. People in the pews jumped to their feet, and everyone became frantic to put the fire out. The funeral parlor had become a flurry of hysterical commotion.

By now, my friend was laughing so hard as he told the story that tears were running down his cheeks. I was stunned. "But this is your Mother's funeral, what can be so funny?" But he couldn't answer, he was helpless with laughter.

I stared at him awhile, but then shrugged. It must simply be English dark humor, I decided.

But, well, enough of that. My R&R travels had finally arrived, and I was on my way!

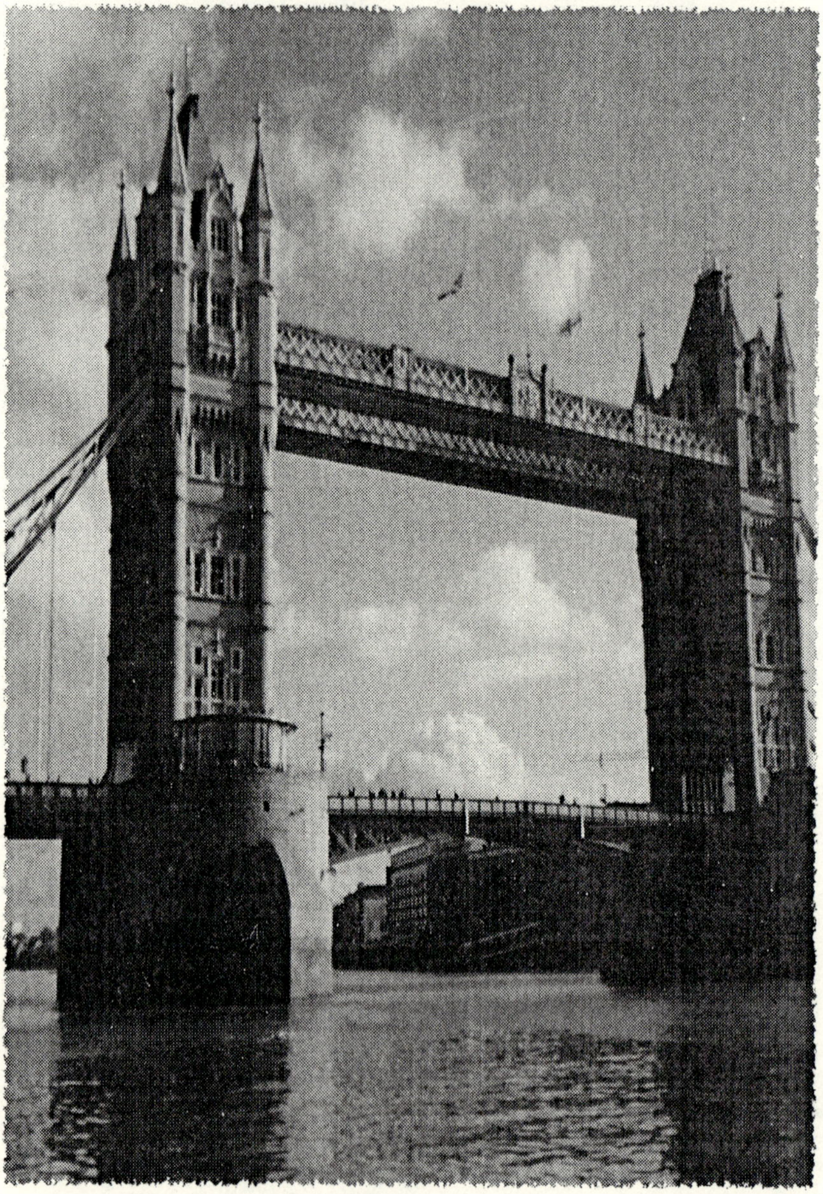

7
By Jove—I'm in England!

The boxy black taxi cab drove through London traffic, and I stretched my neck to gaze out the window. Red double decked buses passed by, a policeman in a tall black hat was blowing his whistle as he directed traffic, and pedestrians strolled along the avenues.

We entered streets lined with lovely Victorian houses, tall and narrow as they connected together. Small gardens of wild flowers fronted the houses, fenced in by fancy black wrought iron.

It was almost dark when we pulled up in front of the small hotel. The street was pleasantly lit with old fashioned streetlamps, and there was a chilly nip in the air. A wonderful fragrance of chimney smoke filled my nostrils and, from somewhere, I could hear the chiming of church bells. London is filled with churches.

The hotel resembled a tall, narrow house. I climbed up a few stairs and noted the friendly glow of a lamp in the window near the entrance which lit up the shingle, telling me that I was at "London House." Just where I want to be, I smiled.

Inside, the foyer was cluttered with antiques and a wooden staircase wound upward to higher floors. A grandfather clock was in the process of a Big Ben jingle, and dinner aromas from an unseen kitchen reminded me I was hungry. I set my suitcase down, and said hello to the fat cat watching from the stairs.

At the sound of the bells as I closed the front door, a slender elderly lady emerged from some other room to greet me. In her lovely

British accent, she told me I was expected, gave me a key, and explained about breakfast. Breakfast, she said, is served in the dining room on the first floor each morning between 7:00 and 9:00 a.m. Then I went to my room on the second floor, and unpacked.

Being in a civilized country again where people speak English, where there are telephones and other modern amenities that I did not have in Khartoum, made me feel alive again. I bundled up with mittens and a warm knit hat and set out in search of dinner.

Oxford Street was just a few streets away and I walked in that direction, careful to set a landmark so I would not get lost.

(Setting landmarks was a lesson I learned many years ago when my brother and I were hiking through the forest around Big Bear Lake in California's San Bernardino area. Norm would set little landmarks as we hiked further into the forest. On our return, we retraced our steps and the fun was in seeing how many landmarks I would remember. When I missed one, he would say "Ah ha!" We were only playing a game, but it became a useful one.)

Christmas was a month away, but Oxford Street was already bright with festive lights and décor. A scattering of people lingered in the shops before closing hour, and pedestrians in the streets were coming and going. The English chatter around me instilled a sense of connection.

But enough walking, already. I was starved. I settled myself into a corner by the window of an Italian restaurant, and ordered a pizza. Outside, those church bells were chiming again. I rested my chin in my hand and watched the people walk by the window.

The waiter set a hot pepperoni pizza in front of me. I smiled at myself—in England, and ordering a pizza?! Why not Yorkshire Pudding, or Liver Pie? Everything was amusing to me this evening—it was impossible to dampen my high spirits.

Karen was also a guest at the hotel. She had recognized my name in the guest registry, and called my room. By very strange coincidence, Karen had been part of the USAID evacuation in Khartoum—although I did not know her—and was in London for a brief visit.

For a few days Karen and I explored London, experiencing together the pulse of this fascinating city. Look—there's Scotland Yard, over there Piccadilly Circus, and there the Houses of

Parliament and Big Ben! Straddled across the Thames River is the Tower of London, and beyond an immense park a crowd at Buckingham Palace had gathered to view the stiff and pompous changing of the Royal guards.

Much of what we were seeing was purely accidental as we roamed wherever our whim took us. We snapped pictures, ate French fries and mayonnaise, and had High Tea at four in the afternoon.

Westminster Abbey and Saint Patrick's Cathedral were the beginning of my fascination for the great cathedrals of Europe. People have said, "If you've seen one, you've seen them all," but I never tired of the beautiful cathedrals and found them all unique.

Those holy sanctuaries, with their masses of lit candles, could be a simple sparse house of worship or an immense, awesome creation filled with ornate holy relics dating back a thousand years or more. On occasion, chanting or singing could be heard within the holy walls.

Stone saints gazed down with unseeing eyes as I meditated quietly by the flickering candles, lost in the spiritual world and the stillness of my reveries in the wonderful European cathedrals.

Up early and dressed, I was among the first of guests to the dining room. The room was warm and cheerful. There were pots of winter greens on the window sills. A sideboard dominated a wall, filled with dainty porcelain dishes and English bric-a-brac.

Urns of piping hot coffee await the guests, and a long buffet is set with platters of sliced meat, baskets of fresh rolls and croissants, boiled eggs, jellies and fruit, and fresh creams. A few other guests were quietly eating as I filled my plate and took a seat by the window.

This morning I have some personal business to take care of in London. I lingered for awhile with a second cup of coffee, and then set off for my mission. In my purse was a piece of paper with an address, and I had called for a cab.

My business was to purchase airline tickets into Israel, the second country I would visit on my R&R. Because of conflicts between Sudan and Israel, and other odd circumstances I did not understand, I was unable to book reservations to Israel from Khartoum. It had to be done in England or other neutral country.

The cab arrived at my hotel at the precise appointed moment. I love those spacious black London cabs! A sliding glass door separates the driver and me from my seat in the rear, but I slide it open and have a brief conversation.

Taxi drivers in London receive 3 years of training and apprenticeship before they can qualify to drive their own cab. They know the city like the back of their hand, and are efficient and courteous drivers.

I was taken directly to the location shown on my piece of paper, but it hardly resembled a travel agency and, in fact, was a dress shop! Did I have the wrong address? Confused, I inquired at the shop next door where I was told to just ring the buzzer by the door to the dress shop.

Timidly, I pushed the buzzer. After a brief moment of waiting, a voice came faintly over a crackling intercom asking who I was and what I wanted? I introduced myself and explained that I wanted to purchase an airline ticket to Israel. For a moment there was no response, but then a buzzer sounded and the voice told me to enter.

Once inside, I looked around at a fairly empty room, feeling somewhat uncomfortable. The only occupants, a woman who sat at a counter and a guard armed with a rifle, were both watching me.

The woman at the counter called me to her, and began questioning me about my reasons for wanting to go to Israel. She asked for proof of my identity. She closely studied my black diplomatic passport, and looked me over cautiously as she did so.

Finally, she stamped some tickets for my flight to Israel and handed them to me. I paid her, the guard opened the door to let me out, and I could hear him lock the door behind me. Such were the precautions of a country on constant guard.

Paddington Station was bustling with morning activity as I waited for a train to Bath. It was Thanksgiving, and I was acutely aware that other people all seemed to be working! This is a Big Holiday, why are people working, I wondered? For a few moments, I was entirely baffled.

It never occurred to me before, but Thanksgiving is, of course, only an American holiday! Amused by my naive assumption that the whole world celebrates Thanksgiving, I thought about this American holiday for a moment.

Thanksgiving is a day to be especially mindful of the bountiful good of our country. It brings to mind visits to grandmother's house . . .through white and drifting snow . . . for turkey dinner with all its trimmings . . . and homemade pies baking in the oven. We may even have the first snowfall of the season on Thanksgiving Day, enough snow to build a snowman or go sledding before dinner.

But I am in England, and today I will celebrate Thanksgiving with an authentic dinner of Yorkshire Pudding. It was not turkey and it was not at grandma's house, but it turned out to be—jolly good!

The top portion of the train window was pulled halfway down, and I stretched out as far as I could with my camera without falling out. Like a snapping fool, I snapped pictures of everything I saw.

Bath is about an hour's train ride from London. The train made frequent stops at rural and country stations, many of them very old. We sped through open green meadows and picturesque country with cows and sheep grazing, dark tunnels, and small villages. It was a delightful journey, but soon we pulled into the small train station at Bath.

The small abbey town of Bath surrounds the remains of a Roman bath, thus its name. It is a stone town throughout, climbing the North bank of the River Avon. The public spas with their healing thermal waters were built largely between 1760 and 1810, and Bath was at its greatest popularity in the eighteenth century when it set a fashion for spas.

During the great age of town building in the late eighteenth and early nineteenth centuries, England had sagacity for planning whole streets and towns as opposed to a single house. Nazi bombing of WWII had not destroyed the character of Bath, considered today by some to be the most complete 18th century small city in Europe.

What I remember most fondly about Bath is Haven House where I stayed for a full wonderful week. It was my first experience with the comforts of a bed and breakfast establishment as opposed to a hotel. This B&B was a mom & pop venture, a "very English" house, cozily small with only three guest rooms.

To reach Haven House from the center of Bath, my taxi drove up a steep hill. The house overlooks the small city and has a lovely view at night of Bath twinkling in its night lights.

The first thing I saw when entering the front door of Haven House was another huge Persian cat—twice as big as Nipper—on the stairway, purring and licking its paws. A fireplace was visible and crackled from the living room beyond. Being late November and quite chilly outside, the fire was inviting.

A very English living room was filled with stuffed sofas and chairs, little tables piled neatly with stacks of magazines, books, today's newspapers. Large picturesque windows looked out over the small city.

My room was upstairs. It had polished wooden floors and a large four poster bed with thick feather blankets. A fireplace and a few choice antiques gave the room a touch of ultimate charm and comfort. In the corner, an electric pot sat atop a table with a basket of hot chocolate and tea bags, cookies and crackers.

A low stone wall ran alongside the woods opposite the road beneath my window, and curled uphill to a village. It was a scene right out of a Beatrice Potter fairytale. So—so—English!

I walked uphill on that charming road the first evening, a nice hefty hike along the stone wall. The smell of chimney smoke mingled with pine from the woods, and all was quiet. The small village at the top of the hill appeared quite suddenly, a simple, unpretentious place most likely unchanged in years.

There in the village, I discovered the joy of the English pub—meaning, of course, public house. The pub originated as a pleasant gathering place for neighbors to eat together, visit, play chess. The specialty on the menu of this particular pub was homemade stew and fresh bread. And beer, but of course. The locals call it bitter. I wondered how a German visitor would handle that—"Ein bitter, bitte (please). Bitte, bitte (thank you)."

Returning to my cozy boarding room, I lit a candle and ran hot water for a bath of lavender oil which I had packed in my suitcase. Then, I curled up under mounds of goosedown with an intriguing mystery novel. Contentment couldn't be greater.

Simple mollycoddling when we're away from home adds a little sugar to the adventure.

Breakfast in the small cheerful dining room of my B&B, with its three tables covered in fresh linen, is a nostalgic gastronomic experience.

The lady of the house is hidden away in the kitchen, cooking while her husband serves a full course English breakfast. I can still see him with the white towel folded over his arm as he carried platters of food to my table. There were generous portions of whatever your heart desires—juice, ham, bacon, eggs, pancakes, or toast with homemade marmalade or jellies.

Plenty of piping hot coffee or tea crowns the table, to sip leisurely and enjoy the garden just outside the window. The English gardens, so charming in their natural, untidy profusion of color. Even in winter, the season brings to the garden its own version of that careless hodgepodge of nature run wild.

Bath is not a big place, really. Countless antique shops are at every turn, and I sometimes lingered in them to purchase old lace or a lovely needlepoint I fancy someone's grandma made a long time ago. I fell in love with the English furniture, the old polished wooden pieces. How could I ever get one back to Khartoum?

When my feet became tired, a nineteenth century ice cream parlor was my retreat where I could rest, gain a pound with a hot fudge sundae, and watch the men go by.

The not-to-be-missed highlight, of course, is the ancient Roman Bath. Its healing waters were once a haunt for kings seeking privacy and pleasure. Today it resembles a swimming pool within decaying stone walls and pillars, statues of Roman royalty overlooking the deserted ruins.

Adjacent to the Roman Bath is the world famous Pump Room, a large elegant room where one can have a fairly good meal—the English are not famous for their cuisine—while a violinist softly moves his bow over the strings.

At the end of a day filled with walking and soaking up the atmosphere of Bath, I climbed the winding hill back to Haven House. The front door was always unlocked. The proprietors were never far from sight, but always out of sight.

The hearth in the living room snaps and crackles gently, throwing a soft glow from the fire. I liked to sit for awhile at the end of the day, to read or daydream by the fireplace. Often I fell asleep on the sofa, and was never disturbed. When I awoke, the fat cat was always curled up beside me.

Very reluctantly, I departed Bath after a lovely week and continued my journey North to York. The train smoked and whistled its way through the Yorkshire Dales and countryside of the English veterinarian, James Herriot.

James Herriot exemplified the virtues of hard work, family life and simplicity. He saw the humor and joy in everyday living.

In Darrowby where James Herriot had lived, I could almost hear an old farmer say, "Tell 'im aye got a cow wot wants borin' out. If we don't do summat, she'll go wrang in 'er ewer."

Then there is Tristin, giving a pull on a Woodbine and watching with tender concentration as he slowly blew out a circle of smoke. Siegfried, Herriot's eccentric, loveable partner, had such little concern with money that he simply stuffed his notes in a jar on the mantle. I thought briefly of my own badly neglected budget book with its empty pages. Maybe I'll try the jar system.

These are real people who lived, and still live, in these rolling hills, country villages and towns.

The names of the various towns—Thwaite, Muker, Askrigg, Hutton-le-Hole—bring a smile to my lips. As we passed through the tiny villages and towns that day, I was leaning out of the top half of the train door just as we passed a sign saying "Horsehead Station." Love it!

The train pulled into York in the late cold, grey and drizzly afternoon. In the distance, I could see the tall spires of York Cathedral towering above this small ancient city in northern England.

In the quiet center of York my room reservations were at Victorian House. This B&B was also a mom and pop business, recently renovated. It had barely opened up for business and I was not only the very first guest, but the only guest!

Fifty small rooms on five floors filled the house. My room was on the top floor, tiny as a closet but clean and comfortable.

In my room, a picture window overlooked rooftops so close I could touch them. Patches of snow on the roofs and chimneys from a recent snowfall glistened in the moonlight, and smoke from the stovepipe chimneys curled up into the dark sky. As I stood gazing out the window, I could almost see the fiddler on the surrounding roofs, slowly and forlornly playing his fiddle in the dusk of evening!

The bed was comfortable. A tellie hung from the corner ceiling on one of those movable racks. There, on an old wooden table in the corner was the familiar electric water pot and a basket stuffed with packets of coffee, chocolate, tea, and crackers.

Down the hallway and around the corner was a loo, to be shared by all guests on this floor. Since I was the only guest, I was Queen of the Loo. Frilly little curtains hung on the window and the walls were papered in a flowery print. An old fashioned floor radiator hissed with noisy steam. It felt good in the chilly night air. Finally, the large bathtub had little feet—how charming!—and the bath salts left by the proprietor's wife released a sweet scent in the air from the radiator's steam.

I was tired and opted for a quiet night in my room. The proprietors, who lived on the first floor of the house, had plans to go out for the evening. I took a hot bath, ordered a sandwich to be sent to my room, and settled in with the local newspaper.

About an hour later, I laid down the newspaper. It was too quiet in this huge house and I was keenly aware of my aloneness. I decided to take a little house tour, having noticed earlier the interesting antiques everywhere.

Making my way through the hallways in the semi-darkness, I felt eyes following me as the old portraits hanging on the walls came alive. Old men with long beards, somber faced women dressed in black and wearing silly looking hats. Who were these people, anyway? Were they long gone ancestors of the proprietors? Had any of them lived in this house at one time? Are they still hanging around?

The antiques cast odd shadows on the walls, firing my imagination. Wandering from floor to floor, I strolled around studying pictures and collectibles placed on polished tabletops, bookcases, and fireplace mantels. A clock ticked hauntingly from somewhere.

I began to feel spooked in this very large, silent and dark house, and wondered if there might be ghosts living here. It felt that way.

Each floor had a window in the foyer with colored stain glass, and the moonlight through the windows gave a surreal effect. Suddenly, from somewhere in the house, the loud screech of an angry cat heightened the spook in me. I ran back through the shadowy halls to my own room on the top floor, quickly closed and locked the door.

Can you believe it! There were only four stations available on the British tellie. I had turned it on for company, and although the programs were a little boring the noise broke the silence of my room.

By midnight, I could hear the faint opening and closing of the front door on the ground floor and the voices of the proprietors, who had returned home. I finally fell asleep.

The morning brought bright sunshine—not common in England. Downstairs in the warm cheery kitchen, I visited with the lady proprietor. Together we had coffee and a bite to eat. It had felt good to have another woman to chat with and break the long aloneness of my journey.

But the winter days are short, and the morning was slipping away. There was a lot to see. Bundling up with warm clothes and good walking shoes, I set out to explore York.

Famous landmarks, local cuisine, and old world architecture are fascinating, but more appealing to me were the small personal experiences and ordinary everydayness of the locale. Whimsical street names. The way local people dress and talk. A chance conversation. The quiet eerie ambience of a very old cemetery. The witty snob appeal of some locals.

That's not to say the famous sites must not be visited. Not to say that at all.

York is largely a medieval city with Roman walls and other historical wonders. The famous York Cathedral is the largest medieval church in England. Within its exquisite interiors, I studied for awhile the fifteenth century illustrations of the Book of Revelations depicted in stained glass. A masterpiece!

In Europe, one can walk into a cathedral at any time of the day or night and find the doors always open. It was that way once in America.

Several narrow alleys led off High Street, or Market Place, to the oldest parts of York, relics of the age of carts and country fairs. I wonder—why is it that these small towns have such a hold on me? Why am I so intrigued by the old churches and cemeteries, the gardens and narrow streets, snooping in antique shops? Could I be a reincarnated small town Brit?

Walking instills a deep sense of connection to the environment. One can stop at will and study the intricate carvings of an ancient wooden door on a ruined abbey or priory, notice the sawdust on a butcher shop floor, linger by a wild flower garden. An old lady walked toward me with ages of deep creases on her face. From inside the window of an antique shop, a cat was curled up sleeping.

More secrets are revealed to one who stands and listens than to those passing quickly by, whose thoughts are intent on other matters.

My grandmother liked to sit on the famous green benches of St. Petersburg, Florida and watch the people go by. I can see why. People watching is interesting. Note their manner of dress, the expressions on their faces, and listen to their chit chat. In our modern day we often hurry here and there, anxious to be on time, to accomplish more, to get in yet one more errand.

But sit for awhile on a garden bench, be still and listen. Imagine the English language of, say, the year 1307:

> *"And who in time knows whither we may vent*
> *The treasure of our tongue, to what strange shores*
> *This gaine of our best glorie shal be sent,*
> *T'inrich vnknowing Nations with our stores?*
> *What worlds in th' yet nvformed Occident*
> *May come refin'd with th' accents that are ours."*
> *Unknown*

Call me Morbid, but I love the old cemeteries. Now that is a site I can spend hours in, the older the better. Such beautiful resting places are found in Europe. The gardens are filled with flowers and benches. Stone crypts are immense and ornate, worn with age. In the stillness, a warbler calls from his perch on the tree branch.

The residents of the cemetery may have been here for hundreds of years, their headstones barely discernable for the passage of time.

"Here lies Abigail Droeshout, born 1495, died 1540."

Who was Abigail Droeshout?

I followed a narrow alley along backyards of stone houses and English gardens, now covered with a light blanket of snow. Church bells could be heard, a monk hurried by on his way to—where? Then, an old lady opened her gate and looked up as I pass by.

"Good morning", I called to her.

"Aye, an tis a good morning," she responded, with a large toothless smile.

The further North one travels, the stronger the brogue. Soon one wonders if these people are still actually speaking English!

A short day trip from York to nearby villages by train is a right jolly outing, I say. Each village or town has something of interest—and don't you love it! Wharfdale and Wensleydale are famous for cheese;

Sheffield for its cutlery; Teeside, the cradle of the railways, for coal and iron.

The sleepy village of Bradford Upon Avon is about twelve minutes by train from York. Has history left this town behind? People in Bradford Upon Avon were most likely born here and will probably die here—simple, good folk who seldom wander far from their birthplace.

It began to rain—really rain hard! I had no umbrella. Up the narrow winding cobblestones I climbed, wet and chilled to the bone. Why is there no umbrella vendor around when I need one?

The streets were slippery and glistened from the rain which has melted the snow into soft slush. This town seemed almost deserted. Some of these tiny spots on the map which people call villages can feel very isolated. A charming place to visit but I wouldn't want to live here, thank you very much.

Ah, good—on a corner ahead, the warm glow of a light shone through windows of an antique shop, and I hurried inside. The bell jingled when I opened and closed the door, and a lady arose from a chair where she sat crocheting.

It was snug inside and I strolled around admiring the array of English antiques and doo-dads. What stories these relics could tell of days gone by, if only they could talk. I hung around the pot bellied stove warming myself, and then purchased a small porcelain dish, an embroidered pillow case, and a discolored but lovely lace collar.

The dimly lit pub in Bradford Upon Avon was cheerful with its fire blazing in the huge stone fireplace. The pub had a lively trade among the local men who had gathered to drink bitter and play chess. A tellie hanging over the bar was largely ignored, providing background noise only.

    I sat by the fireplace warming myself, enjoying the friendly atmosphere. Nobody bothered me. The bartender brought some hot coffee and a sandwich, and as I ate I watched the old men playing their game of chess. As one of them scored a point, he looked over at me and flashed me a wink.

Local trains are a favorite way to travel. Choo-chooing through the Dales and English countryside, clickety clacking in and out of dark tunnels, every once in awhile the train will let out a loud mournful wail as it passes through small villages.

    I am a witness moving through the world around me. My nose is pressed to the window, as I pull a sandwich from my knapsack and flip open a can of Diet Coke.

    Historic Stratford Upon Avon once knew Shakespeare who frequented the streets and drinking establishments. I joined a tour group to visit the cottage of Anne Hathaway, Shakespeare's wife, with its famous thatched roof and picturesque flower gardens. The interior of the cottage contained simple furnishings and small collectibles once belonging to Anne.

    There is something to be said for joining a tour group. While it has its drawbacks—slowness of the other travelers, feeling like part of a herd—still, one can learn much from the guide and not be concerned with getting lost.

    My first visit to England was coming to a close. Did I have time to go further north into Scotland? No, it would have to be for another occasion.

    I would return often to England in the future, and always felt at home there. Ah, yes, England. Tis a right jolly good country.

    Cheerio, England! See you.

8
The Holy Land

El Al Airlines' security checks were tightly rigid at Heathrow Airport in London. Passengers going into Israel were detained in slow lines while El Al Security questioned us by not just one agent or two, but by three different agents.

They were asking the same questions over and over. Why are we going to Israel? Who packed our luggage? Who did we know in Israel? Where will we be staying in Israel? What political groups were we associated with?

Once aboard the plane, however, the flight was the very best in service, food, and comfort. But the same clearing process awaited us upon arrival at Ben Hur Airport in Tel Aviv.

We arrived in Tel Aviv close to midnight, and again waited in slow lines to show passports and answer the same line of questioning by several Security agents. Finally, I was cleared and left the terminal.

It is an hour's drive by taxi into Jerusalem from Tel Aviv. The night air was cold and filled with the fragrance of incense. As we approached the center of Jerusalem, we passed olive trees, date palms, and mosques whose rooftops stood grandly in the moonlight. An old man slowly rode his donkey through the shadowy streets.

The Colony in Jerusalem's Old City was a plantation-like hotel with large rooms, high ceilings and stone stairways. The hotel was sparsely filled. A young Arab clerk took my suitcase and I followed him up the stairs to a second floor where he led me to my room. Was it my imagination or was he scrutinizing me? I began to feel uncomfortable.

He set my suitcase on the floor. I gave him a tip and closed the door behind him. Somehow, the hotel was ominous and disquieting, but I couldn't put my finger on why.

The following morning arrived with sunshine and cheer, and I felt rested, anxious to see Jerusalem.

My knapsack was filled with a bottle of water and a map as I set out for a day of walking. The city was quietly going about its early morning business in the streets of the Old City. I made my way to the Gates, about a ten minute walk from the hotel.

Stepping inside Damascus Gate, overwhelming awe and exhilaration swept through me. The scene quite literally took my breath away! I could only stand and stare, immobilized with wonder. Had I stepped backward through centuries to another time zone of long, long ago? It seemed so.

Narrow musty passageways stretched before me, noisy and dirty. The hubbub was heavy with Oriental mystique. Strong musty odors of Turkish coffee, incense, animal excretions, and potent perfume filled the air.

Over baskets of fresh vegetables and fruit, ribbons of bright sunshine fell from the overhead roof shingles and flooded the marketplace in the open courtyards. Donkeys, camels and dogs mingled with the people. Burlap sacks on the dirt floors were filled with olives, dates, cheeses, souvenirs, fabrics, pottery.

Arab women wearing colorful toabs mingled with

Orthodox Jews with long curls and dark suits, little children and animals. Although the hour was early, already the market inside Damascus Gate was crowded.

Vendors called out loudly in Arabic, their voices echoing through the passageways. They recognized me as a tourist and began to pull at my sleeve or briefly follow me, rambling on in words I could not understand. I imagined they were saying, "Come see what I have, come here, I have good buys for you."

I strolled slowly through the passageways, enthralled with my surroundings. Just outside the Jewish Quarters I found the Wailing Wall where a group of Orthodox Jews stood praying and talking. For awhile I sat on a step staring at the Wall. Jesus himself may have sat here and looked upon the Wall a few thousand years ago.

Jerusalem is a pleasant city, not terribly big. Bells chimed from nearby mosques or churches and every few hours I could hear the familiar call of the muezzin, the summons to prayer.

At the Garden of Gethsemane ancient olive trees still stood. The garden is small and simple. There was nothing to indicate its important place in history

---

Women traveling alone in Israel were generally viewed as loose and easy targets. Everywhere I walked I was plagued with unwanted stares and come-hither looks from dark, foreign looking men. They boldly followed me and approached me in the streets.

I found the aggressiveness in the Holy City offensive, the worst I had ever experienced anywhere. Try to overlook and avoid it, I told myself. Focus on the experience of seeing this ancient city, and ignore the crudeness.

I returned to the hotel and climbed the huge stairway leading up to my room, and again had the feeling of being followed. Indeed, a shadow appeared at the landing in the stairway, but stopped when I did. As I continued, the shadow continued. I quickly slipped into my room, closed and locked the door.

From within my room, I sat on my bed and watched the small crack at the bottom of the door as the silhouette of shoes appeared and paused. I had been followed ever since my arrival in Jerusalem and I was beginning to feel very afraid.

Someone in Khartoum had given me the name and phone

number of a friend. The friend, Felix, was an American architect who lived in Jerusalem with his German wife, Helena. Felix was also an AA member. I called them, and they invited me to their home.

Felix picked me up at the hotel and Helena prepared some delicacies for us to eat. As we visited in their comfortable living room, I told them of being followed and of my fears. They said that in Jerusalem certain unscrupulous men are after a woman's passport or body or whatever they can get, and it makes no difference if she is nine or ninety.

My new friends helped me to relocate to St. Andrews Hostel, a part of the Church of Scotland, located on a hill overlooking Jerusalem. It was small and resembled an abbey. My simple and pleasant room had shuttered windows opening onto a garden filled with weathered clay pots. I felt safe in the hostel.

A shabby, comfortable library was filled with old and rare books, stacked on tables and the floor. Pulling out a few books of interest, I curled up on a window seat with tattered soft pillows. It was quiet and serene, my eyes became heavy, and on my night of arrival I was soon asleep.

Getting sick on vacation is no fun. A sudden, severe bout of the flu kept me confined to bed for days. I simply slept and read, miserable that I was wasting my precious visit to the Holy Land. The kind proprietor of the hostel brought food and drinks to me.

A small AA group in Jerusalem had several English speaking members. I did not know them, but thanks to the efforts of my new friend, Felix, these members called at the hostel to wish me a speedy recovery. One woman invited me to her flat for dinner, which I accepted after my health improved. AA people are among the best in the world.

From my room in the hostel, I could hear singing and piano playing. The voices were soothing, letting me know I was not alone, and I drifted off to sleep.

The other guests of the hostel were a group of about twelve traveling nuns from China. After recovering from the flu, I began to join them in the dining room. The dining room was large and barren with long crude tables and chairs for family style dining. Candles were lit on the tables, and an immense wooden serving buffet at the side of the room held platters of food. The food was always simple, but nobody ever left hungry.

I liked the group of smiling nuns who were always kind and friendly. Sitting with them at their tables, I enjoyed their lively chatter, although only a few spoke English. In the early mornings, it was the nuns whose voices I could hear chanting or singing in the chapel.

I continued exploring Jerusalem and nearby Bethlehem, Nazareth, and Galilee. There were numerous tour buses and I took advantage of a few.

On a tour bus to Bethlehem, I socialized with the other travelers and enjoyed the sights. Bethlehem lies about five miles from Jerusalem in a range of hills. It is modern and clean, looks much like any small desert town. What had I expected?

Christmas Eve in the Holy Land is highly commercialized, and a visit to Bethlehem by tourists is capitalized on by opportunists who take busloads of people there for an evening church service.

I knelt down at the Manger and placed my hand on the Silver Star of the Grotto of the Nativity, the spot where Jesus is thought to have been born. The Silver Star is surrounded by fifteen oriental lamps, donations from various Christian communities.

Over the highly polished marble floors of the Grotto, a monk carrying a lamp of smoking incense quietly moved across the room, hung the lamp, and disappeared. The fragrance of the smoking incense drifted through the room and for awhile I closed my eyes and tried to imagine 2000 years ago.

Stone fortresses, walled cities, guarded grave sites, wonderful old basilicas and churches with age-old traditions still practiced—the city of Jerusalem is a museum of history.

Modern archeology has unearthed ancient relics so precious as to have no price. A stone had been found in Caesarea, worn with age, but still visibly bearing the name of Pontius Pilate. Chipped pieces of marble with names like Solomon carved into them had been unearthed, and fragmented temples—even whole cities—were buried under centuries of accumulated dirt and rubble.

I stood one evening at dusk near Mount Calvary, The Skull, where Jesus was crucified in the year 30. His ministry is said to have lasted about three years.

Jesus predominantly preached about the greatest commandment of all, that we love each other and our enemies.

Love my enemy? I like people, I love a few, but love my enemies? I was only beginning to learn that love is an action as well as a feeling. Loving our enemies could also mean loving parts of ourselves which give us so much trouble.

9
Farewell, Khartoum

Returning to Khartoum, Nipper forgave me for not taking him with on my trip. He sat on my lap as I fed special treats to him and told him about England and Jerusalem. I just knew he understood every word.

The final few months in Khartoum had arrived. I had survived Khartoum, after all. Or rather, like a fine wine, I had improved because of it! Yet, I could not see this until much later when I was able to look back on the bigger picture.

Serving at hardship posts is a preference for some expatriates who like the exotic life, the increased income and career enhancement, the luxuries it can afford which are paradoxically harder to come by in affluent societies where our money slips away quickly. But me? Give me modern civilization, thank you very much!

The so-called "period of transition"—that pocket of time between Foreign Service assignments—is always charged with emotion. Think of it: Several major life changes are taking place at once—home, job, friends, country—all are left behind as roots are pulled up. It can be painful as well as exciting.

But I was still relatively new in the Foreign Service, and thought only of the little picture. I found myself humming little German polkas and daydreaming about my new assignment to Bonn, Germany. I was a happy camper those last few weeks.

"To-Do" lists were drawn up, scratched off, and revised often. A job was winding down, a home being closed, travel plans confirmed, classes in D.C. signed up for, hotel arrangements made. A running list was vital.

The itinerary always includes some time in Washington, usually for training and consultations. Training may last a few days or a few years if, for example, a certain level of competency in a foreign language might be required.

Home leave—leisure time of four to five weeks in our home state—is actually mandatory. Imagine! This is much like saying hot fudge sundaes or popcorn or a holiday by the ocean is mandatory! But home leave is mandatory in order to reconnect with our own country. It has some serious reasoning behind it.

It was early spring when Nipper and I spent our last night in Khartoum. My house was bare, job finished, and everything on my To-Do list scratched off. We would spend this last night sleeping on top of a roof in the desert with friends.

Our friends lived just outside of Khartoum. Lying under the great sky loaded with stars in the quiet African desert was exhilarating. Because there was no smog in the desert, nothing to veil the cosmos, the brilliance of the heavens was dramatic.

The evening was quiet and relaxed, and the Spring air held a hint of incense. For awhile, we sat on the roof eating and visiting and laughing. Then, we spread our thick blankets out to lie on and gaze up at the stars.

And that's when it happened. As we laid there on our backs looking up at the sky, thick now with the absolute fullness of starlight, one lone star went streaking across the heavens. A shooting star! "Did you see it," we asked each other? "A shooting star!"

For awhile we were quiet. Then—someone—someone began to hum the tune. Someone else put words to the hum, and soon we were all quietly singing.

"Catch a falling star and put it in your pocket, never let it fade away . . . save it for a rainy day."

The day of departure had arrived. Up to the very last minute in this country of confusion, there was—confusion!

Careful arrangements I had made on Friday with Embassy drivers to accompany me to the airport were forgotten by Monday—

our departure day. Sitting on my suitcase by the gate at the appointed hour, I waited. Where were they?

An hour later, they arrived in front of my house, babbling little apologies. But now, we were really, really on our way to the airport.

Goodbye little house. Goodbye Musa. Goodbye Rita. Emotions ran high, but I focused on the one thing that simply had to be done—taking our leave of Khartoum. There was one plane out of Khartoum each day and I would not rest until we are on it.

The airport terminal was crowded. Women and children sat in groups on the floors, and men stood here and there, watching. There seemed to be an ominous feeling in the air. The embassy driver asked me to wait while he spoke with airport officials.

Ten minutes later, an official asked me to follow him. Stay close behind, he told me. We picked our way through the thick mobs of people who were watching us with some measure of curiosity. The air was stifling hot. Danger was felt, though I did not know why.

I was escorted to the plane and, after climbing in, the door was pulled shut. Inside, the cabin was empty, and I wondered why I had been given this special treatment. What was going on? I would never know. Half an hour later, a few other passengers began to board.

The plane was old and rickety, possibly a discard from a previous war. We lifted up off the ground, circled over the rooftops of Khartoum, and then began to climb in elevation. With a sudden sharp turn, we were on our way toward Cairo.

An odd sense of numbness settled in. I had no heavy thoughts of what I had left behind in Khartoum, no thoughts of the many life changes just ahead, or of the unknown future.

Instead, my thoughts were oddly frivolous, as though reality was yet denied. Shall I order the chicken or the beef dish for lunch? Did I remember to pack a book in my handbag?

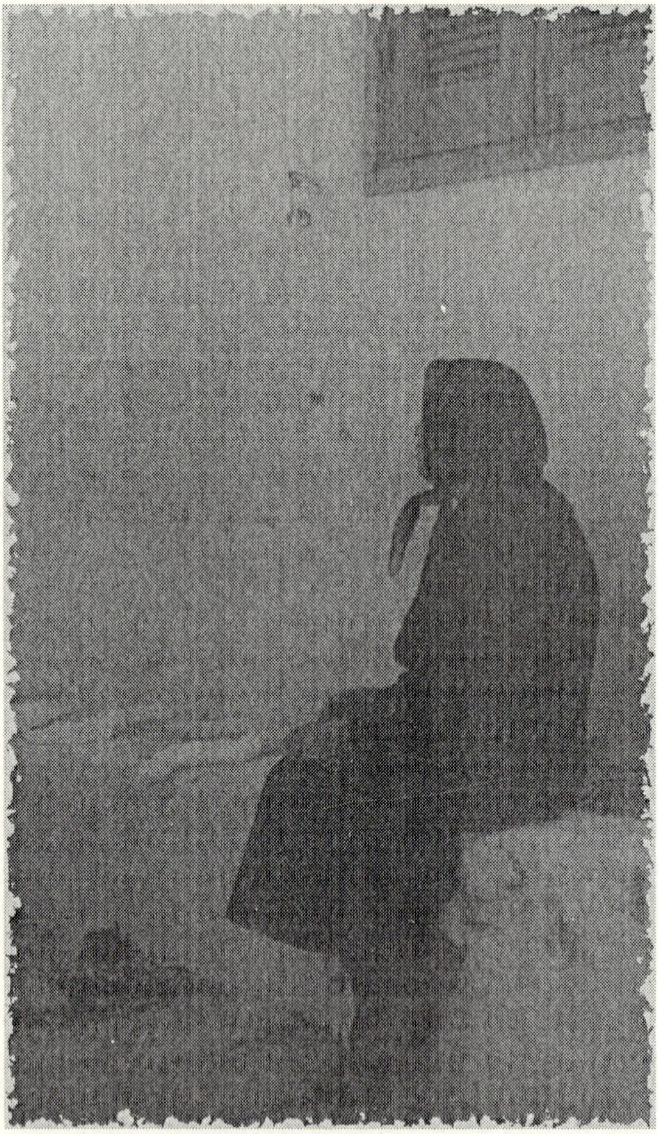

10

The Greek Islands

With over a thousand islands, Greece is a colorful land of primeval calm, white washed buildings with coral roofs, transparent blue skies, boats tucked in remote picturesque bays.

Considered to be one of the oldest and most splendid of civilizations—over 6000 years—Greece is rich in history, relics and ancient ruins.

We landed in Athens where we had half a day's layover before continuing on to Rhodes. I searched for a taxi cab driver with an honest face, and hired him to be my chauffeur for the afternoon.

The luggage went into the trunk. Nipper sat on my lap. We were off to see the Akropolis, speeding through interesting sections of Athens along the way.

The Akropolis is perched high on a flat mountain bed, a hefty climb for Nipper and me. I stood on the ancient ruins of the Akropolis and looked below, thrilled with the significance of the site and the views of Athens in the distance.

We made a brief visit to the nearby temple of Zeus and the Odeon of Herodes Atticus, but this was all we had time to see. Returning to the airport, we passed through a small village and stopped to purchase ice cream. Old ladies dressed in black with babushkas tied over their hair were sitting on low stone walls displaying their handmade lace as they crocheted.

For many of these women, once their husbands have died it is traditional to wear black for the balance of their life.

During the short flight to Rhodes, I flipped through a small tourist book. Thousands of years ago, it said, the noble ancient torch of the first Olympics had been carried by a young Greek athlete for the first time.

Many Greek sages from ancient days originated from the Egyptians, Babylonians, Assyrians, and Chaldeens. To name a few tongue twisters—Kleoboulos of Lindos (one of the Seven Sages) and the painter, Protogenes, of the 4th century BC.

Hippokrates (450-377 B.C.), the Father of Medicine, is thought to have had the most brilliant medical mind in the history of mankind. Try and convince Your doctor of that.

Aristotle (384-322 B.C.) felt that men—and women—can achieve anything if he or she believes deeply and steadfastly in their aspiration.

That evening, perched on the small balcony of my hotel room in Rhodes, I gazed out at the Aegean Sea. Nipper was sound asleep after a special dinner of chicken over rice. Now, close to the midnight hour, I wanted only to sit alone and collect my thoughts.

The sky was loaded with stars, and a giant moon threw its glow across the waves splashing in from the sea. As if in a trance, I sat in the chilly evening air wrapped in a thick warm sweater and stared at those waves as they rolled in, one after another, after another.

The reality that I was no longer living in the harsh conditions of Khartoum had not fully surfaced. A part of me was still in Khartoum. Yes, that's it—and who can understand this but another who has experienced it? I was here, but not here.

I had felt the need for a cigarette so that I could think more clearly. Last week I had quit, but that was last week.

In the concession shop of the hotel downstairs, I bought a pack of cigarettes and returned to my perch on the balcony, to smoke and think. Virginia Slims, my choice, was unheard of in Greece. Just try one of these foreign brands if you really want to give up smoking. Dreadful!

I wanted to savor the fact that I will never have to return to Khartoum. Never. It is over. Finished. Kapoot. I lazily blew a smoke ring into the air and contemplated my new freedom. Somehow, smoking enhances serious thinking!

Yet, I could not seem to think of anything but the richness of the experiences just ended, the culture we had lived in for two years so foreign from my own, the house which had been home for Nipper and me.

I lit another cigarette, blew a smoke ring and watched it drift into the night air, and tried again to feel and enjoy my new freedom. But it was not to be. My thoughts returned again and again—not to my new freedom—but to the friends I had left behind.

The name Rhodes—or Rodos—was developed out of a mythology and derived from Rhodon, the sacred flower of Apollo. Rhodes is a small island and considered one of the loveliest, afloat like a flower in the Aegean Sea and drenched in sunshine.

For miles Nipper and I walked along the Aegean Sea, often seeing nobody for long stretches. The water and sky were crystal blue and a soft wind seemed always to blow. It is spring and not yet tourist season.

I took off my shoes and walked barefoot in the sand along the shore, sent some pebbles skipping across the soft blue waves, collected seashells—lovely shapes and pastel shades of pink—and put them in my knapsack.

My mother told me that if we go home with a little sand in our shoes, we will return one day. I believed her, and would always put a little sand in my shoes when I left a country I liked and hoped to see again.

Around the docks by the sea, pigeons, seagulls and other wild life flocked together looking for food. Fishing boats returning from the sea were filled with lobsters and crabs. A group of fishermen sat on the pier repairing their nets, sharing a joke and laughing.

Wild flowers and brilliant yellow fields led to tiny villages where farmers' wives were gathering their goats together, throwing feed at the chickens, or just looking out their windows. The people were friendly, but not overly so. It was an unpretentious society, not given to fuss of tourists.

Greek cuisine is very, very good. A variety of fresh fish is prepared delectably in imaginative ways, and the salads are fresh and wonderful.

I studied a lunch menu in Greek one day, and pointed to a picture when a polite waiter asked for my order. The price was certainly reasonable. Within minutes, the waiter set before me a traditional Greek salad with black olives and feta cheese and a basket of freshly baked bread. Not too filling, just right.

As I prepared to leave, the waiter appeared again with a large tray—the main course of freshly baked fish! I didn't realize there was more to my lunch, but I sat down and continued eating.

My compliments to the chef, indeed! I again collected my things to leave, but yet again the waiter appeared, this time with a tray of desert and coffee.

By now I was amused. I had not realized that I had pointed to a 3-course luncheon on the menu. "But I have no room left in me for desert," I protested to the waiter! Yes, you do, yes, you do. I sat down and once again ate every bite.

When I finally got up from the table to leave, I paused and looked for the waiter. But this time, he was not there. I paid my bill and left.

Fur is a specialty in the markets, at very good prices! I purchased a white mink hat for my mom which would give her many long winters of warmth in Chicago—not to mention that she always looked good in a hat, and knew it. I had not yet become the strict animal lover I was to become. Still, I'd like to think that Mom's mink hat had merely died of old age.

It is fun to stroll among craft shops and see just what flair the locals have, and what their specialties are. In addition to fur, pottery with its unique colors and designs is popular in Greece.

Small replicas of Greek goddesses caught my eye. I purchased a particularly pretty one which I lovingly protected all the way to the United States.

Simi Island is two hours by boat from Rhodes. The open sea and big sky were relaxing in this pristine Mediterranean weather as I sat on the deck and let the breeze blow through my hair.

At Pedi, an island so small there is almost nothing but one small tavern serving soft drinks, we stopped for half an hour to stretch our legs. I walked around for awhile and then sat on a green bench overlooking the docks. The bench had been freshly painted and was still wet! Bright green paint stripes ran across my back and rear end. I was a marked woman, condemned to the stares of others for the day! But people simply smiled or inquired, and the incident became fun.

A pleasant elderly man stood next to me on the boat's railing as we leaned over and watched Pedi Island fall away from us. The English gentleman was from London, dressed in a tweed suit and holding a walking cane. He told me that he was a widower and he enjoyed traveling. I listened well as he told me of lands he had visited, and we became companions for the day.

Simi is one of the prettiest of the Dodecanese islands, historically home to skilled sailors from fleets as far back as the Byzantines of the 12th century. As we approached the main harbor, we could see a young man sitting on a wooden crate playing his harmonica to flocks of seagulls huddling around his feet.

Clusters of white buildings and colorful bougainvillea were surrounded by the brilliant blue sea. Beyond the small picturesque harbor, stone steps rose steeply upward to a village where we climbed to have lunch at an outside café.

The air was heavy with the scent of fresh spices. Vendors were selling bags of dried basil, oregano, rosemary, and thyme along the harbor. The Englishman and I strolled as he gave me a lesson on how to use the various spices. The spices of Greece, he told me, are among the very best in the world.

A large, open air sponge shop is a literal museum of everything you've ever wanted to know about sponges, but were afraid to ask. The sponges were alive once, actual living beings from the sea! I had not known this. We listened with attention as the proprietor—who spoke to us in heavily accented English—gave us an enlightening lesson on the humble sponge.

Greece is one of the most relaxing countries I will ever visit with its sun and wind and beautiful blue water.

It was time to depart Greece and continue on to the United States. I had forgotten to put a little sand in my shoes—only seashells in my knapsack. Still, maybe seashells will suffice to warrant a return visit.

11
Germany's Little Capital

The terrifying thunder rumbled angrily across the skies as the wind and rain beat against the plane. From somewhere, a few seats over, a lady was screaming.

After having departed Khartoum a few months earlier and indulged in some leisure at the Greek Islands, Nipper and I had taken home leave in the United States. But we were on our way to Germany now for four years, my second Foreign Service assignment.

There had been a long delay in takeoff from Dulles International in Washington. I wondered if we've still been allowed to take off too soon, the weather is so turbulent.

Another rip of lightning flashed across the sky, followed a moment later by sudden deafening claps of thunder as the big plane moved through the storm.

Overhead, a compartment door loosened and fell open. Suitcases and handbags tumbled out into the aisle, hitting a few heads on the way. The lady began to scream again.

The passengers were otherwise very quiet. There were a few—seasoned travelers, no doubt—who continued to nonchalantly read their newspaper.

But I was petrified. The unnerving reality of dangling vulnerably in the air thousands of feet above solid ground at the mercy of a ferocious storm, swept over me in waves. The very air became stifling, and I felt I could barely breathe.

Rigidly clutching my armrest, my knuckles white, my eyes tightly shut, I knew my time had come. And so young yet! Well, not so old. I was praying intently when the man sitting next to me by the window said, "Look!"

He was pointing to a fireball streaking downward from the sky to the ground. In fact, the fireball was an airplane on fire, and about to crash! A moment later it did crash, but our own plane kept moving—shaking but relentless—through the driving rain in the direction of Germany.

Back to my prayers, I considered trying to strike a deal with God. Don't be silly, I thought, you're in no position to bargain. But I did pray, and my entire body ached from the rigid stiffness of fear holding me in its grip.

When we finally moved beyond the storm into clear skies and the stewardess began to serve us coffee and breakfast, the relief I felt was immense. But the experience had taken from me the fun of flying, and a small seed of "fear of flying" had been planted.

In Frankfurt, we boarded a train to Bonn. The small capital of West Germany would be our new home, and my favorite Foreign Service assignment, for the next four happy years.

From my compartment in the train, I could hear singing. A group of German school boys sat with their schoolmaster in another section of the train singing songs of their Fatherland, their young voices clear and angelic.

Two double seats face each other in the train compartment where I sat with Nipper next to me. A tray of hard rolls, sausages and coffee had been served by a train hostess and were propped on my lap. Though the train sped at 189 mph, it was smooth and quiet.

Sharing our compartment was an elderly German couple. We sat in silence trying not to bump each other's knees. Occasionally our eyes met and we exchanged a polite smile, but they seemed more interested in watching Nipper as he sat in his red tee shirt eating his sausage.

Germany is my ancestral land, and I was full of curiosity about this country where my grandparents migrated—from Hanover and Hamburg—to the U.S. when they were young children.

The train windows were dusty, but the views still wonderfully picturesque as we sped through tunnels, slowing down in the villages, and sometimes making a stop at a small station. A few passengers got off, a few more got on.

Traveling ever deeper into the Rhineland, castles began to peek out from the mountaintops bordering the Rhine River. Some of them, they say, long abandoned and fallen into decay, could be bought for one dollar.

For a moment I considered the possibilities of owning my own castle. One dollar? Only five Deutsch mark? There must be a catch. Yes, of course, the purchaser must agree to refurbish the castle within a certain timeframe. One dollar, indeed.

As I pressed my nose to the window of the train, legends and folklore began to fill my head. The Grimm Brothers wrote their fairy tales on the "Romantic Road" running from Wurzburg to Augsburg. Their tales were thought to be violent in their day and for awhile were outlawed, but I loved them as a child.

We were speeding now along the Rhine, and the German couple noticed my intent focus on the scenery beyond our window. They pointed to a large flat rock jutting out into the water on the other side of the river where the mermaid, Lorelei, had lived years ago. From her rock, she would lure passing sailors to their deaths.

Two castles perched high on the opposite banks of the river were barely visible from our train below. The castles, explained the old couple, had belonged to the legendary and long gone "Feuding Brothers." What was the feud all about, I asked? Of course—a woman!

Everywhere my eye fell, picturesque scenes unfolded. What a train ride!

We arrived at the Bundesbahn, Bonn's small town train station, slowed and came to a stop. Stepping from the train and onto the platform with Nipper in my arms, I knew at once that I would love Germany.

Bonn is a university town. Clean, stately, charming German architecture surrounds the main market Square just behind the Bundesbahn, dominated by a large cathedral and a tall stone statue of Bonn's most celebrated son, Ludwig von Beethoven.

An embassy driver and

sponsor were waiting for us—they held up a wooden stick with my name to the strangers on the platform.

It is only a few miles from Bonn to Plittersdorf, the tiny community where we will live. July is a lovely time of year in Deutschland and the trees were in full bloom. Geraniums in reds and pinks hung from windowsills under short lacey curtains. I was struck by the cleanliness of everything.

The Rhineland

A tiny woodsy community of Americans and Germans and a sprinkling of other nationalities, quiet and serene on the banks of the Rhine with church steeples, woods and walking paths, describes Plittersdorf.

The scattering of two-level apartment buildings were tucked pleasantly among the thickness of trees. We climbed to the second floor and entered our new German home.

The apartment was spotless with a pleasant old fashioned feeling, spacious and quiet. In the bright cheerful living room large windows were touched by tree branches, reminding me of a birdhouse. Squabbling birds just outside the windows pleasantly broke the stillness of the summer afternoon.

Exploring the apartment, I noticed that European rooms do not have closets. This is odd to one who has lived with closets all her life. Instead, an armoire stands against one wall of the bedroom. On another wall, a door opens onto a balcony small enough for only two chairs. Here I could look out at a long stretch of woods and parks leading all the way to Bonn. Cologne is twelve miles beyond.

The tedious travels had exhausted Nipper and me. Stretching our legs and getting fresh air were what we needed, so we left the apartment and walked toward the river.

A large expanse of an open meadow with high yellow grass led to the Rhine. Caught up in the exhilaration of the beauty and the fresh air, we ran toward the meadow and fell into the grass, rolled, and lost ourselves in the summer day.

For awhile, we lay in the grass and looked up at the sky, listening to grasshoppers and a meadowlark, a distant church bell. The soft sunshine on my face and the fragrance of the grass and wildflowers caused me to doze for a few moments.

Directly across the river, a church steeple in the village of Neiderdolendorf rose high into the sky. Half timbered houses were scattered along the river and through small villages, interspersed with stretches of woods. A railroad track ran along the opposite riverbank, and every so often a train clickity clacked, letting out a mournful wail.

Musical chiming of nearby churches rang over the Rhineland precisely on the hour. We walked through short patches of woods and a profusion of rose bushes growing wild, and I stopped to pick a bouquet. "For Me", I said. "Welcome to Germany"!

"Zaire gute", I answered. "Danke Schoen"!

The U.S. Embassy is located four miles away, an hour's walk along the Rhine. What great exercise to walk eight miles each day. Life takes on new meaning as one mingles with nature and sees what cannot be seen from a car. New life in the spring, the fullness of summer, autumn's color and harvest of acorns, the snow in winter as it lies upon the cone.

Located at the halfway point to the embassy and encroached right on the riverbank is the old Rhineland Hotel, standing sedate and grand. It was a favorite of Adolf Hitler when he visited the area during the war. Here, too, is the landing for the ferry which goes back and forth across the river to Neiderdolendorf, Koenigswinter and Rhondorf, carrying people, bikes and automobiles.

The embassy was a large white sprawling building surrounded by woods near the river. Though one of the largest in the world, it had a small, country atmosphere. The red, white and blue flag waved near the entrance, the Marines stood guard, and the portraits of the U.S. President and Vice President greeted us.

Inside, the embassy halls were always quiet and pleasant, almost suggestive of a country hospital. Work days were immediately busy, a hubbub of activity behind the office doors which were typically closed or locked.

My assignment was in the Office of Science and Technology with a small group of three Americans and four Germans. The S&R office researched aerospace technology and AIDS. My work was diversified, interesting and heavy.

In fact, I was an astute and hard worker in those days—loving the frenzied pace. I thrived on the fun of dashing across the halls of the embassy, pressed to meet several deadlines at once, stacks of projects piled neatly all over my desk. No lazy sluggard was I!

In 1987, Helmut Kohl was Chancellor of Germany. The Berlin wall had not yet come down, and most political activity centered in Bonn. Long limousine processions with flags from many nations were led by motorcades, and were a common sight in the streets of Bonn. Interesting events were taking place in the diplomatic community.

My days slipped into weeks and then months. Adjusting to the German culture came easy for me, and I was happy there.

In a day, one can walk in and out of countless villages and towns in the Rhineland. Walking and biking paths are everywhere, and walking is an especially old favorite German pastime. On Sunday afternoons, whole families are seen together in the popular Volksmarch among the vineyards and along the promenades of the river or in the parks.

I decided to purchase a bike. A basket with soft pillow was attached to the handlebars for Nipper, and thus began four years of countless enjoyable excursions and companionable hours together touring the Rhineland.

Nipper had not been on a bike before, and he had his misgivings. So did I. Placing him in the basket, I whispered reassuring words in his ear and held his leash firmly in my hand. Ever so slowly, I began to ride the bike. Good, I thought—and picked up just a little speed. But he panicked and jumped out of the basket, landing on the ground and barely missing the wheel. He screamed!—I screamed!—and I screeched to a halt.

We tried again. Back into the basket he went, despite the look of distress on his face. He stubbornly resisted with his legs stiff against the basket, then slowly relaxed and began to show interest in the surroundings.

Soon we loved our excursions on the bike. Sitting at the helm in his basket, Nipper enjoyed the wind in his face as his ears blew behind him while we rode. If I went too fast, he gave me a look which told me to slow down. We had learned teamwork. Biking along the Rhine River and in and out of nearby villages was exhilarating, and often filled our weekends.

My blue and white Hercules was useful as well as fun, particularly on Saturday mornings when I rode the three miles from Plittersdorf to Bad Godesberg where the farmers' market is held every Saturday morning.

In Bad Godesberg, the streets are lined with stalls filled with fresh vegetables, fruit and flowers as early as 7:00 in the morning. Local housewives shop early since on Saturdays everything closes by 1:30, not to open again until Monday.

Upon entering the sweet smelling bakery, a bell tinkles and the proprietor greets the visitor with a "Gutentag." There are over 125 varieties of homemade German bread, including the delicious muesli filled with nuts and raisins. A generous selection of hard rolls is always available since Germans traditionally serve rolls and cold cut meats for breakfast each morning.

There is a gaiety in the streets among the shoppers. Strong coffee brewing in nearby cafes fills the air. A shopkeeper with his window open grills spicy bratwurst, delicious with mustard on a hard bun.

On one of my first visits to Bad Godesberg a Saturday morning sale was about to take place at Herkie's, the only department store in Bad Godesberg. I chained the bike to a tree and joined the crowd of housewives gathered at the entrance. After a brief linger, the doors opened at precisely 9:00 o'clock and with a big whoosh I was swept from behind as the women rushed inside to the waiting sales tables. It was every woman for herself.

Early visits to the produce section of a grocery store were also intimidating. After picking out some vegetables, I approached the scale and politely waited my turn to weigh in. But the German women pushed in front of me, time and time again. I found myself standing for long spells on the sidelines, shyly waiting for a chance at the scale.

Finally, I took a deep breath. My turn had arrived. I stood my ground. "Enchuldegen!" I said, loud and clear, as I persisted against the woman who was trying to elbow me out. It brought me a dirty look, but the scale was mine. I had won. I began to weigh my vegetables. A naughty thought overcame me and I slowed down, leisurely weighing the tomatoes, then the potatoes, then the . . . stealing a glance at the others . . . as they waited.

Another early supermarket incident comes to mind. As a newcomer to Germany, a mistake I sometimes made in the supermarket was in miscalculating the amount of Deutsch mark in my purse. This happened one particularly busy Saturday in Kaiser's market.

I selected my groceries and stood in line, not realizing I had only a tenth of what I needed to pay my bill. When I handed the clerk my currency she looked at the Deutsch mark, then at me, and then—in front of the entire line of shoppers behind me—scolded me without mercy. The manager came running, and escorted me out of the store! My face was red, but shame on You, Kaiser's.

The three miles between Plittersdorf and Bad Godesberg is a treat for the eyes—a picturesque bike ride through winding streets of gingerbread houses and gardens. Herr Tiede has a butcher shop on a corner enroute home, and I often stopped to pay a visit.

"Gutentag, Herr Tiede, it's a good day today?" "Ya, ya, dahlink, gutentag. It's a good day." His display case is usually filled with sliced cold cuts and cheeses, big fresh chickens, sausages, and pickled olives. But my eye immediately searches for his sauerkraut.

Herr Tiede's homemade sauerkraut is unrivaled, but the local women shop early and left none for me. He was all out of sauerkraut. I was genuinely disappointed, and told him so.

He winked. "For you, dahlink, I save a little in the backroom." Then he would disappear and reappear from the backroom with a large package of his sauerkraut for me. "So! Today you will try my bloodwurst, ja? I tell you how to cook it, and you will come back to thank me!" "No, no, Herr Tiede. No bloodwurst today. Next time for sure."

It would be two years before I tried Herr Tiede's blood sausage. It was so good, I wondered what had taken me so long! Maybe with a different name I'd have tried it sooner, I thought, something less . . . bloody?

As a young girl, a foster family I had lived with for a few years taught me how to count in German, and a few simple sentences have stayed with me. "Du bista dumkof"—"You are a dumbbell"—is not acceptable if I hoped to make friends in Germany. A stronger grasp of the local language was needed.

I decided to do something about it. The embassy offered language classes, so I signed up. But ultimately, I found that living and working among the people was my best teacher.

Learning a foreign language is cruel agony for me. My official orders sometimes required me to attend a fast course at the Foreign Service Institute in Arlington—a lovely new college built in the late 1980's exclusively for government workers—prior to a new foreign assignment. I have attempted Arabic, French, German and Spanish, and in each case suffered immeasurable stress.

From the beginning, the class of usually six was expected to speak in the language being studied! No English allowed. For the teachers, who all had the native tongue, the language obviously came easy, and they seemed to enjoy watching us squirm. They moved exceedingly fast. By the end of three classes, the teachers had us on lesson 9 while I was still struggling with lesson 2.

Finally, a kind instructor took the time to explain to me that not everyone has the capacity to grasp foreign languages. It has something to do with the brain structure. All people are talented, but not necessarily in the same areas.

I noticed that the Germans at the embassy have a terrible time with the English W and V. My colleague Dieter Schnitzer told me a story which included the word "velvet." I could not understand. Patiently, he repeated. It wasn't sinking in. "Welwet, welwet" he said, becoming irritated with me. "Ohhhhhh, I said," finally getting it. "You mean Velvet." "Ya," he said, "I mean welwet!"

Dieter worked across the hall from my office. His job was to translate local news reports from the daily newspapers. His office was always a storehouse of newspapers and magazines, stacked in piles on the floor, spilling out from the bookcase, thrown neatly atop chairs, and stacked so high on his desk that he himself was seldom visible.

I often walked into Dieter's office and assumed he was not there, so simply walked out again. But then I began to inquire before I walked out. "Dieter? Are you in here, Dieter?" I would ask. Silence. Then, from somewhere behind a stack of papers—"Ya, I am here."

I was picking up the ways of the Germans, just by working with them. Methodical and organized, their project is laid out carefully, performed, and then when it is finished a loud "So" puts the final touch to their project. No work is complete without that final "So!"

I, too, finished up some work one day and found myself saying "So!" It was spontaneous, but yes, somehow I did feel that now the work was officially done!

Leo was a German embassy colleague who became a friend early after my arrival. She was blond and petite, and always smiling. I liked her immediately.

She could knit sweaters like nobody I had known, and in the winter months often wore them to the embassy. The designs, color and quality of workmanship were exquisite. I expressed my admiration at such talent and skill but she brushed off my compliments, telling me anybody could do it. She decided to teach me how to knit.

Together we went shopping and purchased yarn and needles. Our lunch hours became the appointed time for our new classes. We rolled the skeins of yarn into balls and were ready to begin, concentrating on the very basics. She told me how to count, but that's where the rub came in. I couldn't remember from row to row how many stitches I had counted, so I had to pull out the stitches and start over. I became frustrated.

But Leo was patient. Gradually, my knitting began to evolve into a sweater without the sleeves. Knitting sleeves requires a lot of counting, and in time I decided that the sweater should instead be a vest. It was, in fact, a much larger vest than I originally planned. I decided to send it to my mother. She loved it! Or, at least she said she did.

We eventually abolished our knitting classes, but in the process Leo and I had bonded. She became my German sister.

Friendships blossomed as well with American secretaries in nearby offices. Ann was a "cut up", pretty and outgoing. Barbara, tall and southern, was friendly and always smiling. Shirley, insightful, possessed a tremendous sense of humor. Gail was down to earth and folksy. Pat was to become a very good friend in later years. Louise was motherly, and also my neighbor. She frequently gave Thanksgiving and Christmas dinners in her home.

"Quick. Put the money away, here comes Jeanne!" That's Ann. A tray of cookies is left on my desk in the morning by Barbara, who did some baking last night. Someone placed a rubber mouse on my chair, which squeaks and scares the shhhh out of me when I sit on it. Shirley sometimes sticks her head in my office long enough to tell a joke and leave me laughing. We all genuinely liked being together, outside as well as inside the workplace.

The spook who worked in our office was a CIA agent incognito. We had become friendly because of our mutual love for our Miniature Schnauzers. Sharing our most recent dog tale with each other was fun.

My spook friend and his wife were Italian Americans and invited Nipper and me to their home for an occasional spaghetti dinner. Their dog, Zig, was much older than Nipper and a pampered pooch with a closet full of little designer coats, jeweled collars, name plate water bowls.

Ziggie was ill, and the vet could do no more for him. The spook told me how he had held Zig on his lap Christmas Eve, gently stroking him throughout the long emotional night. By morning, little Zig had passed away. It was the first time I saw a big man as torn up as the spook when he told me this last tale of the dog he loved.

Nipper inherited one of Zig's coats. It was red plaid corduroy with a fleece collar and a belt buckling at the waist. He looked dashing in his new coat. "Ahhh, Nipper," I said, "little Helga will be impressed!"

Little Helga was also a Miniature Schnauzer who lived in the German community, somewhere. We often saw her running along the river with her master, Hans Joachim, who rode his bike. Helga was small, round and chubby, with long eyelashes.

Nipper's ears always perked up when he saw Helga coming toward him on the path by the river. They happily sniff each other and then dash off to chase geese or bark at other dogs. Hans Joachim and I gave them time together while we practiced our English and German languages on each other.

August is often warm and humid in the Rhineland. Air conditioning was uncommon and the heat spells could be wilting. In August, the Germans—and English, Belgians, Swiss and French—

disappear for vacation for the entire month. Businesses and shops close down, and the streets and neighborhoods become deserted and quiet.

But by September, the locals return. Trees begin to change into a blaze of brilliant colors. Cherries and olives are ripe and cover the grounds. The air takes on a nip.

Sitting on a bench by the Rhine, I was lost in my thoughts when I was suddenly hit in the head with a stone! I jumped up and looked around me, but I was alone.

I sat down, but again I was hit in the head with a stone! Okay, what's going on! Was someone hiding and playing tricks on me? Barbara or Ann, perhaps? It would be something they would do. But no, I was definitely alone.

Another hit in the head followed, but then I began to smile. Of course! I am sitting under an acorn tree! In autumn, acorns cover the grounds and sidewalks everywhere! People are seen in the parks and woods, bending over and picking up acorns and cherries to fill their baskets.

Large "V" formations of geese in the sky follow their leader for the journey south. Talk of the Oktoberfest, the beery madcap festival of Munich, is heard in October as the Rhinelanders made plans to go.

Other simple events marked the season. My feather blanket from the U.S. had arrived, warm and cozy during the cold nights. Americans begin to think about Thanksgiving dinner in November. The days become short—as early as 4:00, it is already dark. Walking home from the embassy in the cold dark evenings, small lights twinkling from the villages across the river took on new sensations and pleasures.

With the last few days of November, workmen are busy setting up the Christmas stalls in every Square of every village, town and city. The Kriskringlemarkts begin to spread their seasonal magic across Deutschland.

The Kriskringlemarkts are clusters of tents adorned with evergreen branches and tiny lights. The tents are filled with German wooden ornaments, nutcrackers, smokers, tins of spicy gingerbread and other age old German delicacies. Neighbors and friends gather to shop and visit, to enjoy a tiny glass of hot wine, a bratwurst from the grill. The air is frosty and the atmosphere festive.

Wreaths decorated with holly, candles, and long red ribbon streamers hang like chandeliers in the German homes. Traditional holiday wreaths are also placed on tables as centerpieces, with four candles representing the four Sundays before Christmas. As each Sunday arrives, a candle is lit.

In Plittersdorf, a tall steepled red brick cathedral stands alongside its small, 17th century cemetery by the river. The beautiful shrines and headstones are worn with age, and I lose myself in thought as I stroll and read the names and dates of people buried there.

During December, Christmas evening concerts are held in the cathedral. The high ceilings provide quality acoustics, and the voices of German singers, strong and pure, resonate across the cemetery and over the moonlit Rhine as the old carols are sung once again, not in English but in Deutsch.

A package had arrived from the U.S. addressed specifically to Master Nipper. Underneath the brown paper, the box was gaily wrapped in Christmas tissue and ribbons. I placed it under our tree in the living room, but then noticed the tag said to "Open before Christmas."

With Nipper sitting at my feet, we opened the mysterious gift. Lifting the lid of the box, we saw within four shiny black rubber goulashes—boots for the snowy winter—nestled in colored tissue. How cute, I thought, but it took me five minutes to get a boot on each foot. Once done, I got out the red plaid corduroy coat Nipper had inherited from Zig. Then I reached for the leash, something which normally brings eager enthusiasm from Nipper.

But he simply stood and stared at me—rigid and awkward—in his coat and new boots. Then, slowly and with exaggerated effort, he made a feeble attempt to walk. His legs were as stiff as sticks as he toddled across the floor like a small robot with clothes on.

Until he came to the front door, that is. Then he had second thoughts and stopped. He sat down and refused to budge. Nothing could coax him into a nice walk outside until I took the boots off.

And off they came, back into the Christmas box and onto a closet shelf—where they were soon forgotten. But we appreciated the thought!

Christmas bazaars at Ramstein and other Air Force bases are held in huge tents and draw European artisans from many countries who bring to the bazaar a feast of beautiful international crafts.

The bazaars also gave the Marines a chance to hold a cookout where they set up their grill just outside the PX and bazaar tents. Who can resist those thick, juicy American hamburgers and hot dogs sizzling on the outside grill in the cold winter air?

On a particularly grey drizzly Saturday morning, a friend and I visited the bazaar and then decided to drive to Nurnberg.

Nurnberg is a protestant city, the first to support Martin Luther in the 16th century Reformation. It houses the turreted castle of the emperors of the Holy Roman Empire, and is sometimes referred to as the treasure house of Germany. For good reason, I might add. Nurnberg can lay claim to many famous sons like Peter Henlein who made the first pocket watch called the Nurnberg Egg.

But we came to see the Christmas decor and Kriskringlemarkt, reputed to be one of the biggest and best. The festive stalls are laden with peanut brittle, strudels and sweetbreads. Spicy gingerbread is crafted into whimsical children with clothing of colored frosting. The Nurnberg tins depict historical German scenes and script, and are works of art.

I purchased a Nurnberg Doll in a red velvet dress, to top my Christmas tree. A true story, the doll originated during the war of 1914 when a poor family living in Nurnberg had no money to buy their young daughter a gift for Christmas. The father decided to make a doll for her. He crafted the doll in straw—the original version—and his wife sewed a dress for it.

Other families saw the doll and asked if the father would make one for their own daughters, and soon there was a great demand throughout Germany for this angel doll, known today as the Nurnberg Doll, placed at the top of Christmas trees.

Snow at Christmas in Germany is not uncommon, but in the Rhineland it is usually light and soon melts. An occasional good snowfall stays awhile, picturesque as it covers rooftops, church steeples, roads, and giant pine cones on the evergreens.

Being stuck in a snow storm is a good way to deepen a friendship. Traffic was moving at a snail's pace, and for three hours Leo and I crawled along in her car going home from the embassy. The road was slick with ice and snow.

It was a few days before Christmas and the snow was especially beautiful as it covered the Rhineland. Inside the car, Leo and I amused ourselves by telling each other ghost stories. Soon the ghost stories became events from our own pasts, sharing parts of ourselves we normally would keep private.

As we inched along the icy street in the dark snowy night, we began finally to talk of our ghosts from Christmases Past. And what came from all this sharing? When Leo finally reached my home I hugged her good night, and felt I knew my friend considerably better because of the snow. It was a Christmas gift of friendship to both of us.

January and February usually bring dismal weather with slushy snow. The days can be so relentlessly grey as to start a plague of depression. Maybe that's why the fun of the annual Carnival takes place in February, a week of celebration all over Germany and many parts of Europe.

The partygoers don colorful, outrageous costumes and masks at carnival time. Parades take place. Serious beer drinking and singalongs with friends fill the local discotheques. The Germans take their carnivals very seriously.

Leo invited Nipper and me to join her with some of her friends at one of the Carnival's disco parties. My simple mask of white feathers and rhinestones was fun, and Nipper wore his dark Batman cloak. The room was crowded with masked Germans, the beer was flowing, cigarette smoke grew thicker as the evening wore on.

About six or seven of us were squeezed in together around a table, with Nipper and I the only Americans. For a moment or two, the group chatted in accented English—a nicety to make me feel welcome—but as the great pitchers of dark beer flowed, I was forgotten and they were talking and laughing together in their German tongue.

The celebration became rowdier as midnight approached. Large groups of people were holding hands and dancing in a ring, and the bizarre masks and costumes lent a surreal effect to the dimly lit room.

I do not drink beer. I could not understand the German jokes and conversation. The noisy band and boisterous singing of the Germans were giving me a headache. The smoke burned my eyes. I felt out of place. Everybody was having fun but me!

"Come on, Batman, let's go home."

During the Middle Ages, more than 20,000 castles were built in Germany, Switzerland, Austria and northern Italy, and many of them still remain intact.

Immense gateways led into the drafty hollow castle courtyard of the military castle known as Marksburg. Up the old dimly lit stone stairwell we climbed, Leo and I, our footsteps echoing eerily. Small open lookout windows allowed for a peek at the Rhineland below. The narrow stairwell opened eventually onto the highest landing where military exhibitions were displayed—armored uniforms, documentaries of wars, cannons and cannonballs.

Up there—so high it felt we were in the very sky—we could hear only the stirring of the wind and an occasional hawk.

Marksburg Castle is a fully preserved stronghold on the Rhine, one of only about 200 castles to have fully survived. Lived in continuously since the 12th century, its interiors contain many old German relics, the Knights' Stairs, torture and punishment instruments, and the weaving and spinning room. More than 170 different plants and spices are grown in the castle's surrounding garden—many of which were used by witches.

Castles were built largely for either royalty residences or military defenses. The cannonballs in a military fortress, Leo tells me, were shot out the open windows from the heavy cannons—which are still sitting on the floors today. As the cannonballs went rolling down the mountain, approaching enemies were mowed to the ground or knocked back to the flatland. I was intrigued.

But I don't get it. How can the heavy iron cannonballs be lifted into the cannons to begin with? Leo told me not to get hung up on details. She must not know the answer.

Sometimes starvation was the "weapon" used by the enemy to flush out the castle occupants. To avoid the cannonballs, the enemy waited at a distance below the castle and prevented delivery of food. The castle occupants eventually either starved to death or surrendered.

Since castles of long ago had no wash closets, pans were placed in each room, and the chambermaids were tasked to periodically empty the pans. Picture, if you will, a gentleman guest of royalty coming down the immense stairways after having just used a pan, and passing a young chambermaid—maybe one he had noticed and found especially pretty—going upstairs on her regular pan cleaning rounds!

Body odor was an aphrodisiac. Rotten teeth was common, or no teeth at all! That may explain why beautiful ladies of that era always had their mouths closed when their portraits were painted. Hmmmmm....

Spring had arrived, and the yellow crocus and other wild flowers were pushing their tiny heads up through the soil. The birds returned from the south.

In the marketplace, women happily and with intense purpose

selected flowers and bulbs for their homes and gardens. The parks and woods were filled with masses of flowers.

New families of geese and swan were seen under bushes, sleeping, or sunning themselves on the river bank. Little babies paddled together in the lake, trying to keep up with their mother.

Nobody had ever forewarned me not to mess with a large mother goose or swan, especially when they have young to protect. Nipper and I found this out the hard way. We wanted a closer look at a mother and three baby swans sleeping in the grass by the water.

Not knowing what our intentions were, the large mother swan charged after us. We didn't know they had such a bite, or that they could run so fast!

But Nipper and I ran faster, and we had learned a thing or two about the swan.

The famous Kierkenhof Tulip Festival is held every April, and Barbara and I decided to go to Holland.

Along the way, windmills rose silently in the farmlands, their large blades quiet now. The windmills seem so "Dutch", but other countries, too, have them. Even in the U.S., I had fun as a child climbing inside a deserted windmill. At the top, the open pigeon holes and glassless windows gave me a wide view of the surrounding quiet countryside below. I am sure the old windmills must be left standing for kids to have fun in.

On our way to the Kierkenhof Festival, we stopped at a clog shop where an old man and his son make wooden clogs. Nobody visits Holland without buying a pair of wooden clogs, do they? The clogs are also so, so—Dutch! And they are quite comfortable to wear, if one doesn't mind the cloppy noise.

While I would visit Holland often, that day was devoted to Kierkenhof. It was a day of paradise among the flowers, especially the thousands of colorful tulips which must be the prettiest in the world.

It was drizzling at Kierkenhof and visitors to the gardens had all brought their umbrellas, except us. You can always tell who the true natives are in Europe—they're the ones with the umbrellas!

It is Easter in the Rhineland. German shops are filled with artfully designed, hand painted eggs—insides removed, of course—delicate works of art! And in their homes, German women decorate for Easter by placing a bundle of branches in a heavy vase to hang painted eggs, little ornaments, and ribbons.

Spring weather is cool, but still brings the people out. Germans like to walk along the river promenade on Sunday afternoons, stopping now and then for a mid-afternoon snack. A sweet smelling cafe can always be found for a slice of Black Forest cake, and stout coffee.

The long flat barges moving up and down the Rhine River transport goods between towns and cities. Whole families live on these barges and could be seen hanging out their laundry or working in a small garden they have planted right on the barge! It is their life. They are river people!

The tiny town of Adendorf is highly unique in that its main livelihood is pottery. With a population of probably only a few thousand people, the narrow streets of Adendorf are filled with shops of the unique grayish blue German pottery. The potters often live above their small shops, and work in the studio to the rear.

Each spring, Adendorf holds a pottery festival in the streets and courtyards. Artisans' studios are wide open where visitors can watch them molding their clay or painting the designs. The pottery is displayed on shelves or the floors, and we only have to decide whether to purchase a new pot for flowers, a little kitchen jug with holes to hold onions or garlic, or one of the many other choices.

The women of Adendorf set up tables in the outside courtyards on that festive Sunday with platters of homemade cakes and large silver urns of hot coffee and tea. If you're not into pottery, the homemade German baked goods alone are worth the trip.

My friends and I never missed this special day in Adendorf and, although it rains a lot in Germany, that day seemed to always bring out the sunshine. We sat on the crude wooden benches with our stout coffee and slice of cake and visited or simply watched the people.

The advent of an enormous flea market begins for one weekend each month, April through August. The tables and tents of the flea market trail on and on through the woods and park beyond my apartment, quietly bustling with festivity.

On one of my strolls through the fleas, I came upon a vendor selling old German and Jewish passports from WWII, of all things! One wonders how such items were ever acquired by the vendor. Everything imaginable appears on the tables, and it is a day of great fun for all scavengers who appreciate a treasure hunt.

Reminders of WWII are not hard to find. In Cologne, where most of the city was bombed to rubbles, the treasured thousand year old cathedral was relatively untouched. Within its dank immense interiors, holy relics, crypts, and some of the world's finest examples of gothic art still remain.

Goslar, a town located high in the Hartz Mountains, has a lovely but lonely old cemetery for German soldiers of both WWI and WWII. Row after row of identical tombstones, tightly squeezed together, depict the name, birth and death dates, and a small portrait of each fallen soldier. With my morbid fondness for old cemeteries, I spent many evenings among the tombstones of Goslar during a holiday there.

A bombed out cathedral in Hamburg has intentionally been left standing, as is. Abandoned, overgrown with weeds, bordered by a fence to prevent people from entering, the eerie remains of the cathedral are a grim reminder, lest the memory grows dim.

In Bavaria, a friend and I visited Dachau, the concentration camp in the town of the same name which was seized in 1933 after the Nazis had gained power. Citizens from almost every nation were imprisoned and died in Dachau during the war.

Rows of long barracks resembled chicken coups, and my friend and I walked slowly through them. The camp was larger than it appeared initially, and still held a prevailing sense of death.

We left Dachau a few hours later, quiet and pensive. The concentration camp had instilled reality to something previously seeming surreal.

If Dachau was a walk through a house of horrors, a trek to the

Eagles Nest—Hitler's Berghof in the Bavarian Alps where he actually spent very little time—was a visit to heaven.

A wild drive upward through the Alps with a busload of noisy tourists was like a rollercoaster to the sky. The road was narrow and steep, and snow hung heavy everywhere. Below us, the beautiful Alps stretched as far as the eye could see.

The lodge of the Eagles Nest is accessed by entering a cave with an elevator going upward to fairly unimpressive interior rooms. But a wide deck outside the lodge literally overlooks the mountaintops of the Bavarian Alps. There is nothing above but the sky. The air is raw and cold. There is no sound but the wind.

In late 1989, the embassy had been filled with talk about government plans to pull down the Berlin Wall which separated East and West Germany. Such an event would have its impact on everyone, and drastically change many lives.

It was a Saturday morning in November and I was deep in my thoughts as I leisurely enjoyed my croissant and coffee in a Cologne café. After a long week at the embassy, Saturdays were a special day of relaxation—time for myself.

Near the café window, just feet from the Cologne Cathedral, a man was sitting alone at a table reading the newspaper. The headlines shouted out, "Berlin Wall Comes Down!"

"History is being made today," wrote my boss on a postcard from Berlin. He often traveled there on business, and was witnessing the tearing down of the Wall. After fifty years of separation, East and West Germans were being reunited.

The media and newspapers were filled with stories and pictures of joyful crowds climbing over the Wall, bringing a hatchet to it, chopping off pieces for souvenirs. On the surface, the reunification seemed a happy event, a positive move.

Helmut Kohl's popularity in the East had risen dramatically, but his optimistic promises soon appeared premature.

Kohl hoped for a quick economic union. A likewise speedy political union might have a favorable outcome for him in the elections of the West German Bundestag. But the headaches that he faced were astounding. Uniting two countries is a big undertaking.

The West Germans worried about their economy, their jobs, and the retirement benefits that they would have to share with the East Germans. Thousands of misplaced Germans will migrate back into West Germany from the East, from Czechoslovakia, Soviet Union, Romania. Crime will likely be on the rise. The estimated costs for unification may prove to be too modest as compared to the realities to follow.

The East Germans were afraid, as well, and had their own concerns. Many were born behind the Berlin Wall into the communistic Soviet occupation of the German Democratic Republic. They had lived their entire lives in the GDR, and it was all they knew. Older East Germans remembered life before the Wall went up and divided them from their families, but their West German families were strangers now.

A walk through Saxony, Dresden, Leipzig, or Berlin would show a contrast so different from the West. Decaying buildings. Massive dumping grounds of rotting garbage. Pollution surpassing the worst worldwide.

In the café that morning, I watched the man sitting at the table nearby with his newspaper. The concern on his face seemed to speak of the anxiety felt by all Germans.

Still, the German people are inherently industrious and hard working. I believe they will make it work.

War was taking place between the U.S. and Iraq. Because of the conflict, threats toward American embassies were again on the rise.

The grounds surrounding the embassy began to fill with daily anti-war demonstrators. The local authorities allowed demonstrations for as long as they were peaceful.

Near the embassy and along the river, anti-war demonstrators set up a camp where they lived day and night for several weeks. Their camp was comprised of scarecrow soldiers strewn along makeshift graves, and signs stuck in the ground depicted various horrors of war. While they never made remarks to passersby, their presence alone made their statement.

It was refreshing one morning to arrive at work and see the old German woman—a one-woman demonstrator—with a sign on her back which said, "Danke, USA". Maybe she was remembering 1945.

On the following morning, yet another old woman was demonstrating alone. She approached the Marine on duty and handed him a yellow rose, saying "Danke." The Marine returned her favor by kissing her hand as he accepted the rose.

It was during this time that an act of terrorism occurred in the embassy by the splinter group called the Red Army Fraction. For many of us, it was a narrow escape.

Just minutes before 7:00 in the evening, I left my office for the day and began walking home along the river. I knew nothing of the embassy attack until the following morning.

The RAF had a statement to make to the U.S. Embassy, and they had their own way of doing so. Across the river, they waited for the appointed moment of 7:00. Their attack came abruptly and without any warning as they fired 125 rounds of ammunition through embassy windows!

Not many people were still working when the firing broke out. A few officers talking together in a doorway narrowly missed the bullets as they dove under a desk. Bullets were lodged in the walls and furniture, and one tore a hole through a chair and stuck in the screen of my computer.

By morning the embassy and grounds were still scattered with police. People were lingering inside the offices and halls, inspecting the various bullet holes and talking about the events of the night before. I sat quietly in my own office, staring at the bullet holes in the windows and walls.

A small group of about 12 members of Alcoholics Anonymous met each week for an English-speaking meeting. We were a mixture of Americans and Germans, and we soon bonded in that special way.

The Bonn Group, as we called ourselves, met in the basement of a small church in Plittersdorf. As an Alanon member, Nipper liked to attend the meetings with me. The group sat around a large table, proverbial coffee pot and cups in the center, and Nipper sat on the floor by my side.

I could always tell when Nipper—who made the rounds under the table to each member—was getting his ears scratched. The member would lean to one side, a hand under the table and a smile on the face.

It was at one of these meetings that I first realized Nipper snored! It was winter, and I had placed my coat on the floor by my chair so he could have a soft spot to sit on. The meeting began, and one of the members was "sharing." She paused for some moments, gathering her thoughts. The group quietly waited, and one by one we began to smile as we noticed the quietness broken by the sound of "zzzzzzzzzzz" coming from the floor under the table.

I had attended AA meetings in many countries—Khartoum, England, Jerusalem, France, Germany. While they all followed the basics, I was beginning to notice certain differences in the meetings. For example, if an American member has a "slip" and admits to it, the member is praised for having the courage to admit his mistake. He or she is encouraged by other American members to "keep coming back."

In Santiago, a Chilean AA meeting is one of folksy, all-is-well sharing. As each member speaks during the meeting, nobody admits to personal failings or fears, to having a bad day, to wanting a drink, to facing any kind of dilemma. Sharings are happy little musings of unimportant events.

On the other hand, should a German member have a slip and have the courage to admit it in a meeting, the other German members give him a good scolding: "Dumkof! Dumbhead! What is wrong with you!" (It is their well-meaning way of helping the one who strayed.)

Germany's location in Europe makes it ideal for touring. Alsace, Provence, Lichtenstein, Switzerland, and Germany itself were just a few of the beautiful places to visit. Country roads beckoned, picturesque villages and vineyards waited to be explored. Come on—grab your walking stick!

When the Rhine reaches Koblenz it connects with the Mosel River where winegrowing villages and vineyards unfold. The vineyards grow along shady sides of the low mountains on both sides of the narrow Mosel, and in the villages wine vats are kept in dark cellars as they age. Sampling the local wines is a popular activity in the vineyards.

If you reach Trier at the end of a long winding stretch on the Mosel before getting too tipsy from wine tasting, you will have reached the oldest town in Germany—well over 2000 years old—picturesque and full of history.

No matter where I wandered I felt the pure joy of being in the awesome beauty and history of the old world, of seeing sights I had not seen before.

While I enjoy excursions with others, there is something to be said for traveling alone. Often I did this by train. As a lone traveler, I was free to pick and chose what I wanted to see and when, to sleep late or get up early, to eat when I alone felt like it, to chat with other travelers.

Sometimes I simply want to be alone, to hibernate by the window of my train, and watch the picturesque scenes unfold as I let my thoughts wander at will.

Rigidly structured itineraries do not appeal to me, but some planning is worthwhile. A mental idea of what I want to see or do, and then perhaps change my mind if I am in the mood for something else.

Meandering through ancient villages, shopping in a foreign city, sitting quietly in an immense old cathedral with masses of flickering candles, walking through a German forest—these experiences set my soul free from the cobwebs of confinement in an embassy office. I return home with a slightly better concept of who I am.

It is said that to travel is to broaden one's horizons. This is so true, I have found. Like a kaleidoscope, my ideas, values and understanding of life gradually changed just a little. With each experience, each exposure to paintings by the masters, each conversation with a foreigner, I am enriched as an individual.

Of course, traveling can be broadening in other ways! I always seem to eat too much!

12
My Ancestor Was A Hamburger!

A special personal memory is mine of a business trip to the city of Hamburg, the home of my great, great grandfather. I am a descendent of a Hamburger.

On occasion, the large U.S. Embassy in Bonn sends assistance to one of the many smaller embassies and consulates located in Europe. Such was the case when I boarded a train one morning for the U.S. Consulate in Hamburg, a 5-hour journey from Bonn.

I had never given much thought to my great, great grandfather until the train began to enter this old seaport city—once the shipping artery of Central Europe. What was he like? What was his life like? Genealogy is difficult to trace since so many records were destroyed in fires and wars.

That entire week was mildly busy within the small, quiet consulate. In the evenings I lingered over dinner or walked along the seaport or through old neighborhoods. My business trip was as much pleasure as work.

Industrial Hamburg is an interesting city of medieval guildhalls, ancient warehouses, the Krameramtswohnungen, houses built for the widows of officials in 1670. Still the major German port, the Port of Hamburg is involved in trade with some 1,100 ports worldwide.

On a Saturday morning, a breathtaking boat tour began off the St. Paul wharf to the gigantic harbor. The boat wound through narrow canals sided by the ancient warehouses, high and narrow and sootie with age. The experience was awe inspiring and I was entranced. What a ride through the past!

My final evening in Hamburg was also my birthday. Leo had arranged for her friend at the Consulate to take me to dinner at a famous seafood restaurant by the water at the Grand Harbor. My

German companion and I had a table at the very edge of the pier where we watched the giant sun set over the water of the Elbe. It was a spectacular sight.

As we dined, immense ships silently floated by our table on their way out to sea. A charming gesture of the Hamburgers was to play a musical farewell from nearby loudspeakers of each ship's national anthem as they sailed for their homeland in China, India, or who knows where.

13
The U.S. President Visits Prague

Before Czechoslovakia became the Czech Republic, Prague was expecting its first visit ever from a U.S. President. This high level visit required additional support from the embassy in Bonn, and my colleague, Pat, and I were selected.

Rumor had it that about 700 people were in the President's entourage including the press, speech writers, bodyguards, and administration support. The expenses were staggering. By contrast, many years earlier when President Thomas Jefferson traveled, he was accompanied by only one or two people!

Shirley Temple Black—at one time, the child actress with famous curls—was the U.S. Ambassador to Prague at the time. She was well loved as an ambassador by the people who worked in the embassy—an embassy tucked unobtrusively among picturesque old buildings in Prague.

Pat and I arrived in Prague in the late afternoon and taxied to our hotel where we had adjoining rooms. It was November and already dark outside. We were hungry, and left the hotel to have dinner and see some of the city.

Only a year and a half earlier, Prague had been liberated from its communist occupation and the deprivation was still evident. Buildings were dark with soot, although some were already in the early stages of restoration. Despite the decaying condition the Soviet occupation left it in, Prague was still one of the most beautiful cities of Europe with its span of ancient bridges arching now and again over the Vitava (Moldau) River. The city is dominated by the Prague Castle.

We crossed over the 600 year-old Charles Bridge. This unusual structure of the 14th century was built according to the order of Charles IV and still stands in its original shape despite several damaging episodes throughout the years. Enormous statues tower over and along the expanse of this very long stone bridge.

Bohemians, gypsies, artists and musicians hang around the bridge selling their paintings and crystal, or playing a harmonica. A woman was selling crystal and we stopped to purchase some cobalt blue Bohemian pieces. Crystal was cheap, but the winds of change would take care of that.

Leaning over the center of Charles Bridge, we gazed out in the darkness over the many lighted distant bridges which seemed to cascade one after the other down the river. In the distance, rooftops and cathedral spires of Gothic and Baroque architecture were silhouetted in the moonlight. Lovely.

We could not find a restaurant. Our search was becoming frenzied, and we could find nothing! Was there a scarcity of restaurants because of the Soviet occupation ending just a year and a half ago?

Finally, a dim light from within a small cellar window caught my eye. It appeared to be a restaurant, but was so inconspicuous. There was no sign, but yes, this was indeed a restaurant. We entered. Inside, the waiter spoke English with a heavy accent, and told us that they would accept U.S. currency. We were in business!

The underground cellar was hundreds of years old and had been a medieval dungeon for prisoners until recently—before dungeon settings were fashionable atmospheres for restaurants! The room was quiet with only a few other guests. Candles were mounted on the stone walls and sent flickering shadows dancing through the dungeon. It looked and felt very, very old.

We ordered from a Czech menu and the waiter translated the selections for us. Still, we did not realize our order consisted of four courses! It was delicious, but would prove to be the only nutritious food we would eat for the next week.

When our bill was brought to us on a tiny silver plate, it said five dollars was due for two meals. No, there must be a mistake. Five dollars for two wonderful four course meals? But our waiter confirmed that the bill was correct. Pat and I looked at each other in puzzlement.

"I wonder what a bowl of soup would cost—they would probably

The Heydays / 143

pay Us to eat it!" With that from Pat, we broke into peels of helpless giggles, paid the bill with a generous tip for the waiter, and left the dungeon.

Throughout the week, Pat and I alternated shifts to provide round-the-clock coverage for the President's visit. We worked and slept, and worked and slept.

A suite of hotel rooms for the detail working group had been set up as temporary offices with secured phones, fax machines, and direct lines to the White House. People were in and out of the rooms, writing speeches, receiving and placing phone calls, sending faxes.

The food in the hotel was surprisingly of poor quality. After days of sporadic work pattern, poor sleep, and low grade food, I began to feel tired and rundown.

Mr. President, George Bush, Sr., arrived. We watched the events of the state visit on closed circuit television in the detail rooms. Although weeks of preparation and 700 supporters went into that visit, the President was in Prague for a brief four hours. Suddenly, it was all over but the clean up.

A small incident caught my eye and left an impression on me the last morning as we began to clean up. A young woman with the White House task force walked into our "office" where a table had been set up with coffee and platters of fresh rolls. She picked up a sweet roll, took a bite, then tossed it back on the platter and left the room.

The little sweet roll was not expensive, but the wasteful attitude of the young, supposedly well educated woman was obscene. In a city like Prague where food was so scarce, I was embarrassed for the young woman's behavior.

Pat and I returned to our hotel rooms at the end of the clean up day, exhausted and hungry. My phone was ringing. Someone from the working team had tickets to Prague's National Theater to see Mozart's Magic Flute. I was invited to go with.

We took a cab to the theater, passing through the lovely city and under the apartment windows of Czechoslovakian President, Vaclav Havel.

The National Theater, a neo-Renaissance construction, is tiered with worn seats surrounding the stage, ornate with heavy red velvet drapes and gold rococo.

On the wooden floors by each seat was a small old fashioned foot heater to warm our feet by. I felt myself grow relaxed and even drowsy as the beautiful opera unfolded, entrancing with soft colored lights, elaborate costumes, and the beautiful music from Mozart's Magic Flute.

Pat returned to Bonn, but I remained in Prague for several holidays and rented a room at the home of a Czech woman.

The weather was cold but sunny as I left my boarding room and walked downhill through a wooded area toward a tram stop. The tram will take me into the center of Prague, but I could not find it. Then, I noticed a woman walking in my direction. She looked poor with her tattered coat and worn shoes.

I stopped the woman and tried to ask in English where the tram stop is, exactly? She did not say a word, but pointed me in the right direction and as I started to walk again she stopped me. From her jacket pocket she took out one coin, a tram token, and placed it in my hand. "For the tram," she seemed to be saying. I was so touched by this gesture of friendly kindness, and it has forever endeared me to the Czech people.

A small vegetable stand near the tram stop held a skimpy selection of carrots and potatoes, poorly shaped and gnarled. There was not much to choose from. Prague was poor then, struggling to recover from its recent occupied past.

The old tram ride was fun. It took me through a panorama of morning activity as the Czechoslovakians began their day. I jumped off the tram and found myself in front of a department store. What, I wondered, would a department store in Czechoslovakia be like?

The department store was very old fashioned inside, reminding me somewhat of the 1940's of Chicago. The lights were dim, but several people were quietly shopping. Merchandise was scarce, the selections meager. I stepped onto a slow moving escalator which carried me to the second floor.

On the second floor at the ladies' toilette, a tiny line was waiting by the entrance and a woman sat collecting a coin from each of us for use of the toilette. It was my first experience of having to pay to use a public bathroom!

Still in line, I gave the woman my coin and in return she gave me one small square of toilet paper. One small square! This made a great impression on me. Normally I would use at least five squares! Nobody else in the line seemed to find it unusual, and so I thanked the woman and waited my turn. One small square!

Walking through the picturesque streets of Prague, I was ignoring my enormous fatigue from the past five days of erratic work and poor diet. I did not want to miss one day of being in Prague by giving in to sickness.

I stopped at a fast food chicken restaurant, ordered a chicken plate, and brought it to a tall, empty table. There were no chairs. People stood while they ate.

I set my plate on the table, but suddenly I was overcome with dizziness. My vision blurred. There was no place to sit down, and I groped my way toward the door and out of the restaurant. Surely I looked drunk to those around me.

The Czechs did not speak much English, the city was foreign and unfamiliar to me, and I was ill. Not a good situation to be in. Someone kindly noticed and helped me to a chair in a nearby shop where I sat long enough to recover, and then a taxi returned me to my boarding house.

I could not ignore my ailing health any longer. In my very quiet room, I climbed into bed. The soft tick-tock of a clock lulled me to sleep, and for almost two days I did little else but sleep and occasionally eat.

Once recovered, I left my room to explore Prague. Despite the dirt and grayness of the city, and cold sunless weather, the breathtaking treasures of Prague filled me with awe. The grayness, in fact, lends its own mood to the atmosphere.

I visited the Little Quarter Gothic and Baroque churches. In the Old Town over Charles Bridge were the picturesque 13th century gardens of Petrin Hill and Strahov, the Baroque Strahov Monastery, and Prague Castle from the Romanesque era with its precious works of art and culture.

Along the Golden Lane, tiny houses from the 16th-19th centuries still stand. The people who lived in these small row houses were workers at the castle hundreds of years ago. What was their life like without electricity, running water, automobiles, or telephones? Very simple, I would think.

When I left beautiful Prague to return to Bonn, I knew I would be back one day. But again I could find no sand for my shoes.

14
Enchantments of Germany

Ludwig van Beethoven was born in Bonn around 1770, and his two-storied childhood home with its flowered courtyard stands on a side street off Bonn's Square.

Ludwig was a short and stocky man with pock marks on his face and a lot of hair. He was a romantic man who loved women, and was loved by women, but he never married.

In 1793, Beethoven moved to Vienna where he wrote most of his music, and where he died in 1858. Throughout his life he suffered from many illnesses, and in time he became deaf. Yet, Beethoven wrote some of his most beautiful music with a deaf ear. His music was a highlight of Bonn's 2000th birthday party.

On a Sunday afternoon in the summer of 1990, my friend Shirley and I stood in Bonn's Square waiting for the birthday festivities to begin. Special celebrations and concerts were taking place all year long in the Rhineland in honor of Bonn's birthday.

Happy chatter and laughter filled the Square, children were playing and running, and the locals were in a festive mood. Before long, the crowd was thick and tightly squeezed together as it filled the Square and side streets.

Finally, the first loud notes of Beethoven's Fifth blared through the many loudspeakers of the Square—"Da da da—daaa!"—resounding throughout Bonn, and over the Rhineland. The effect was moving and beautiful.

The crowds were suffocating me. My phobia of mob madness was resurfacing as the people pressed tightly against each other. I could not move or breathe. I began to panic, pushing desperately between people who would not budge. "Enchuldegan, enchuldegan," I said, but nobody noticed. The sights and sounds became dim and, once again, I passed out.

When I opened my eyes a short while later, a group of concerned faces were looking down on me. Someone had carried me from the crowd to a bench, someone else was rubbing my arm, and a glass of water was offered.

I will not soon forget Bonn's special 2000th birthday party. But I began to avoid crowds, and seek out the country instead.

―∽⚘∾―

The countryside and small villages were more to my liking. Nipper and I packed our bags and set off for several weeks in Bavaria and Austria.

Nipper is easy to travel with. He enjoys sitting by the window of a train to watch the outside flow by. If it is a long journey, we will briefly hop off the train at one of the small station stops so he can take a wee behind the caboose.

In Freiburg, Bavaria's capital, pretzels were first tied into knots. And, America was born—it was the birthplace of a geographer named Martin Waldseemuller who, in 1507, credited Amerigo Vespucci with discovering the New World. Freiburg is also "the place" to buy cuckoo clocks.

Mittenwald in Bavaria has provided the world with its beautifully crafted violins for centuries. The trade still takes place in its 300 year old violin school. Watch as a craftsman works and allows the visitors to witness a violin in the making.

Ulm, Munich, Baden-Baden, Landshut—we stopped here, and we stopped there. The Passion Play in Oberammergau takes place only once each ten years. This village beauty has little houses painted with folk scenes or writings on the sides or over the entryway. The writings depict the year in which the house was built, the names and a description of the family who originally lived in the house.

We passed through the Black Forest to Berchtesgaden, where we stayed at a chalet. The spa village chalet was cozy in the winter and from its balcony I had a panorama view of the snow capped Alps. Pine, cedar and wood burning from fireplaces scented the air as Nipper and I followed a walking path through the forest. The sounds of wildlife—birds, the call of an elk—broke the silence of our walk.

Bavarians still dress in lederhosen, felt hats with feathers, boiled wool jackets of dark drab green. All over Bavaria, there are cobble stoned villages, farmland and flowers, chalets, cows with bells hanging around their necks. We could hear yodeling and music in the villages.

In Bertchesgaden, we boarded a bus for the twelve miles down a forested country road to Salzburg in Austria. An occasional local climbs on or off, a housewife with a basket over her arm or an old man going—to church?

Innsbruck and Salzburg have their own individual charms. Wherever I visit, I want to live there—in all the fairytale magic—never to return to the reality of the real world.

A parade was about to begin in Salzburg. Austrians were dressed in traditional costumes of their various locales as they marched in the parade. Their colorful banners were hoisted in the air by school children, and young freuline carried baskets of flowers. Trumpets blared and drums beat loudly as the parade moved through the streets of Salzburg.

Nipper was wearing his new tee shirt—black and red with a small white edelweiss flower—and I held him high during the parade so he would not be stepped on. But he doesn't care for the loud music which hurts his ears, so we moved on.

We stumbled upon a walled rose garden in the center of Salzburg. Within the garden, little paths meandered between rows of colorful roses, and for awhile we sat on the benches to enjoy the beauty and morning sun.

Stone stairs led up to the apartment in Salzburg where Wolfgang Amadeus Mozart was born in the late 1700's. The stairs are worn to a dip in the center from centuries of footsteps. Inside, the apartment is sparse—sheet music exhibited in a glass display case, a few pictures, a piano, and a few violins.

Mad King Ludwig II (1845-1886) committed suicide in a lake near one of his famous castles. Some say he was just advanced for his era, and not mad at all. He was immensely rich, never married, and preferred the life of solitude, away from crowds. I can relate to that. His three lavish creations are all located in Bavaria.

Herrenchiemsee was built on mountain rimmed Chiemsee, and is known for its elaborate mirror halls designed after the French Versailles of Louis XIV.

Linderhof is the smallest of Ludwig's castles, the richest in ornamentation. It sets just under the towering Austrian and Bavarian Alps. Visit this one in winter, as I did.

Ludwig designed his fairytale castle Neuschwanstein with the swan and peacock in mind. Neuschwanstein reaches into the heavens, and looks down at thickly forested mountains. Here I could visualize knights in shining armor astride their white stallions.

I was told to take a ride in the skiers' cables of the Zugspitze, the highest snow skiing point in the Alps near Garmisch-Partenkirchen. Could there possibly be anywhere in the world to rival the loveliness of this snowland?

My friend and neighbor from Bonn, Lou, did the driving on a later journey to southern Germany. We spent a few days in

Rothenburg, and then drove south to Garmisch-Partenkirchen where we boarded a farmhouse cabin nearby. It would be our home base from which to explore our surroundings.

Every season dresses this beautiful wonderland near the Austrian and Italian border with a new look. In winter, the snow was not yet heavy. The air was fresh and invigorating, and the scenery breathtaking. We did a lot of driving through the Alps, stopping now and then. Nipper slept in the rear seat—the rhythm of the car quickly puts him to sleep.

Our small rustic cabin was owned by farmers who lived across the road in the main farmhouse. We awoke each morning to views of the snowy country around us, the smell of coffee in the kitchen nook, and the sound of yodeling from a radio station quietly reporting the skiing conditions throughout Bavaria.

A walking path curled around the big farm, snaking in and out of the woods and through the open countryside. Here in this remote farmland, Nipper in his fur jacket and I in my warm boots and heavy socks work up a good appetite before breakfast. We encounter no people, only deer and rabbit.

The farmhouses in Europe are commonly attached to their barns where the animals live, making them one long building. The air smells fresh and good with the scent of pine and breakfast from the nearby farm.

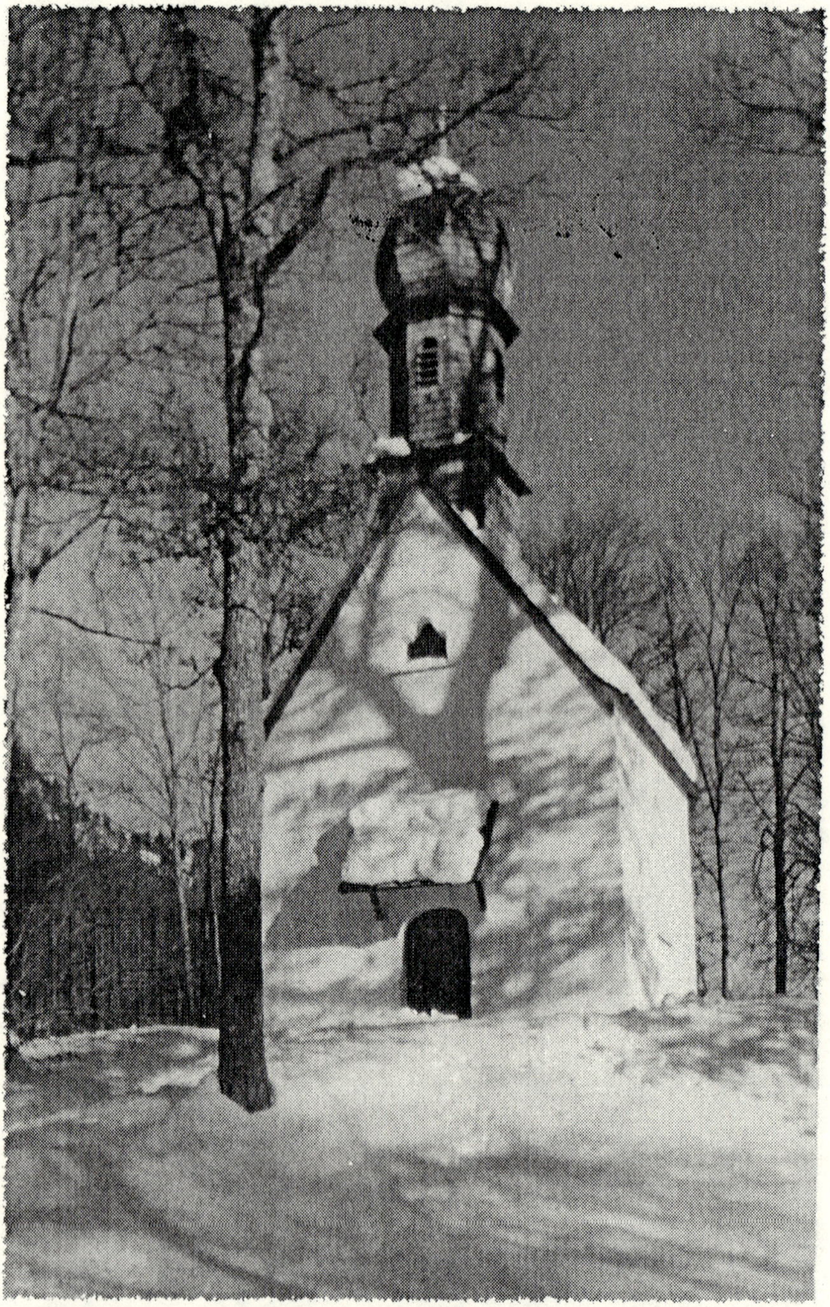

My friend prefers to stay inside the cabin in the early mornings and study the weather conditions. She is not a walker like Nipper and me.

Lou became the "photographer" as she pressed her new movie camera against the window just as the slow rising morning sun moved over the snowy Alps. It was a spectacular sight, to be sure, but watching twenty minutes of the sun coming up on a video could be—well, uh, like boring! Don't give up your day job, Lou!

The Wies in Bavaria is one of the most beautiful churches of human creativity. It is a masterpiece of rococo art, built in the 1730's as a pilgrimage. From all over Europe, pilgrims journey here to worship.

Our days were carefree. We lingered in small villages, visited an abbey or hunting lodge, walked through the woods, and ate German food.

A small shack caught our eye one evening on our way back to the farm. It had a shingle over the door—something about homemade food—and friendly lights shown from within. Chimney smoke drifted upwards into the darkened sky. "Let's go in," I said.

A large stone fireplace was crackling inside and good smells of sausages, sauerkraut and baked bread were mouth watering. Three old men sat around a wooden table with pitchers of beer, engrossed in their game of cards. A doorbell jingled as we entered and they looked up at us with mild curiosity, nodded a greeting, and returned to their game.

But more often than not, we dined evenings in Partenkerchen at a restaurant serving homemade German dishes. Long wooden family style tables were set up and the three of us—Lou, Nipper and I—always found a good spot near the front. As we ate, we were entertained by a little round German dressed in lederhosen. He played polkas for us on his accordion, while Lou caught it all on her new movie camera.

I would have to say—if I have to—that Rothenburg au Tauber was my favorite getaway. No matter what the season, medieval Rothenburg captivated me. It was my own private, heart-hidden fairytale hideaway.

The closely packed half-timbered houses tower over narrow streets dating back to the 13th and 15th centuries. In Rothenburg's charming Square, a clock strikes on the hour and a tiny wooden window opens to re-enact a whimsical scene of the Meistertrunk. Miniature mechanical figures drain huge mugs of beer.

I rented the same room each time I visited Rothenburg. It was a very old, small hotel, once a house, just off the Square on a side street. My room was pleasant and comfortable. Wooden shutters opened onto a courtyard below where tables and chairs and large pots of geraniums were scattered.

The hotel contains family heirlooms and old portraits hang on the walls. Downstairs, one must pass quickly through the bustling dining room to reach the front door. I say "quickly" because the home cooked German food always smells good and making it to the front door without stopping to eat each time requires great willpower.

If I returned to the hotel after eleven at night, I used my key to let myself in the front door. But first, I visit the hunting lodge restaurant next door for black forest cake and hot tea. This always gave me sweet dreams!

Rothenburg sits on top of a hill overlooking farmland and the Tauber River below. On the stone wall encircling Rothenburg, in a large garden filled with trees, benches and a scattering of artsy statues, a violinist sits and moves his bow to the strains of Wagner and Bach.

The summer's scent of flowers and the soft violin music lulls me into reverie. "Oh, feed my soul, thou bow of life. Strum on my heartstrings. Caress me with your kiss of melodious passion, and leave me, at peace and loved."

Four years in Germany passed, and I felt sad at the thought of having to leave.

The old shadowy staircase of the tenement house where Leo lived was filled with delicious aromas of dinner as I climbed upstairs. It was my last evening in Leo's cozy third floor flat in Bonn, and she was preparing a farewell dinner for me. A handful of other friends had been invited.

Leo was single then. I smiled to myself as I climbed the stairs and thought of how, recently, two men had both asked her to marry them. One was much older than she, the other younger. She said she cared for them both and didn't know which one to chose, but it would be the younger one she eventually married.

After the reunification when the capital reverted to Berlin, hundreds of embassy people stayed behind in Bonn rather than uproot their families and relocate. Leo and her husband moved to a distant town where they bought and renovated a house.

My farewell dinner that evening was special in Leo's cluttered apartment with its wooden floors, mish-mash of antiques, old screened porch over the flower strewn garden, and huge cat.

She entertained us with songs in German—what a lovely voice!—as she played her guitar. I can still hear her . . . "Ich Liebe Dich," she sang, as softly and as clearly as the beauty of German crystal.

Auf Weidersehn, Deutschland. Ich Liebe Dich.

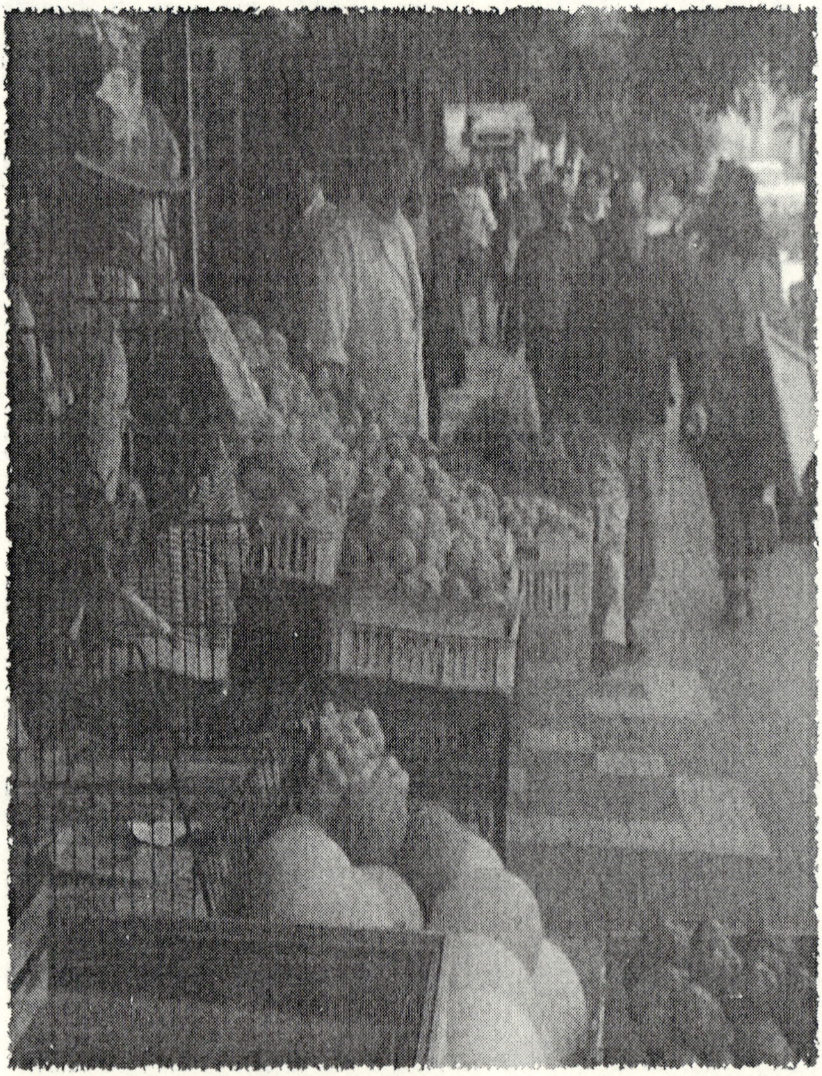

15
Santiago, Chile

A small Chilean boy had a drum tied around his neck as he pranced in front of our table and banged on his drum. He was making a pathetic attempt to entertain us—hoping for a coin—as we sat dining at an outside restaurant in one of Santiago's side streets.

I had recently arrived in Santiago and was with two new colleagues that evening. "Don't give him a coin," my colleagues told me, "or he will not leave us alone." So I slowly ate my dinner, and watched the boy.

He was barefoot, his clothing was tattered, his face dirty and his nose running, and he plainly did not know how to beat on a drum. His young eyes already hinted of seeing too much of the harder side of life.

Suddenly, the boy lost his balance and fell into the gutter with his little drum. Nobody paid any attention to him and as I started to get up from my table to help, my colleagues objected. "He is only pretending and wants our attention," they told me. "Ignore him."

That small drummer boy would remind me a little of myself during the ensuing three years in Santiago, trying to beat my drum and make a living but falling into the gutter.

Nipper and I had arrived in Chile in late August, following two months in Washington where I was subjected to a torturous fast course in Basic Spanish. Its not that I didn't learn Anything, but in the process I lived under immense strain.

Now I do have to say that the class started out with seven

students, and only two of us endured the course. Say what you will of my fluency in Spanish, but you can't deny my stick-to-it-iveness. The two of us remaining, and the lovely older instructor who originated from Nicaragua, became three peas in a pod—really good friends in the end.

Anyway, it was my first weekend in Santiago and I was familiarizing myself with the downtown streets. Seasons are reversed from that in North America, and the dismal winter weather was all but gone. Spring and summer in Chile are quite beautiful, I was told. Lush and enchanting, with soft sunny days.

Downtown was not the best of Santiago, but interesting nonetheless. It did have a Latin flavor, somehow. The streets were fairly crowded with noisy traffic and olive skinned, dark haired pedestrians. In the arcades, shoeshine boys were bent over their work, polishing shoes to a spit shine. Fashionable shops filled the arcades, and prices were very good.

A certain aroma filled the morning air coming from an open vendor—Chilean "fast food," you might say. Curious, I had a closer look at what was similar to a Mexican enchilada. Quite tasty!

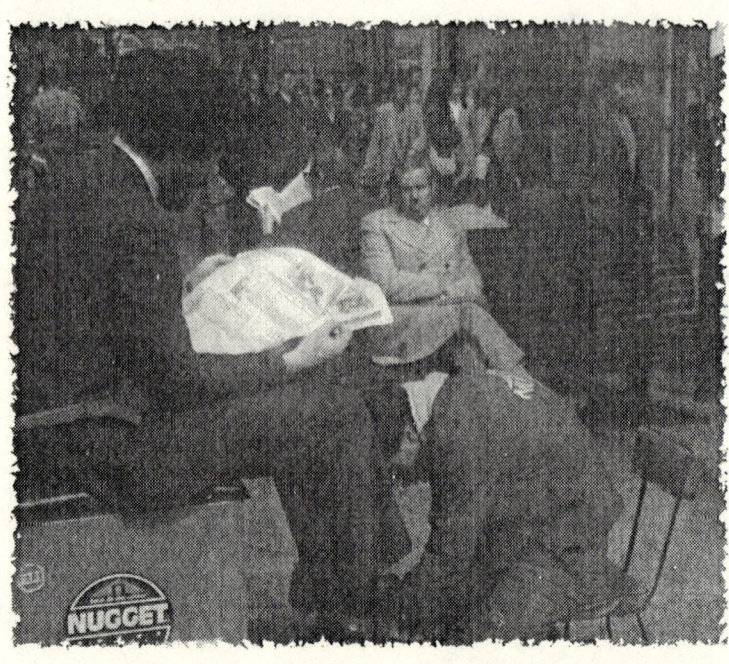

Speaking of Chilean currency, a fistful of Chilean pesos amounted to only a very small value. Never have I seen so much actual currency amount to so little.

As I strolled along the downtown streets that Saturday morning eating my Chilean enchilada, I became aware of an odd noise growing louder and louder. It was, in fact, a commotion much like a herd of animals rushing toward me.

A mob was running in my direction. Ordinary citizens were on a stampede, frantically running from a small handful of police who were spraying strong teargas at them!

Stunned at the scene in front of me, I ran for safely in a doorway where I stood and watched. Immediately, I felt the teargas myself, stinging my eyes and causing painful blurred vision. Since I could not see well, I stayed in my safe spot for a good while.

I never knew what caused that stampede—possibly a controversial demonstration of some kind—but the experience left me with a small insight into what Chileans must have been living with in police brutality.

In an old office building in crowded downtown Santiago, the U.S. Embassy was located adjacent to Chilean President Pinochet's palace. The large palace was fronted with an open courtyard, and two guards stood at the entrance with rifles.

Political unrest still lingered in Chile, and I soon began to hear the sordid tales of Pinochet and his murderous regime. As I began to make Chilean friendships, stories relayed by them sometimes conflicted. Some people felt Pinochet did much good for their country.

The palace grounds always appeared peaceful, and I often sat on a low stone wall nearby on my lunch break, eating my sandwich as I watched the activity around the palace. On occasion, I saw Pinochet himself, always protected with bodyguards.

The embassy was housed on several upper floors of a very old building, a veritable fire trap. A fire did break out one night, causing extensive damage and leaving the building reeking with smoke soot for a very long time. While a new American embassy was in the planning stages, it would not be ready for occupancy until 3 years later, after my departure.

My job assignment was in the Political Office on the ninth floor—dark, cluttered and crowded, with a manager given to dark moods and yelling. The entire embassy, in fact, was filled with gossip and low morale.

In a corner with poor ventilation and dirty walls, my desk pressed against that of a colleague, an older woman who did not like me. She was called periodically to assist in other offices and, while this gave me some reprieve from her scorn, her work was added to my already heavy load.

I soon loathed going into the embassy each morning, and this unhappy scenario continued for my entire 3 year assignment.

It was about this time—the early 1990's—when the new Clinton Administration began trimming fat in Washington from the government budget. The State Department placed a freeze on hiring, and began to abolish many Foreign Service positions. Since the work remaining still had to be done, it was divided and added to our already heavy workloads.

(In later years, I attended a 3-week workshop at the Foreign Service Institute in Arlington. A State Department inspector was a guest speaker, and he admitted to our group that the abolishment of positions had been overdone. But getting those positions reinstated, he said, was no easy matter.)

Recognition for the professionalism of the modern Foreign Service Secretary was absolutely behind times. Yet, much was expected from the position.

Foreign Service Secretary is just a name. The position itself is a demanding, often draining, one. A leading American magazine ran an editorial on the most difficult jobs in America, and interestingly, the "secretary" was number one on the list!

The modern Foreign Service Secretary must be proficient with the computer, maintain and operate numerous modern office machines, be adept in foreign diplomacy, keep up with a myriad of details and a heavy workload, risk foreign hazards, and deal with cultural adjustments as well as anyone.

A group of secretaries from one of the American embassies

launched a campaign in the early 1990's to increase job promotions and opportunities and to change the name of Secretary to Office Management Specialist (OMS). It was hoped that a name change might relieve some old stigma from the days way back when secretaries did little more than file papers, answer the phone, and take a little dictation.

Input from secretaries in worldwide embassies was solicited and combined for a strong campaign. The results brought certain improvements, but still, apparently a rose by any other name is still a rose. The true professionalism of the OMS continues to receive only a token nod.

What I have observed over the years is that the greatest respect and recognition received as an OMS actually comes from the highest caliber of associates. Not those necessarily holding a higher position or title, but those who themselves are genuine professionals. They seem to possess a sense of personal confidence which allows them to freely accept the important place others also have in the work world.

Chile is a country of natural abundance and beauty. I am told that if you begin a trek from Arica in Northern Chile and travel downward to Puerto Williams in the South, you will have moved through parched deserts, snow covered mountaintops, ravines, jungles, sand dunes, rivers and valleys, prairies and lakes. I should think you would also be very tired!

Resembling a long ribbon, Chile lies between the Pacific Ocean and the Andes Mountains, the highest mountains in the world after the Himalayas. The beautiful snowcapped mountains surround Santiago, and the ocean is only an hour's drive from the city.

Lying near the bottom of the world, Chile's seasons are reverse from those of North America. This intrigued me—at the Bottom of the world, in reverse seasons. Without gravity, we would fall off! Several years later I would live on Top of the world, in Finland.

Chile's rich soil produces those big black sweet grapes in January and wonderful juicy strawberries in the summer. A large bundle of flowers costs little, and I purchased fresh flowers regularly. In fact, the U.S. dollar went a long way in the affordable economy of Chile.

Winters are cold and rainy. However stunningly beautiful the Andes Mountains are, in winter the landlocked Santiago is imprisoned in bad air from the exhaust fumes which have no escape. Santiago has the worst smog in the world, rivaling even Mexico City, and Chileans often wear gas masks in winter.

Because of the serious smog and the high threat of earthquakes, Santiago is on the hardship list of the State Department. This entitled diplomats serving there to extras, including an R&R to Rio de Janeiro. But the heavy workload at the embassy made it difficult to take time off, and I never did see Rio.

The earthquake faults in Chile cause frequent tremors, but a major earthquake had not occurred since 1985. My first experience with tremors came shortly after arrival in Santiago.

I sat alone minding my own business one evening, a plate of dinner on my lap, watching the evening news on television. Suddenly, the ceiling chandelier began to sway, the floor beneath my feet vibrated, and a picture fell lopsided on the wall. For a moment, I froze, staring and waiting to see what might happen next, but the tremor soon passed. On many occasions, tremors shook my bed as I slept.

The unnerving part was in not knowing whether we were experiencing just another tremor, or the beginning of something bigger!

Santiago is a mixture of both Latin and European influences. It has wide boulevards, modern shops and apartment buildings, large fountains, and thick trees and gardens. Old haciendas in the city were being torn down and replaced with apartment buildings. A pity, if you ask me, though nobody did.

Nipper and I had settled into an attractive neighborhood of mature landscape lush with trees. Consignors and live-in maids were customary, and Carlos was the senior consignor of our apartment building. He lived on the premises to the rear, and could be seen sweeping, working around the grounds, or opening doors for people. Carlitos was his younger assistant.

The maids dressed in uniform dresses and aprons of pastel blues and pinks, and sometimes wore a small maid's hat. They lived with the family, cleaning, cooking, and taking care of children. Apartments were built with a bedroom and bath specifically for the maid, usually off the kitchen.

While my own apartment had a maid's room and bath off the

kitchen, I did not want a live-in maid. The maid's room became my pantry, and the bath was kept closed and never used.

It was in my pantry where I saw the ghost. I was staring at the canned goods one Friday evening, very tired after working all week, and wondered what to make for dinner. Then I noticed that the door to the maid's bath was open and the ceiling light on! This was very odd, because I had not been in that room in many months.

A strong feeling that I was not alone caused me to turn my attention to the window. There, the silhouette of a man—transparent like a sheer curtain—was watching me. His smile was kind, even loving, and I did not feel afraid, just fascinated.

For a few moments I simply stared at the image by the window. I gave myself a chance to "wake up," to realize it was surely only my imagination. But the image did not dissipate into the air. It remained, watching me in a friendly manner.

I left the pantry and sat a few moments in my living room. A mysterious peace had washed through me, so intense I felt I had been tranquilized. When I returned to the pantry, the image was gone. But the door to the bathroom was still open—and the light still on!

I wondered if the ghost image may have been meant to somehow bring me some measure of comfort and encouragement, since I was experiencing immense stress in my workplace. The lotus came to my mind, which is said to blossom in the mud, a reminder that we can blossom wherever we are planted if we try hard enough.

It was the stalking by an old man that actually had me afraid, but only for awhile. I met him in the neighborhood one morning while walking with Nipper.

He walked slowly toward us, leaning heavily on a cane. My attention had been on the loveliness of our walk—the gardens, flowers spilling out from wrought iron fences, Spanish railings winding upward to a balcony, the scent of corn dishes baking from someone's oven. "Gute mohnink", he said. His English was thick with a German accent, and he stopped me for a brief conversation.

In the weeks and months ahead, I found myself running into the old man, and he always tried to engage me in conversation. Not taller than five feet, he had no teeth and wore a felt German hat with small feather. Possibly in his 90's, he claimed to be an ex-Nazi. "Many

Nazis," he said, "had fled to South American countries after the second world war."

It seemed the old man was intentionally lying in wait for me as I took Nipper for his daily walk. He hid in the bushes and behind trees, followed us home, hung around my apartment building. Sometimes I saw him in the street below, looking up at my veranda on the first floor.

Coming out of the grocery store one day, a short distance from home, the old man suddenly sprang from behind a tree! Horrified, I quickened my pace, but he was remarkably fast on his cane! Imagine—stalked by a 90-year old ex-Nazi on a cane. And I was afraid of him, of all things!

The stalking was bizarre and offensive. Before long I was no longer afraid, but annoyed. My firm objections to him did not put an end to it, nor did the consignor or the local police take the matter seriously. The old man stalked me to my very last day in Santiago.

In a small Anglican church, only one of two English-speaking churches in Santiago, I gradually made friends. The members were largely British and Chilean.

A cozy library in the church was a gathering place for fellowship and study groups. Its worn wooden floors, shelves filled with old English books, the piano in the corner, became a comfortable place for me. I began to attend Saturday's used book sales and Sunday's study groups. It was there that I became better acquainted with Valerie.

Valerie is British, with a Chilean husband whom she had met in Spain many years earlier. They have lived in Santiago ever since with their son and daughter and a live-in maid, a few dogs and a cat. Valerie shared her family with me and we became close friends. The roughest spots of my assignment to Chile were softened by her friendship.

Ken and Lena were from the church, and often invited me to their home for dinner or a Sunday outing in the lush Chilean country. Ken was originally from Wales. Lena was born in Russia, grew up in Japan, and lived in Chile for most of her married life. She spoke five different languages! This always impressed me tremendously.

On occasion, Ken and Lena took me with them for a weekend in Peechidangi, a pristine fishing village by the Pacific Ocean. It was a paradise where one could walk along the shore for miles without seeing another living soul. At dusk the sun settled over the shore and turned the land into a colorful fantasy. We watched the fishermen come home at the end of the day, their buckets heavy with shrimp and lobster.

Our rooms were just feet from the water's edge, in a modest but clean boarding house. Chilean pesos translated into only five U.S. dollars a night for a room! Yes, of course, it was modest, no frills, but only five dollars a night!

Rolf and a few other friends joined us one memorable weekend at Peechidangi. As the morning sun broke through the dawn, Rolf and I went horseback riding along the ocean. The horses were gentle, and the joyful exhilaration of riding in the open air along the ocean was very special.

In a nearby village one day, Lena and I stopped for lunch and watched as the proprietor made bread. The recipe is old as the bible, but I will share its secret:

Made without yeast, mix flour, water and a dash of salt together and throw the dough against the wall of a large, very hot, old-fashioned oven. When the bread has fully baked, it falls off the oven walls. Add some butter—and it is Umm-Umm Good!

Now, if you do not have a very old iron oven, do not attempt this recipe. Throwing dough against the wall of a modern oven will only make a yuckie mess in your oven.

Chilean women must be just about the most beautiful women I have seen anywhere. Most impressive is their long silky dark hair, light olive complexion, and beautiful Spanish eyes.

The Latin men, now, are altogether irresistible. Masculine. Come-hither. Flirty. Smiling, teasing eyes. I first noticed their playful nature in the street one day where two husky men were engaged in a wrestling match. One had a tight armhold over the other's neck as they grappled around on the sidewalk kicking and yelling. A small crowd had gathered to watch.

I also stopped to watch, and expected the worst, that one of the men would be shortly knocked out cold! The crowd didn't appear concerned. I looked anxiously down the street for a policeman, but there was none.

Then, the two men suddenly broke out laughing, slapped each other on the back, and helped each other up. The crowd also began to laugh and clap their hands. "Bravo. Bravo", they yelled.

A favorite pastime of mine on a Saturday morning was to indulge in the Turkish bath, Latin style.

Located in large secluded gardens, the bathhouses resembled long wooden chicken coops. There was a separate house for women and for men. After the bath, one can sit in the sun on stone benches and enjoy the garden where, nearby, a small cabin-like dining room served tasty vegetarian meals.

Inside the bathhouse, the steam is so thick one can barely see all the nude women in their individual wooden stalls. We are given a towel by the Chilean woman attendant and a stall where, once immersed, only our heads are exposed.

Eucalyptus leaves give a heady scent of nurturing balm in the steam. Its branches are beat against the skin to stimulate. Five to ten minutes in the hot steam bath is followed with a towel soaked in icy water from a nearby bucket and pulled over the body in a downward pattern. That done, we return to the steam bath to repeat the procedure.

Quiet time in the gardens after an hour in the Turkish baths sums up a wonderful way to restore aching muscles and a tired mind.

There seemed little leisure time for roaming around the South American countries, but shorter treks were possible. The nearby ocean was always delightful. A visit to Valparaiso or Vina Del Mar was fun, or a drive through the countryside sprinkled with Spanish settlements, little pottery shops along the way, and old missions.

Farmers markets were filled with an abundance of beautiful fruit and vegetables. Also, many of the local crafts go back through the centuries, and Chile is one of the few countries excavating the lapis lazuli, an azure, opaque semiprecious stone. Artisans turn the blue lapis into lovely pieces of jewelry.

Departing Chile meant leaving with diminished health. The stressful 3 years in a highly dysfunctional embassy had taken its toll on me.

Yet, if we should experience an unpleasant assignment, there is always hope in the Foreign Service that the next assignment will be a better one.

It was time to go. Despite all, Chile remains in my memory a truly lovely country and I especially remember with fondness my Chilean friends.

And so—Adios, Santiago. Ciao!

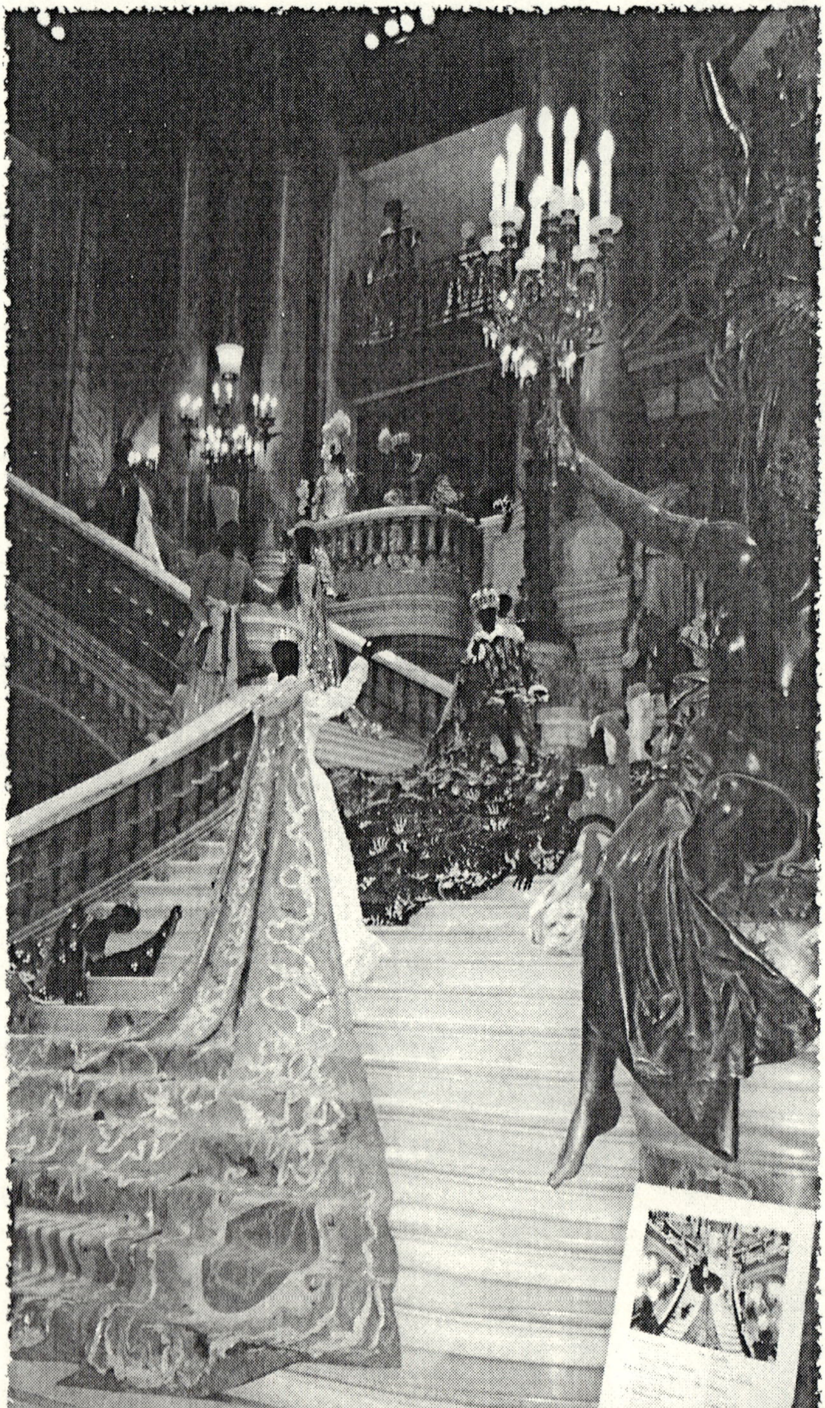

16
Paris

I was Christine, running through the old opera house of Paris in the shadowy halls, across the stage and past the scaffolds. Images of colorful dancers wearing outrageous, bizarre masks and costumes were dancing—without music—in the flood of intense colorful lights.

As I was about to descend the massive red carpeted staircase, a strong hand in a black leather glove caught my waist and gently turned me around to face him. He wore a mask over dark penetrating eyes which smoldered with passion into mine as he pulled me provocatively to him. He was, I knew, the Phantom of the Opera. And he was in love with me, Christine.

Then—as he kissed my face—and just as our lips were about to blend in madness—I woke up! Nipper was licking my cheek, trying to rouse me to take him out for a wee.

It was only a dream. I was not Christine, but I was indeed living in Paris now.

It was September of 1995 when Nipper and I arrived in Paris for my 3-year assignment. It rained daily for the first two weeks, but nothing could dampen my spirit for having been given an assignment to Paris. I was delighted!

Chestnut trees along Avenue Mozart were still full, and half covered the shops lining the street. A very old streetlamp stood just below my living room windows, casting a soft glow across the wet Paris sidewalk and trees.

In the 16th Arrondissement, where Amy and I lived on Avenue

Mozart, the heavy front door at the street unlocks with one of those large old-fashioned keys. Note the deeply carved, ornate door—a thing of beauty in itself. Passing through a foyer, walk to the rear hallway and take the lift to floor two. On floor two, large French doors open to my roomy 19th century Parisian habitat.

The rooms were large and airy, with French windows looking out to the street. Each window opened onto small wrought iron balconies, too small for even a chair but with railings just right for trailing geraniums.

Intricately carved borders along the high ceilings had motifs of cherubs and flowers, and the wooden floors were worn with age. Who had walked on these floors during the past century, and slept in the room we now sleep in? What conversations had these walls quietly listened to over the years?

Four fireplaces were in our Paris home, with each main room having its own. These fireplaces were works of art, ornately carved and crowned with a large overhead mirror.

Wood is expensive in Paris, but who cares? As a lover of candles and fireplaces, it was my little indulgence—and I deserved it!

A wood delivery service was available outside of Paris, and I contacted them. When the first batch arrived (complete with wood bugs), I hurried to the hearth with a log under my arm, and matches in my hand. I actually knew nothing about building a good fire, and time and again the tiny flame fizzled out. Great disappointment settled in as I watched the last little flicker go out.

For awhile, I was forced to use the artificial logs available in grocery stores. They were better than nothing, but I longed for the scent and crackle of fresh wood—the real stuff!

It was my brother, Norm, who taught me how to build a great fire. He came to Paris for a visit, and soon I had my first lesson. "The trick," Norm said, "is in the kindling wood and a bit of crumpled newspaper to get the fire started. Make sure the logs are very dry, with good ventilation between logs." We added some pinecones for a fragrant aroma. That done, we sat near the hearth and watched as the lovely flames began to crackle and pop.

For 3 years, I would enjoy many cold mornings and evenings with those lovely crackling fireplaces.

Norm and I spent a week in Bavaria together. We were driving through the beautiful countryside on our return to Paris, when we noticed a huge pile of wood stacked along the side of an old farmhouse. The farmer was working nearby, so we stopped to inquire whether he would sell us some of his wood. He agreed, and we stacked the wonderful firewood into our trunk.

As we were about to climb back into the car, Norm goodnaturedly ran back to the farmer to give him a can of his American beer. It was a friendly gesture, but I smiled to myself as I wondered how the farmer would compare the weak American beer to the very dark stout German stuff.

Off my kitchen, a side door led to a stairwell reminiscent of a medieval prison or something from a Stephen King movie. The stairwell had thick white dust, and cobwebs hung from the ceilings and covered the railings and stairs.

The stairwell appeared to be abandoned, but was actually still used regularly by tenants to carry down garbage or access their "cave" in the basement. The cave—storeroom—was a small room with dirt floor. Each cave had a padlocked wooden gate.

Down there, where a dark narrow pathway led to the caves, a timer allows ten minutes of light once the button is pressed. If you are still in your cave after ten minutes, you'll be in utter darkness as I was one day. It was a spooky, frightening experience! I avoided my cave—I knew without doubt that urchins and ghosts lurked down there, just waiting for someone to linger longer than ten minutes.

The other questionable feature of my apartment building was the wrought iron elevator. Since there were about eight floors to the building, the elevator was useful. But it was also old, slow and unreliable. If it should stop between floors—as it sometimes did—one must yell loudly for Madame, the proprietor living on floor one. Madame never came running, but she will eventually come to the rescue—if she hears you.

I preferred using the wide staircase. Sweeping and graceful, the stairs wound upward with their worn Savonnerii carpets. They had surely been affluent once, and I sometimes fantasized Greta Garbo or Ernest Hemmingway descending those stairs.

In Paris, the ground level of a building is the prima level and not floor one, as it should be. The second level is considered as floor one, and so forth on. While this seems trivial, I felt it was wrong. How can I direct guests to my apartment on floor two by telling them to go to floor one? However, nobody seemed confused but me.

Since it rains a lot in Paris, dampness penetrated the rooms of our apartment when we first arrived in the chilly autumn of 1995. Madame controlled the heat for the entire building—and she believed in being frugal where electricity was concerned. Nipper and I shivered and rattled around the bare apartment for our first two weeks, awaiting my household shipment with warm clothes and personal furnishings.

Settling into a new country, a new apartment, and a new job takes many months of frequent adjustments. But one of the first things I like to do in my new home is make it pleasant and comfortable, personalize it, and make it mine.

Early one Saturday morning, the sound of rain outside my window placed me in "the mood." Throwing a log in the fireplace, I made coffee and curled up to survey my little kingdom as I let my mind run free with decorating ideas.

Interior design is my personal passion, and what better way to give creative vent than in a Paris apartment?

Everyone has a special living room chair. Mine had big goose down pillows, and I moved it closer to the fireplace, with a view to the window. A few velvet and silk throw pillows. Pictures of one's family on the table. A large vase of fresh roses to adorn the mantel. When the spring weather arrives, I thought, I will plant boxes of geraniums on the balconies. All day long I moved from room to room, making our new home cheerful and cozy.

When had I fallen asleep? I could not remember, but by midnight I awoke to the steady beat of rain in the courtyard and soft French voices from a neighbor's adjoining building. My table lamp was still on, and a platter lay on the floor by my bed of a half eaten apple and slices of cheese.

Possibly one of the most beautiful of Paris interiors is that of the American Ambassador's Residence located on the fashionable Faubourg Saint-Honore, where expensive boutiques and jewelry shops make for an interesting afternoon of browsing. The present site of the Residence goes back to 1710 and has a long colorful history, including the Nazi occupation in 1941.

An estimated 70,000 people visit the Ambassador's Residence annually for a wide variety of events. Guests are greeted formally by doormen within the large sweeping elegant courtyard.

Inside, a grand central staircase winds two stories high to upper guest suites and sitting rooms. Protecting the stairs is a Louis XV of intricate wrought iron grillwork, and overhead are Greek bas reliefs depicting such artistry as "Diana and Ceres" and "Apollo and Iris."

The magnificent chandelier in the entry hall highlights marble floors where two flags flank a bubbling fountain, the flags of the U.S. and of the Department of State.

Each room is filled with eighteenth and nineteenth century French furnishings and paintings, and at every turn an interesting historical story can be told.

Once a month, on a Sunday afternoon, Ambassador Pamela Harriman had Americans to the Residence to view a recent Hollywood film and enjoy some cool refreshments. It was a nice touch by the Ambassador.

Speaking of the colorful Ambassador Harriman, I had the dubious distinction of being an overnight patient at the American Hospital in Paris when she was brought there by ambulance. She had been swimming that evening with a friend at the Ritz Hotel—a man friend, I had heard—when she had a stroke. She died the following day.

Benjamin Franklin was the first American Ambassador to Paris. He was dispatched to Paris in 1776 by the newly declared independent U.S. to secure French assistance in the revolutionary war effort.

Thomas Jefferson's appointment, the second and possibly the most famous of U.S. Ambassadors in Paris, followed. He had a warm relationship with the people of France, as he noted in a letter... "their kindness and accommodation to strangers is unparalleled..."

He forgot to add, "...assuming the stranger has a dog."

The hubbub of the early morning started the workday off nicely. It was an easy twenty minutes to walk from my apartment to the U.S. Office of Economic and Cultural Development (USOECD), where I was assigned to work.

Pedestrians hurried here and there in the streets. Shopkeepers opened up, swept their sidewalks, and placed bundles of fresh flowers in water bins by the doors. Chickens roasted on outside grills, filling the air with tantalizing aromas.

In a handsome 19th century building, the offices of USOECD comprised suites on two floors. It was a bright and cheerful atmosphere. One quickly became accustomed to the sounds of many languages in this building of international hubbub with its frequent visitors who wore formal dark suits, or perhaps Arabic taigas.

OECD is a membership of many countries. Its main purpose is to hold meetings throughout the year for an exchange of information and ideas.

Special meeting rooms hold semicircular seats with nameplates and headphones. Because of the diverse languages spoken, translators sit to the rear behind a glass-enclosed partition. With the flick of a switch, one can receive a translation of the moment's speaker.

The Heydays / 175

In the Paris streets, high-ranking visitors traveled in a procession of cars, the flag of their country mounted on their bulletproof vehicle with its dark windows. French police on motorcycles led or pulled up the rear, and traffic cleared the way for the procession.

My assignment was full and interesting for the first few years. It was unique work for me, assisting various U.S. agencies—such as the CIA, the Justice Department, the State Department, to name a few—who came to Paris for the ongoing meetings.

I monitored many official functions, and managed dinners, luncheons, or receptions from beginning to end for the visiting agency. Numerous details were my responsibility—meeting with the caterer to plan the menu, ordering linens and flowers, drawing up the guest list which often included a mixture of cultures, designing and sending out invitations.

It was all quite demanding, and fun! An unforeseen boo-boo had to be spotted and quickly corrected. Perhaps invitations were printed improperly—send them back immediately! A visitor has an emergency telephone call. The Saudi interpretor is stuck in traffic jams and will be late—arrange for an interim substitute. A prime speaker is ill in his hotel room with a bad cold—dash out to the local pharmacie for medicine. The British Ambassador lost his raincoat, and it is raining like crazy outside!

From beginning to end—when the bills come in and reporting cables were finalized—I worked diligently. Even the lost raincoat was located, and I mailed it to the British Ambassador—who had already returned to London! A bit late, perhaps, but we do try to please!

For my performance those first 2 years, I was honored by the visiting agencies I had helped, and recommended for a promotion. Nevertheless, when a new manager arrived in our office, she decided she wanted to handle what I had been doing quite well, thank you very much—at a considerably higher salary, but of course!

It was a disappointment to have this work—work I had experienced such pleasure in and proven to do well at—taken from me. In fact, it was to be the last work I would truly enjoy in the Foreign Service.

Before arriving in Paris, I had been beside myself with excitement at the promise of three to four years in this quaint lovely city. I had visited Paris several times, and I just knew living there would be a piece of cake. With frosting and ice cream.

But it was not. Living in Paris did not hold the glitz it had always held for me as a tourist. Too much cement—on streets, sidewalks and buildings. Too many crazies on skateboards, too many motorcycles and automobiles on the sidewalks. Too many grey dreary days. Too much rain.

While I could never deny the treasures of this lovely city, or that there was still much I loved about Paris, I simply found it . . . how do you say . . . "tres difficile!" Difficult to live in! Not that I am complaining, mind you, but I want the record to stand that Paris was not my favorite place to live. If anyone cares, of course.

The French have a certain—shall we say "reputation"—but their snippiness and wit is part of their colorful character. I like the French, and learned early that they are friendlier when one has a dog. The sight of a dog transcends the impersonal demeanor of a French face into warmth and charm.

But I admit I was puzzled by the French men. Living in this "city of love" afforded me a first hand opportunity to observe the French man, to determine what it is exactly that earned him the reputation of mmmmmm and Ooooooh-la-la—"the French lover."

I could not see it. All this fuss about being so desirable to women—was it a farce? I decided to find out by conducting my own private study. In the streets, restaurants, office, museums, everywhere, I took careful note of French men. But after weeks into my study, their charms still eluded me.

Perhaps their charisma is subtle and easy to overlook. Yes, that might be it. They did have a cute little way of twitching their nose as if smelling a flower, and the animated hand waving when they spoke was endearing. Also, a few had that certain hard to describe look in the eyes which could be disarming. We American women call it bedroom eyes. But I still had my doubts.

"French policemen"—worth a study, I thought, jotting it in my notebook and underlining it.

It was my day off. I walked along the Left Bank searching for a particular cathedral. When I realized I was lost, I spotted a policeman directing traffic in the nearby boulevard. "Pardon, Monsieur, parlez-vous Anglais?" "Oui, Madame." "Can you direct me to the American Cathedral?" "Oui." (Did I notice a flicker of fun in his eye?)

The policeman gave me instructions—which I followed carefully—but half an hour later, I still had not found the cathedral. It seemed I was going around in circles, and indeed I was! Over there, still directing traffic, was that policeman again!

Walking a little closer, I stood at the curb glaring at him. Despite the crowds of pedestrians, our eyes met and, to my outrage, he gave me a wicked little smile. What nerve, I thought! I would learn later that French policemen simply like to play little games with confused tourists just to add some amusement to their otherwise monotonous work day.

A few notes on this went into my notebook.

I remember well the actual turning point in my study of French men. For weeks a backache had been a problem for me and was getting worse. Someone recommended seeing a Dr. Pierre du Charme, a chiropractor. It was worth a try, so I made an appointment for 10:00 on Friday.

Madame at the reception desk escorted me into a back room, told me to take everything off except my underwear, and Dr. du Charme would be in shortly. She did not offer a cotton gown, or anything. Dr. du Charme was not in shortly. I waited a good while, shivering and feeling awkward and self-conscious.

Then, suddenly, the door opened and in walked the most gorgeous, clock stopping hunk of a Frenchman with dreamy bedroom eyes. And his accent was so beautifully—French!

Dr. du Charme asked me some questions, but I was tongue-tied and inelegantly aware of my telltale grey underwear. He told me to lie down on my back, place my left arm over my head and right leg over the left. Then, with his nose inches from my own, the handsome French doctor grabbed a firm hold of my shoulder and hip, and gave a mighty jerk. Maneuvering me over, he had a strangle hold on my neck while pressing my lower spine, and again gave a brisk jerk.

The appointment over, Dr. du Charme instructed me to come back in two weeks.

As I turned to begin pulling on my blue jeans, I felt a pinch on my bottom! Was it my imagination? Glancing at the doctor as he walked out, I caught a slight smile on his lips as he flashed a wink at me.

Two weeks later, and although my back was no longer hurting, I entered Dr. Pierre du Charme's reception area for my second appointment. Madame was on the telephone and waved me to a chair. I sat down and realized I was a little breathless this morning. The pinch had been on my mind.

Well, that's silly. I am simply here for a follow up. Still, I'm glad I had my hair done and lucky to have found that great lingerie at Victoria's Secret! Madame hung up the phone and said it would be just a few more moments, the doctor was finishing up with another patient.

Noticing a picture on her desk of a group of children—did I count five or six?—I tried small chit chat with Madame and inquired if they were her children? "Oui," she said, and then returned to her work. Finally, the door opened and a smiling woman emerged (looking just a little flustered, I thought).

Madame turned to me and said, "My husband, oh pardon, the doctor, can see you now. Please follow me." "Your husband?" "Oui." "I see. Then, the six children, they also belong to the doctor?" "Oui, Madame."

My study of French men ended about that time. The results of the study were favorable and I gave the French men a "6".

But the Latin men were still ahead, with a healthy "9" on a scale of 1 to 10.

I might mention that the lower rating of the French men was somewhat influenced by what I called the "shoulder pad incident."

One of the stickiest situations for a foreigner to find herself in—even with diplomatic immunity—is an entanglement with French authorities of any level. My own incident was small, but dreadful.

Printemps, a popular department store in Paris, was having a sale. As I browsed among the ladies' dress racks that Saturday morning, one dress caught my eye. It hung in a remote corner with just a few other "rejected" dresses. A button dangled loosely, a shoulder pad was missing, another shoulder pad hung precariously by a thread. I liked it!

Unthinkingly, I pulled the loose shoulder pad off and laid it on a nearby chair. I slipped the dress over my jeans for fit. Yes, I liked the dress and I'll take it. As I took the dress off, a store detective wearing a badge and carrying a gun appeared out of nowhere and told me to follow him—all in French, but I clearly understood. Confused and not knowing what in the world this was all about, I followed timidly behind him.

He led me to a small room in the basement. "Monsieur, what is the problem?" But he totally ignored my questions. Within minutes, another investigator walked into the room, a small skinny Frenchman wearing a yellow raincoat.

With limited English, the skinny investigator told me to dump the contents of my purse on the table. Then, questioning me at his leisure, the investigator slowly and carefully scrutinized my purse contents—a wallet, two keys and a tube of lipstick. And a Snickers candy bar.

Finally, the investigator explained that I was being detained regarding the "damaging of store property." He was referring to the dangling shoulder pad I had removed from the dress. To my embarrassment, a giggle escaped my lips.

I expressed my apology for the shoulder pad and, with a straight face, tried to explain that I had intended to purchase both the dress And the shoulder pad. They were not easily persuaded, but the man with the gun finally escorted me out of the department store by a side entrance.

As we nodded our "good days," I wondered how they treat one who has stolen, say, a bottle of their French perfume. I would imagine that should bring a prison sentence.

In 1996, we had been living in Paris for eight months when my mother had a stroke. I flew to Illinois to see her, arriving on Mother's Day. Although she was paralyzed and confined to bed in a nursing home, Mom looked peaceful that morning. Her head was propped on a pillow, and she smiled at me with her translucent blue eyes. Together we sat and held hands, and watched a Sunday service on television.

She was trying to tell me something. I had to bend over and concentrate closely to her words. "I love you," she said. "I love you, too, Mom." Though she lived for ten more months, these were the last coherent words exchanged between us.

Because of my work, I could only stay for one week, and had little choice but to return to Paris.

Ten months later, I was visiting lovely Burgundy for Easter weekend, a land of vineyards and wine vats, and brilliant yellow fields of mustard. In the small town of Dijon, every shop seemed filled with the famous Dijon mustard, sold in pretty little jugs with ribbons.

It was, in fact, Good Friday as I sat by a splashing fountain in Dijon, watching the sparrows take a bath. My thoughts were about Mom, at the precise moment when she died.

Returning to my hotel room at the end of the day, I found a note marked "urgent" pinned to my door. It was from the embassy in Paris, and I knew without reading it that my mother had passed away.

That evening I returned to Paris. As I waited on the platform in Burgundy for my train, I felt someone watching me. There, on a nearby bench, an old woman with familiar deep blue eyes sat alone. She was smiling, and for awhile we just looked at each other. I smiled back and then my train pulled into the station, blocking my view.

It had been too late to return to the U.S. for her funeral, so I said goodbye to my mother at the American Cathedral of Paris in a private ceremony. I placed a single red American Beauty rose on the altar for Mom, whose name was Ruth Rose, along with her portrait.

The woman priest read passages from her book, and said a few comforting words. She felt Mom's presence, she said, and we turned our heads to look at her portrait.

Right on, Mom, you finally made it to Paris.

Paris is laid out like a wheel, with the center its hub and the city streets spreading out like spokes.

Of course, everybody knows this city is filled with many beautiful buildings. Just to stroll the streets is entertaining, to have an ice cream cone and look at the architecture.

I think I had—accidentally—the best seat in the house one Christmas at the Garnier Opera House where I came to see the Nutcracker. The ticket was cheap because my seat was in one of those side overhangs near the stage, mistakenly thought to be undesirable. It would be my little secret.

Charles Garnier, a French architect, designed the opera house in 1862. It took ten years to erect, and is a masterpiece.

During a visit to Paris by DeAnna, my beautiful daughter, the Garnier Opera House held an exhibition of outrageously dramatic costumes and masks used in the many operas staged over the years. I was certain that the French had scheduled this special event precisely to coincide with DeAnna's visit. A nice gesture, for sure.

Whenever I had the chance, I visited Versailles (when are they going to clean all those mirrors?), the Royal Palace, or the Louvre to enjoy and study the interior design. Many lesser known chateaus and palaces throughout France are also enchanting, each one unique in its own way.

It was a common practice in days of yore for a king to give his guests, or his host, a portrait of himself as a gift, much as we would bring flowers to a host today. It does strike me as a little presumptuous.

The king also, on occasion, allowed the commoners to enter one room of the palace and watch as he and the queen ate their dinner. This was considered to be a favor bestowed on the people by the king.

In the late 1700's, when Marie Antoinette was married to King Louis XIV and both lived at Versailles, most of France was steeped in poverty. Marie seemed hardly aware of the problems of France. She spent lavishly upon herself. Her day to day life was filled with personal comforts and pampering, the latest fashions, and expensive jewelry.

The French people were aware of this and began to rebel loudly. Who wouldn't? The king and queen lived well at the expense of the people, while ignoring their cries for help and reform.

Thus, the French Revolution broke out. The people of France stormed the palace of Versailles and abducted the king and queen who were brought to Paris where they lived with only a fraction of the power and luxuries they once had. Here in Paris, dramatic changes took place with the people in charge.

But none of this came about without much blood shed.

Journeying alone to the South of France, I stopped in Orleans, Chateauroux, Limoges, over to Lyon, St. Etienne, Avignon, zig-zagged to Nice and over to Marseille. My destination was Aix-en-Provence.

I loved those lazy days of being free to lose myself in the wonderful, nostalgic French countryside. The one deterrent was my inability to communicate well in French. But my eyes take in everything I see, and often this is enough.

Aix-en-Provence is known for its sunshine, that magical light which attracted Van Gogh, Cezanne, Picasso, and Renoir. I had grown weary of rain in Paris and looked forward to sunny Provence, but it rained almost entirely while I was there.

Funny the things we remember about a city or town. The memory may appear to be inconsequential trivia, but what I think of most fondly about Aix-en-Provence are two particular incidents.

The first incident was in an artist shop where I purchased a small replica of a Cezanne painting. The proprietor was an old Frenchman who spoke English well enough. It was near the closing hour, and the shop was empty.

He offered me coffee, and engaged me in conversation concerning the life of Paul Cezanne whose studio, small house, and garden are located in Aix. The local people are proud of him, and I listened with interest as the proprietor told tales of Cezanne's daily life. The warm friendship I felt with the old Frenchman stays with me still.

The second incident took place later that same evening in a very old cathedral. A classical concert was about to begin as I strolled by, and I purchased a ticket.

The very high ceilings and immense interiors provide an acoustics unlike any I had experienced. I was immersed in the fullness of those rich voices blending so beautifully, like a chorus of angels. Flickering candles danced upon the old holy relics, and I sat transfixed in the dim enchantment of the ancient cathedral.

In Alsace, Strasbourg is the seat of the Council of Europe, frequent host to the European Parliament representing the countries of the European Union.

Strasbourg is more than just another pretty face. Many diplomats jumped at the chance to attend "business" at one of the modern convention centers in Strasbourg which is flanked by waterways, bridges, and weeping willows drooping among a collection of idiosyncratic 19th century mansions.

There are too many pretty faces of Europe to ever visit, but seeing just a few satisfies me.

Tossing my bag in the back seat, I jumped into Sally's car. Sally is an American friend from the embassy. We were off through the bustling morning shoppers and street traffic of Paris to a weekend in Normandy. Normandy—green pastures, cows, apple trees, sleepy villages, the sea beneath towering cliffs.

In Evreux, we stayed at a remote country chateau. The proprietor lived there alone, and we were her only guests that weekend. She was friendly and talkative, no doubt lonely living there by herself! Her chateau was filled with family antiques and heirlooms.

On the first evening, the proprietor had plans to go out, leaving Sally and me alone. Since there were no near neighbors and the chateau was surrounded by woods, you can imagine how easily spooked one can become.

Sally and I shared a room on the second floor which we reached by a winding staircase in a tower. At the top of the tower, our room was pleasant with twin beds and a toilette down the hallway. Sally immediately fell asleep, but I lay awake listening to all the strange noises.

There were goblins outside in the woods, snooping around the doors and windows. "Sally, are you awake? Talk to me." But she told me to go to sleep.

I laid there in the dark, listening. Tree branches cracked, an owl called eerily in the dark woods beyond, the stairway creaked, and strange shadows moved across our room. I looked over at Sally a few times, hoping to catch her awake. But she slept, peaceful and undisturbed.

Interesting how other people sleep. While I usually have no trouble sleeping, per se, I am one to dominate the bed. I stretch out in all directions, and am never in the same position all night. A sleep analyst may find me to be an interesting subject of study.

Sally, on the other hand, sleeps flat on her back with her hands folded, and wakes up in the same position. I did not see her move once! Not once!

The following morning, the weather was exquisite and the proprietor set up a picnic table outside by a creek for our Sunday breakfast. Here we sat under a shady tree in the midst of two large peacocks, a goat, and a variety of birdlife. It was a breakfast to remember—hot sweet breads, homemade jams, slabs of ham and sausages, eggs, and a big pot of steaming coffee—served to us by the proprietor in a paradise setting.

Traveling alone on a subsequent journey—Nipper stayed behind in Paris with a friend—I made my way to Cote d'Albatre on the Northern Coast of Normandy. Specifically, for a few days in the town of Etretat.

Etretat was quite different from the green grassy pastures and small villages of Normandy. Here the sea air is cold and clear. The high cliffs rise to 325 feet and tower over the ocean below. Along the harbor and coastline are small fishing villages, with Etretat considered one of the prettiest.

The coast along Etretat is famous for its large rock resembling an elephant's trunk. The country is wild and beautiful, and days were spent walking along the shores and among the rocks exploring and wandering. Evenings in tiny Etretat were quiet, lingering over home cooked meals of fish and boiled potatoes while eavesdropping on the casual tête-à-tête of the town folk.

The spires of ancient Rouen Cathedral in the petite capital of Normandy was a favorite subject of Monet's, and he painted over 100 versions of it. Rouen is a short train ride from Paris, and a lovely Saturday outing.

Speaking of that—who could be more French than Claude Monet? His home in Giverny for many years before he died is located another short distance from Paris.

Monet was born in Paris in 1840. It was not until 1883 that he settled in the country village of Giverny on a hillside surrounded by acres of his magnificent gardens and the pond where he painted his famous water lilies. In the spring, the flowers are exceptional, and people from all over the world come to visit. See the row boat and bridge—still there—which were in many of his paintings.

Southwest of Lyon, Annecy dates from the 12th century. It is French, but located on the border of Switzerland's Lake Geneva. Narrow canals wind in and around the little city, and white swans are striking against the greenish canals. I found it to be a lovely place to spend a few days in.

The sun had finally come out in nearby Geneva. Geneva is a main entry point to the French Alps, to skiing and other snow sports. Tucked up in these Alps are the beautiful villages of Chamonix, Les Portes du Soleil, Morzine and Avoriaz, with picturesque chalets and the sounds of cowbells and yodeling.

My friends and I were hiking through a remote village in the Swiss Alps, a gorgeous scenic chip of a place atop the highest elevation possible. It is smart to hire a hiking guide when the terrain is unfamiliar. While I do not claim to be smart, we did hire Hans to be our guide.

The air was thin and crisp. It was winter, and heavy snow lay upon the mountains. The sky was a slate grey, and the only sounds were distant cowbells.

For hours, we followed Hans through the snow, the white stuff crunching under our boots. The scenery was spectacular. By the end of the day—with sore muscles and a huge appetite—we were stiff and cold, and had only dinner on our minds!

We stayed in a chalet. My small room was of highly polished cedar wood. A thick fluffy feather blanket covered the bed. I sat that evening by my window—after a hearty dinner!—and gazed at the snow scene beyond, a candle flickering on the windowsill, and wondered what it would be like to live in a remote and beautiful place like this.

In the morning—Sunday morning—a small rustic chapel across the road was holding a service. The chapel had large windows exposing views of snowy fir trees, and masses of candles were lit by the altar. We sat on crude benches to the rear of the chapel, mesmerized by the chanting of the village nuns.

This is my favorite memory of Switzerland.

17
The Swiss Alps to Italy

One begins to acquire friends around the world after a few years in the Foreign Service, usually other Americans working at the various embassies or consulates. Having houseguests, or being a houseguest, is not uncommon.

I took a train from Paris to Italy to visit Ollie who had invited me to be her houseguest. Ollie lived in Milan and worked at the embassy there. We originally met in Arlington, Virginia when we were both attending classes at the Foreign Service Institute—the State Department's new college campus. I liked Ollie, and looked forward to seeing her.

My train climbed up, up, up into the Swiss Alps. The scenery was breathtaking! It was a crisp sunny morning in early autumn. The snow laden Alps towered above us as we sped by flocks of sheep in grassy clearings, past small villages with Swiss chalets, in and out of dark tunnels, and along stretches of woods.

When the train stopped at the French-Swiss border, Customs officials came through the train asking to see our passports. Passports. Passports? Our passports! No, no, no, it can't be true. I had forgotten my passport.

The Customs officials asked me to "follow them," ominous words I had heard before. In a private cabin at the end of the train, they questioned me at length until they were finally satisfied that I was not an imposter or a terrorist, but simply an American tourist who forgot her passport.

I could proceed to the Italian border, they said, but warned me that it was not likely the Italians would let me into Italy without my passport. My only other option was to get off the train at the next stop in Switzerland and make my way back to Paris. I decided to take the chance and continue on.

At the Italian border, the border patrol refused to give me entry into Italy without my passport, and so I had to make the five hour return to Paris on the next available train.

By midnight, I was back in Paris, and the following day began my journey to Milan once again. With passport tucked securely in my money belt, I once more experienced the delightful fairyland journey through Switzerland.

The train pulled smoothly into Milan's train station by early evening. It had been fifteen hours of traipsing back and forth through the Swiss Alps, but because of the extraordinary beauty of the Alps I had no regrets.

My friend, Ollie, was waiting for me. We both had a good laugh about my passport ordeal—my laugh a little less hearty than hers.

Milan, Italy, I decided, as Ollie and I rode the tram that evening to her apartment, has a staid, engaging charm. The quiet orderly streets were filled with trees, and our tram moved under the evening glow of lamps along the street tracks.

Ollie's apartment building resembled the old structures of early Chicago. An ancient elevator took us up to her apartment, with its very large rooms facing a noisy street. We dropped off my suitcase, and left the building. We were very hungry!

An authentic Italian spaghetti dinner—the Real Stuff—was it any different from American spaghetti?

Frankie's Ristorante Italiano, our choice for the evening, had a sitting bar surrounding an open pit of fire where three chefs deftly prepared our dinner. Here Ollie and I sat on a stool sipping our cool drinks, watching the chefs, and visiting.

Among Foreign Service friends who have not seen each other for awhile, there always seems to be a certain amount of gossip to get out of the way before we can forget it and lose ourselves in the fun of our get-together.

The cozy ambience of the restaurant was relaxing. Tiny lamps on the tables glowed softly, and the fire of the open pit crackled and threw shadows across the ceiling. People huddled together in dim corners, speaking quietly in Italian, laughing. The aroma of pastas and sauces, garlic, homemade breads, made us impatient to eat.

Across from us, a small group of Italian men, their dark hair slicked back gangster style, leaned against the bar smoking cigarettes and talking low among themselves. Suddenly, one of the men broke out in robust laughter and slapped his companion on the back.

The Italians seem to do that a lot, good naturedly slapping each other's faces or pinching cheeks. Pinching cheeks a little lower down is also common. Secretly, I was disappointed when I left Italy and did not personally experience this.

Yes, I thought, everything just Feels Italian to me. The spaghetti? Not bad, not bad at all. Tomorrow I'll try their pizza.

Milano—a city of high fashion, of trams, tree lined boulevards. It was my first visit to Italy, and I was filled with wonder. We sat on the steps of the basilica for awhile, finishing up the remaining bits of gossip as our eyes took in the activity of the Italians around us.

It is a three hour train ride from Milan to Venice where Ollie and I shared a highly expensive, small and somewhat dirty hotel room. In fact, this very old place called Venice, beautiful as it is, impressed me as dirty and poorly maintained. What do the Italians do with all their tourist money? Really, they should clean it up a little!

But of course the architecture and treasures of art, canals and gondolas, and the tremendously interesting history and people, this is what everyone comes to see.

Basilica San Marco was under restoration, so we could not go inside. It dominates the Piazza San Marco, a very huge Square lined with shops and cafes. In the evenings, lamps in the Square beautifully illuminated the old architecture.

We sat at a small outside cafe table, ordered hot cappuccino, and became quietly lost in our thoughts and the solemn beauty of the evening. Small musical groups throughout the Square were playing their violins softly to classical pieces.

The unique charms of Venice at night captured my heart. This city is a museum, an amazing collection of ancient treasures ranging from Byzantine (12th-13th c.), to Gothic (13th-mid-15th c.), to Renaissance (15th and 16th c.) and Baroque (17th c.).

Hundreds of narrow streets snake here and there, opening now to a small square with fountains and statues, then to the Grand Canal. Bridges over the canals were lit by street lamps, casting mystical shadowy images over this ancient city.

It was easy to get lost, and we did. The hour was after midnight, and we had wandered off the beaten track to find ourselves in a dimly lit back street. There was nobody else around. Dark shadows cast eerie impressions and hid . . . what? Little balconies hung overhead with laundry pinned to a clothesline. Tiny lights glowed from a window here and there, but the narrow streets were otherwise deserted and dark.

There was no magic found in these dark watery alleyways and tall tightly shuttered houses. The quietness of the late hour was broken by the screech of a cat and the barely audible babbling of a drunk in his oblivion. A large rat jumped off a ledge and splashed into the canal.

Trying to make our way out of this maze, Ollie and I finally emerged into a small dimly lit Square with a fountain at its center. Two seedy-looking men sat by the fountain watching us. As we passed by, they stopped us, swept their eyes over us with a slow come-hither look, and said, "Buona sera. Come sta?" I mumbled "Si, per favore" and we hurried on past them.

My Italian is worthless, but they tell me the Italians appreciate our efforts to speak their language. Instead, we heard them laugh at us as we hurried on!

In the distance, a lighted piazza with evening strollers and window gazers came into view and I began to breathe easier. Now we were approaching the little shops still open, and saw the people walking and singing.

Its not that I was afraid we wouldn't find our way, its just that—well, for a brief half hour, it seemed that way! We decided to check out the Italian ice cream, then to our room and to sleep. "Mi scusi, Venice, Buona sera."

Daylight returned the fairyland fantasy of Venice, and we strolled among the stalls in the open piazzas and purchased post cards and scarves.

I bought two masks from one of the mask shops, one for my daughter, DeAnna, and one for me. I probably paid too much for them. But—well, itsa only money!

The annual carnival of Venice is world famous, and serious preparations are at work for months before the brief Carnival days. Masks and costumes are often deeply rooted in Venetian history. They become, each year, more lavish and impromptu than the year before.

Speaking of lavish—notice the lavish crowds of pigeons, which flock together and fill the Squares. If I were a pigeon, I would want to hang around Venice. Tourists feed them very well.

The pigeons like to perch on the heads of stone statues, a somber Italian hero, or long gone saint. My photo collection of Europe is filled with snaps of pigeons sitting on the head of a favorite son or local hero, or yet another stone Napoleon. Disrespect, I call it. But maybe Napoleon likes the companionship.

I did not experience a gondola ride until a much later visit to Venice. Our gondolier—whose name was Mario—wore a red and white striped tee-shirt. He paddled down the Grand Canal and serenaded us as he paddled, his voice soft at first, then breaking out into loud emotional song.

The Grand Canal, known to Venetians as the Canalazzo, follows the course of an ancient river bed and snakes its way around the heart of Venice. It was a parade of fine palaces and old aristocracy of faded frescoes and worn marble.

Our gondola slowly passed such sights as Ca' da Mosto, a good example of 13th century Veneto-Byzantine. Alvise da Mosto, the 15th century navigator, was born there in 1432. To our left may be the birthplace in 1454 of Caterina Cornaro, Queen of Cyprus. Just up ahead, see the Rialto Bridge which spans the Grand Canal, and the Palazzo Giovanelli, a restored Gothic palace.

Mario is soon all worked up, emotionally carried away as he sings out "Viene la Sera." They say many of the gondoliers are amateur opera singers, moonlighting with tourists until they can hopefully be discovered.

Oh, puleeze, Mario. Give it a rest, already.

By the time we left Venice, I had decided that the dirt actually enhances the already distinctive character of Venice. I began to like the laundry hanging on clotheslines over the canals, and felt that this charming sight would be shamefully lost if clothes dryers were used.

Pity, though, about the rumor that Venice is slowly sinking into the water. I'm glad I saw it before this happens.

And so, for now, "Arriederaaci, Venezzia." "Placccere di conosceria." Farewell, Venice. See you!

18
Romance in Portsmouth, England

We stood at a Tabac counter in Paris, and Peter was lost in one his long animated stories. When he stopped talking long enough to take a sip of his coffee, I smiled benevolently at him and said, "You Brits have an interesting accent. I like the way you talk." He set down his coffee cup and raised one eyebrow. With a cold eye he said, "You yourself, my friend, also have an accent. A bloody strong one!"

"What? Me? A bloody strong accent? No way." I repressed an urge to laugh as I flicked a fly off the counter. "In my country, we all talk like this."

But his steady eye was still on me. "And in your country you all have an accent." We squabbled over this for awhile, but in the back of my mind I was beginning to believe that he did have a point.

I thought for a moment about this idea of accents. My dictionary says an accent is a speech pattern, a pronunciation, or regional mark. It is always the other one with the accent, isn't it? The person who lives farthest away? It is "they" who have a funny way of talking and thinking.

Romance with Peter was brief, but so nice. I had not fallen in love, but there were some of the earmarks just the same. The feelings took me off guard, and pleasantly surprised me to discover that romance is not just for the very young. In fact, it really does get better with age, like a fine wine.

But we were just friends that morning, drinking our coffee in Paris. Always conscious of the penny, Peter knew that by standing at the counter the charges were less than had we sat at a table. Actually, he saved me a little money since he did not pick up my tab, anyway. Being tight with money was not endearing, but I enjoyed his company and sense of humor nonetheless.

He told me he would be leaving Paris soon and moving to Portsmouth, England, where he had just purchased a Victorian styled row house. On a paper napkin, he drew a simple map of the Southern coast of England and the waterfront town that is Portsmouth.

Peter persuaded me to visit him, describing the water, mild sunny climate, historic sites. "It's only an hour from London's Waterloo," he said, as we picked up our individual coffee tabs and walked out into the street. He did not offer to buy me a train ticket to Portsmouth, I noticed.

The idea of mild sunny climate and the English Channel with its long stretches of sea appealed to me. I was tired of the grey skies and rain in Paris, and I accepted the invitation.

Portsmouth was all Peter said it would be, a charming old English seaport with clear air and brilliant sunshine. His tall narrow house overlooked a dock where boats were tied.

The house had three floors, and my guest room was on the top floor. The windows, which did not yet have curtains, faced a large church steeple and its chimes on the hour were loud but easy on the ear. Brilliant morning sunshine streamed through the room.

But it was not the chimes or the bright sun which woke me that first morning in Portsmouth. It was the loud thumping noise of my friend who had tripped and fallen halfway down the stairway, yelling out the F-word as he fell. I got up and called to him. "Are you okay?" But he did not answer. He had already disappeared into the kitchen to prepare breakfast.

I was about to be treated to an authentic Scottish breakfast of kippers. My host, having come from Scottish ancestry, seemed bent on having me experience this special ethnic meal. With his brows knit in concentration, he happily moved around his kitchen, banging frying pans and burning toast.

The kippers—almost raw and filled with little bones—were cold and clammy, the eggs dry, and the toast burnt. What does a guest do in such a delicate situation? I did not want to be ungracious, but I finally offered a feeble excuse of some kind. Peter just looked at me; he knew I did not like his kippers.

The following morning, I made breakfast—a nice kettle of American oatmeal.

That first morning, a royal tour around historical Portsmouth given by my host himself was interesting and fun. The wonderful fresh air and sunshine soon made me forget my queasy stomach from the kipper experience.

Fronting the English Channel, Portsmouth grew as a military fortress and at one time became both the prime naval base and strongest fortress in the United Kingdom. Here is the port from which scores of ships sailed in Elizabeth's reign, where too many sailors left their lovers on shore, never to return.

The original town, Old Portsmouth, was badly damaged during WWII. Today it is pleasantly quiet with its harbors, boats, docks. From nearby Portsdown, there is a wonderful view of the Isle of Wight, with Portsea Island miles beyond, and a moat to visit here, an abandoned castle there. The smell of saltwater and fish competes with the wonderful freshness of the air, and the sea wind blows incessantly.

We climbed aboard Admiral Lord Nelson's ship, the Victoria. Nelson spent almost two years on board without setting foot ashore. In the most decisive battle ever fought at sea, off Cape Trafalgar, Admiral Nelson was killed. Rather than bury him at sea, his grieving sailors preserved his body in a barrel of icy water and he was returned home as a hero where he would be buried.

It was a long walk to Charles Dickens' birth house on Old Commercial Road. The house was rather charming with its small rooms and old fashioned furnishings, and a tiny museum and gift shop was located on the first floor.

Dickens was born in that house in Old Portsmouth in 1812, and his family moved to London when he was two. Then in 1838, he returned to Portsmouth to collect material for his classic book, "Nicholas Nickleby."

A month later, on an early Saturday morning in June, the sun was shining through the lacey curtains of my boarding house room in London as I waited for the phone to ring. It rang, and the lady of the house announced that I had a "gentleman waiting for me in the sitting room."

I squirted a puff of perfume behind my ear, and skipped down the three flights of old wooden stairs to the sitting room. My friend had come from Portsmouth on his motorcycle to show me around London.

He was sitting near the fireplace, and we exchanged the traditional French greeting. A kiss on each cheek is for casual acquaintances, and the kisses increase as the friendship deepens.

Practicing the French way of greeting is awkward. Not that one must demonstrate proficiency, but as temporary residents of France we do try not to offend anyone. Too many kisses on the cheek could be in bad taste, but not enough kisses may be a snub.

Let me see—as I recall, Peter and I were now exchanging about two cheek to cheek kisses.

To be shown around London by Peter or anyone British, is a privilege. We walked for hours, stopping now and then for a cool drink. We watched the river traffic on the Thames. We often sat on a bench to rest, feeling the sun warm our bones. We were sitting, he told me at one point, under the Queen Mum's apartment!

Peter was in his element as my tour guide. I was to hear the life history of every statue hero we passed, and sometimes the history of the horse they sat on. How can he know so much about all these historical characters, I wondered? I was impressed. Passing an infamous hero, one not well liked, my history lesson was given with heated emotion. Peter took England's history very seriously.

It was a memorable day from beginning to end. My companion's sharp wit kept me laughing. We ate too many fish and chips. Too many cool drinks and too much laughing caused me to wet my pants, but that only made us laugh harder.

As the street lamps began to light up the city, we hopped aboard a red double-decker bus and climbed to the outside top level.

I slid into a window seat and he slid in next to me, a little too close I noticed. When his shoulder pressed against mine, a warm glow crept over me as I pretended to look for something in my purse. We were hardly teenagers, but that day I felt like one, girlish and happy.

Thus began romantic interludes together between Paris and Portsmouth. He made me laugh and, a few times, even made me cry. But it was to be no more than a passing romance.

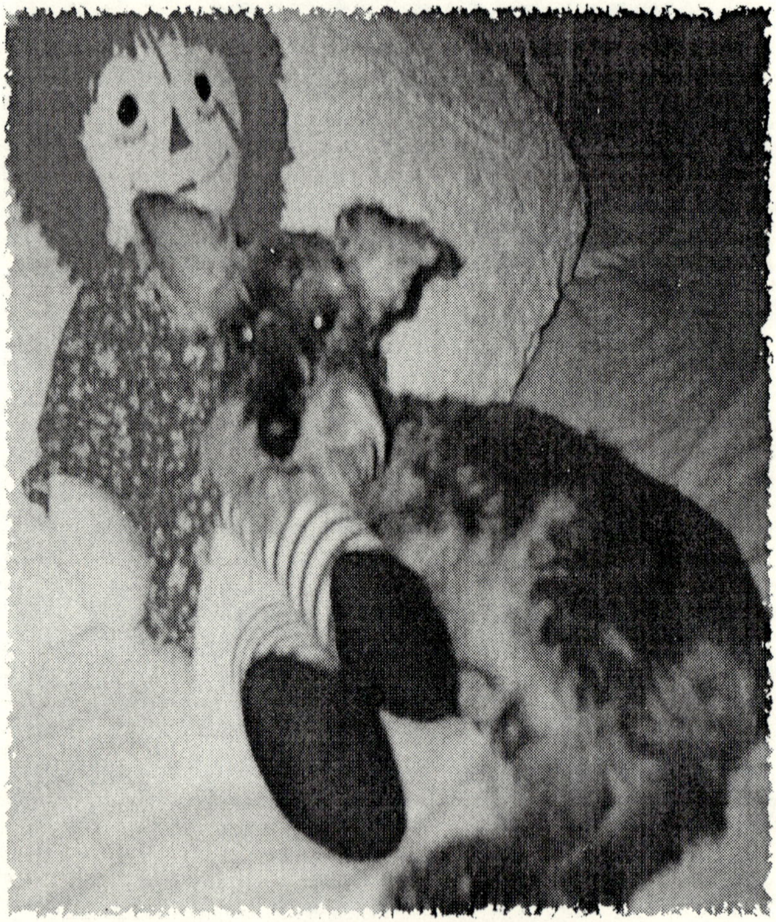

19
Nipper's Special Visit

The veterinarian in Paris advised me that Nipper should be put to sleep. I hung up the telephone after speaking with the vet, and felt a deep sense of devastation and grief flow through me. How can I possibly let go of this dog who had been with me for fifteen years?

I loved Nipper as I never thought possible to love a dog. But he was deaf now, and yesterday had a stroke. My darling dog was in pain and could not even be picked up without crying. I made the decision.

With intense sorrow, I wrapped Nipper, so frail and sick, in my navy sweatshirt and gently carried him in my arms to the waiting taxi outside. As we sped through the streets of Paris, he lay on my lap in the rear seat and did not take his eyes off me.

I was crying hard, and my tears fell on Nipper's whiskers. I did not care what the taxi driver must be thinking, though I noticed him glancing at me kindly through his rear view mirror.

We pulled up in front of the veterinarian's office. It was a beautiful sunny day on May 27 and the chestnut trees were in bloom. I took Nipper for one final walk, holding him still wrapped in my sweatshirt. He took his eyes off me just long enough to look up at the trees and the sky. I sat down on a corner bench and held him for a short while. Then it was time to go.

Returning home later, I was filled with pain. It seemed I would faint from my grief. I removed dog biscuits and toys, and put his little red shirt away. My crying would continue for days, but that night—exhausted from so much emotion—I fell into a deep sleep.

At about four o'clock in the morning, something at my right arm seemed to be trying urgently to wake me up. It was a persistent vibration, or a flapping of wings. "Wake up, wake up, wake up," it seemed to be telling me.

"Is someone there?" I was startled—yet in a certain twilight zone, not quite awake and not fully asleep. But the vibration was persistent.

I reached to my right side and there I felt the soft hair of Nipper's body. He stood upright with his front paws on the bed, no longer frail but healthy and whole.

"Nipper? Is that you?" It seemed incredible. I reached over and wrapped my arms around him. He was smiling, and covered my face with kisses. For awhile I just held him close to me. "Oh, Nipper, I love you," I said to him.

There was another presence with him, a loving presence I sensed but could not see. Was it an angel who had escorted Nipper to me?

"Go now and find T.J.," I finally told him. T.J. had been a dog friend since they were pups, and had died six months earlier. Then Nipper left with the friendly presence, and I did not see him again.

I sat up in bed shivering with goose bumps, and wondering what had just happened! It had not been a dream. Nipper had come to comfort me and to say goodbye. It was just the thing this kind little dog would do.

My grieving for Nipper would continue for many, many months. He had been my friend for a long time, the best kind of friend, and I missed him.

Two months after Nipper died, my assignment in Paris was over. It was time to leave. The movers arrived, two strapping French men. All day long, they worked hard.

The old elevators in these Paris apartment buildings are much too small to transport furniture. Instead, furniture and boxes are moved on conveyer planks mounted into the windows from the street below.

All was going well enough until the movers pulled apart the bed frame. I saw it immediately.
There, under the bed, lay a small forgotten dog biscuit.

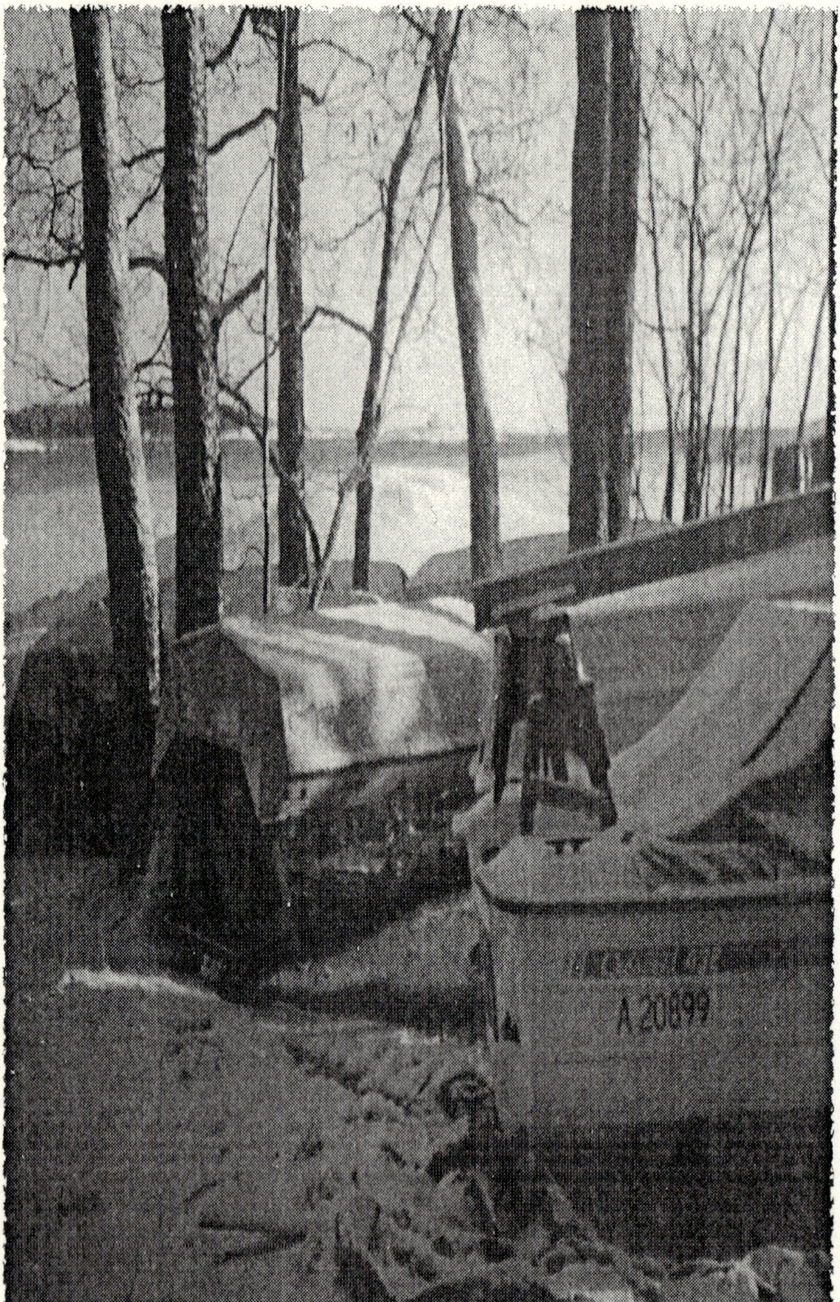
A 20899

20
Land of the Midnight Sun

If you are moving to Paris, bring an umbrella. But if you're moving to Finland, bring lots of warm clothes and snow boots!

Finland is the coldest and one of the prettiest countries I have seen. It has almost 188,000 lakes, vast forests, and extensive archipelagos. The air is fresh and clear.

Finland was quiet and sunny and had a frontier-like feeling when I arrived that late autumn afternoon. A tram wound its way through the small capital of Helsinki and along the Gulf of Finland. Many islands comprise greater Helsinki, and all are connected by bridges and trams.

A particularly long bridge connects Helsinki to the forested island of Laauttassari.

There on my island of Laauttassari, I lived in a lovely rustic apartment in the forest by the sea. The floors were made of light birch, I had my own private sauna bath, and a long veranda faced a stretch of woods and the sea beyond. The country kitchen, like the entire apartment, had huge windows touched by tree branches.

The island was lovely. The nearby forest paths were lit up at night for walkers, which includes just about everyone. Here and there in the forest are the small Mokki, colorful wooden cottages not much bigger than an outhouse, used solely for sauna baths.

The Finns comprise about 98% of the population of Finland, with the remaining 2% being foreigners. Swedish people continue to live here as well since the days when Finland belonged to them. The street signs throughout Helsinki are in both the Finnish and Swedish languages, with whoever dominates the area being noted first.

I quickly grew to like the Finns. They are forest people, quiet and a little shy, unpretentious, possessing a great sense of humor, industrious, and helpful to strangers.

A shopkeeper greets me with a "Hei", and her shop had the sweet aroma of the popular cinnamon rolls. This was the first word and smell I had experienced on my arrival.

The Finnish language is one of the hardest to learn and understand. The quiet spoken, slow, melodious words and accent of the Finn is engaging. Consider trying to find a kansallispuisto (national park). You might inquire at the opastuskeskus (info center). Where can we find a kauppahalli (indoor market), a particular kaupunki (town or city), or a valaistu latu (illuminated ski track)?

Talar nagon engelska? Ja. Lucky for me, most Finns speak English very well. In fact, the Finnish social system is impressive, and almost 100% of the people are literate.

I was also impressed with the great number of Finnish women who have higher education and hold prominent positions in the medical, legal, and other fields. The social system provides well for almost every imaginable need of its society.

Sitting on a hill near the edge of the sea, the U.S. Embassy occupies a few small buildings. The surrounding wooded neighborhood is filled with mansions converted into embassies and foreign companies.

At the entrance to the embassy, the Finnish receptionist, Raiija, worked in her small office answering the main telephone and greeting people as they come in—a position she has held for over 35 years! She is a gentle, happy woman who says she has always enjoyed her job. I found this refreshing, having worked many years now with the driven, rank conscious diplomats.

Also refreshing is Ronald, a very large, somewhat old, sheep dog who belongs to the Deputy Chief of Mission. Ronald sometimes accompanied the DCM to work, and always dressed in his business attire with one of the boss's ties around his neck.

Sitting by the desk or laying under the coffee table, Ronald has attended many meetings. He has the important responsibility of being a conversation piece and of putting visitors at ease. This he does by slowly walking over to the visitor and sitting at their feet to be petted. Sometimes a lick of their hand is helpful.

When the visitor has broken out into a smile, Ronald's work is done and he returns to his spot under the coffee table.

Upstairs, my small office was quiet, the views from the windows were pretty, the work not particularly interesting and there was plenty of it. From the beginning, I was told about the personnel shortage and asked if I would be willing to handle two positions temporarily. The double positions became mine for almost the duration of my entire stay.

Most of my work involved sitting at my desk and handling paperwork. It was routine and grinding, challenging only in my attempts to keep up with a load meant for two workers. When I asked for badly needed assistance, I was told there was none available because of the budget and that we are all in the same boat.

Our office quarters were very cramped. The building was previously utilized with offices on both floors, but a new DCM arrived with other ideas. He ordered renovation of the building. All other offices were moved together upstairs, and the lower level was for the exclusive use of the DCM and the new ambassador, who had not yet arrived at post.

Rumor had it that the newly appointed ambassador—who was still in Washington struggling with Finnish language classes—could not pass the required level of fluency! I understood these things! Eventually, he was disqualified as our ambassador to Helsinki, and a new appointee was ultimately selected.

The reshuffling of the ambassador position took the greater part of a year, during which time the new DCM acted as "Charge d'Affaires." I often strolled through the spacious, quiet first floor quarters, hoping with all my heart that the Charge d'Affaires was truly enjoying his sweet suite.

Up on floor two, meanwhile, the rest of us had to make do with what we had. We were cramped, and cramped we stayed.

My colleague, Frank, and I occasionally broke away in an afternoon for a walk down to the sea and Café Ursula. It sat alone along the shore, and here we could relax with a cup of coffee and watch the sea stretch out to nowhere with its various boats and ships. Café Ursula was a cozy place with glass display cases of gourmet dishes and an old nickelodeon which occasionally played tunes for guests. In any weather, Ursula was a friendly reprieve.

It was common practice in Finland to hold business meetings in a sauna room. Frank was a modest man, so when he told me about his first upcoming business sauna, I could feel his anxiety!

The President of Finland, it was said, often conducted his meetings in the sauna bath. Titles and positions—and inhibitions—were left outside the sauna bath.

Finnish receptions or social diplomatic functions were also kicked off with half an hour in the sauna—in the nude, of course. This can be awkward for the newly arrived, modest American diplomat. After all, he must join a group of strangers—naked businessmen—in a small steam room and try to discuss business! But to refuse such an invitation may be insulting to the host.

The Finns and the Russians both claim to have invented the sauna. Almost every home in Finland has its own, as I did, and whole families may take a sauna bath together. It is not a meeting place for sex, as in some countries. Despite the nudity, the Finnish sauna is very moral and strictly holds to this code.

My own private sauna bath at home soon became something I looked forward to at the end of each day. It was the size of a closet with a tiny window looking out to the forest below. Made entirely of polished wood, there were two wooden bench levels to sit on.

Dribbling water over hot stones in an electric stove creates the steam filling the room. A special sauna bucket with a long handle is filled with water, and a ladle is used to scoop up water and dribble over the stones. Then—I climb up on one of the wooden perches and let the steam penetrate.

As with the Turkish bath, branches of eucalyptus add a wonderful scent to the sauna room and are used to beat against the skin to stimulate, heal and nurture. After the steam, a cold shower or dip in the lake finishes the process.

I had been warned about the Finnish winters, but warnings never suffice for experience, do they? It was September when I arrived in Finland, and already there were patches of snow to be seen here and there.

By October, Laauttassari was covered in a blanket of snow. From my windows I could look out at the forest and the sea. The snow laden branches were lovely to look at.

But by November the snow was piled as high as my waist and the temperature dipping well below zero. Still, I enjoy the snow and often went for long walks. Bundling up with layers of wool and heavy snow boots, I walked the quiet forest edge, my nose and cheeks a healthy red, the scrunch of snow under my boots, and my breath blowing puffs of mist into the cold air.

A slick layer of ice often lurked hidden underneath the snow, and more than once I was to go sliding until I fell. The Finns invented a little gadget which attaches to the bottom of boots much like chains to snow tires. Tiny metal teeth on the gadget help to keep one from slipping on the ice.

Lack of sun in the winter often causes a great deal of depression, and sometimes a sunlamp is used. I tried it myself, but noticed no improvement.

Winter's severity is also blamed for the high degree of alcoholism in Finland, particularly among men. The remoteness of much of the land, the long cold winters, and the natural reticence of Finnish men—all are blamed for the high rate of alcoholism.

In the center of Helsinki, near Stockman's Department Store and the train station, drunks are a common sight. But, I must rush in to say that they were harmless drunks and did not create problems.

Summer in Finland. A beauty so exquisite words do not justify it. Soft clear summer air, lush flora and fauna, the beauty of the sea. From the shoreline of Laauttassari, I often watched with fascination the ships on the horizon and the small boats of countless unusual designs and bright colors.

The fabulous midnight sun of Finland is so called because of its light at the midnight hour. Daylight shines until the peak moment—about two a.m.—when the sun has settled into a golden sliver over the horizon of the sea. This is the eerie beauty of the Land of the Midnight Sun.

The moon in any season is a spectacular sight. Enormous and utterly close—like a giant golden ball of a lantern—I feel I can reach out and touch it. The unusual size of the great moon may be due to Finland's location near the North Pole, literally on top of the world.

From my lovely island of Laauttassari, I watched the changing seasons and never tired of the awesome rugged beauty of this country.

But the island is also remote and isolated. I am lonely here and often tired. And I miss my dog.

21
Amy

The Finns love candles as much as I do, and flickering candlelight is friendly from the many Finnish windowsills during my evening walks. But walking is not the same since Nipper died, and now eight months later my thoughts keep returning to that ad I saw in the newspaper.

"Mini-Schnauzers, 5 weeks old, soon ready to leave their mother." I had an appointment to see the pups, and was expected.

A taxi driver drove me to their home in the country, traveling through woods and small villages along the way. Darkness had already settled in when we pulled up in front of the house resembling a cabin.

A young Finnish woman answered the doorbell. At her side smiling up at me was a beautifully groomed, well mannered and gracious adult female Schnauzer—the mother of the pups.

The young Finnish woman led me into her warm, cozy kitchen where she introduced me to her new husband. He spoke no English, but I felt at ease with these shy and friendly Finns. He brought out a platter of cookies, some hot coffee and dishes, and invited me to sit down next to the box of pups in the warm kitchen. I knew the hospitable Finns were setting me up, but it was okay.

The pups, eight of them in a large cardboard box, were squealing, playing, and squabbling for my attention. Mom jumped up on my lap and together we watched her pups at play. She was obviously proud of her brood.

I asked Mom if, just in case, I were to take one of her pups home with me, would it be okay with her? She seemed to understand and gave me a big lick on my nose. I figured that was a Yes.

About an hour later I left with little Amy wrapped warmly in my long knit scarf and tucked inside the front flap of my coat. The taxi driver had waited, and so we returned to Lauttasaari in the dark cold evening. But inside my heart a little warm spot had already developed.

Amy was a pretty little thing, small enough to sit in my hand. Her beautiful form, black silky coat with white markings, and her brown flirty eyes made her adorable and cute. Everybody who saw her wanted to hold her and play with her. I was a proud new mother.

In Finland, cropping a dog's ears or tail is prohibited. Amy's ears are floppy and her tail long and fluffy. Adopting a dog is also strictly controlled by Finnish authorities, and the process is as detailed as adopting a child. I liked that.

Amy was a stealer. Slippers and pantyhose often disappeared, and I would find them later under the couch. As she grew, her antics became more pronounced. She was full of mischief, and I realized I was less lonely.

Amy made me laugh.

It takes time to make new friends. People can be friendly, but genuine friendship comes slowly. This is where being a member of Alcoholics Anonymous gave me an edge, which other Americans—we call them "normies"—do not have. AA members share a bond. Friendships are almost instantaneous.

I had been attending a meeting in Helsinki each Thursday evening. It was a group largely of Finns, who speak excellent English, and I felt drawn to them from the beginning.

When Amy had been with me only one day, I had reached 15 full years of solid sobriety and decided to invite the AA group to my home for dinner. They all came, dressed up in their best, bringing flowers and small gifts. AA members take these celebrations very seriously!

The most wonderful gift, however, was quite unexpected! As I sat with my friends that evening, the doorbell rang. A special delivery all the way from the United States was coming from my lovely offspring. I was stunned, and touched.

I opened the small gift, with my Finnish guests sitting around me watching in anticipation. Inside was a black velvet case with satin ties. The case contained a gold 'chip' engraved with the Roman numeral XV and the AA pledge, "To thine own self be true."

It certainly was My Day! The beautiful chip lay on its velvet case by my dinner plate for all to admire. My Finnish friends were eating, laughing, and visiting. Amy had found herself a soft pillow atop a nearby chair—it felt so good to have a dog around again.

Through my AA friends, I began to feel attached to Finland and I gained closer insight into the Finnish people. Most enchanting is their unique, special sense of humor.

Consider a typical Finskevitser (Finnish joke): The Finns, whose country had once been occupied for many unhappy years by the Russians, still have cool relations with that country. To this day, Finns claim to use double-ply toilet paper because they had become so accustomed to giving a copy of everything they produced to the USSR.

When severe winter weather finally subsided, I took Amy outside. Tucked inside my heavy coat, it was her first main venture in the outside world. But as still warmer days arrived, we often sat together on the large rocks by the sea or walked down the forest paths past the Mokki.

As in other parts of Europe, bikers on the island were aggressive. They whizzed by, and walkers had to scurry to get out of their way. I barely saw the biker coming, but heard Amy's cry and, horrified, I ran to pick her up. She was whimpering, but otherwise seemed okay. Still, I was filled with anger at the biker—who had stopped—and scolded her severely for running into my dog.

I suddenly realized the woman was crying. She said nothing, but stood by her bike watching Amy, and cried. So typical of the gentle Finn, I thought, to be moved to tears for her mistake.

Hannelie had recently moved into a new apartment, and she was planning a housewarming ceremony. This tradition is meant to bless one's new home and promote a happy, healthy habitation.

An "abundance wreath" made of wheat and wild flowers or dried vegetables is a popular housewarming gift to be hung in the Finnish kitchen. It is believed to attract abundance and good health into the new home.

There were a dozen or so guests at the ceremony, and we sat in a circle in the living room taking turns reading from a book about the qualities of a happy home—safety, comfort, abundance, laughter, love, good health. Although the other guests spoke in Finnish, most understood when I did my reading in English.

Following the ceremony, refreshments are served and for awhile I mingled with Hannelie's Finnish family and friends. What nice, simple, honest, talented people the Finns are. I do believe they are among my favorite of nationalities.

In the Lake District—due north from Helsinki—Hannelie's family cabin was located in an isolated stretch of woods on the edge of a lake. The Lake District, of course, is filled with lakes, and the vast surrounding forest is wild and remote.

Hannelie invited Amy and me to spend several days with her at her family's cabin, and to experience what most Finnish families enjoy doing in the summer—live in the open country. The Finns often have cabins of their own or rent them during the lovely short months of summer.

Outside Hannelie's cabin was a crude picnic table and some chairs, a hammock hung between two trees, and a canoe was pulled up by the edge of the lake. Near the pier, a small Mokki stood alone. It was here where I took my first authentic sauna bath—the way the Finns do it.

Following a hot steamy sauna of about fifteen minutes, we jumped—without a stitch—into the lake! The water was icy cold even in summer and the plunge a gigantic shock. But the body quickly adjusts, and the water became exhilarating.

Amy, who was about six months old, had been watching from the pier and—not knowing what was going on—came running to rescue me. But she lost her balance and fell into the lake. I heard the plop, but she was nowhere in sight. Suddenly her head bobbed up and I saw her—paddling along the pier like a little duck. I reached down and pulled her out of the water.

She was sopping wet, but the large smile on her face as she wildly wagged her tail told me that she had enjoyed her little swim.

After a steamy sauna bath and dip in the cold lake, Hannelie and I would sit on the wooden porch with a cool drink to enjoy the quiet nature around us, our feet propped up on the railings. No radio, no television, no telephone, no traffic, no neighbors—just the sounds of silence, broken only by the breeze or the call of a bird.

I slowly rowed the canoe one evening out to the middle of the lake, alone with my thoughts. It seemed I was the only person on earth in this lovely land as the moon shone over the lake and dusk fell upon the forest. But then—in the distance—I saw a tiny pink body dive with a splash into the lake. A distant neighbor in another Mokki had just had a sauna bath.

The sun began to set low and the forest became very dark indeed. With only moonlight to guide me, I returned to the cabin where Hannelie had started a fire in the hearth.

We stretched out on the floor of the cabin and roasted small sausages and marshmallows in the fireplace, lazily talking about this and that. Amy had claimed a soft pillow by the fire and was asleep.

The knotty pine guest room where Amy and I slept under a pile of blankets—since nighttime was cold—was rustic and cozy. A lantern hung from a nail over my bed, and its candle flickered gently.

From my bed, I could look out the window to the black isolated forest, a forest utterly quiet. Deer, bear, and other animals live in this forest, and I fantasized goblins and forest urchins as well. But the mesmerizing candle made me drowsy, and I soon drifted off to sleep.

These were days typical of a lazy summer in the forest which the Finnish family loves.

The forests in Finland are full of nuts and berries. Each season brings something special to brag about. In summer, strawberries are abundant and farmers set up stands on the street corners to sell boxes full of the fresh beautiful berries.

The wild mushrooms growing in the forest bring out the Sunday mushroom pickers! Raiija invited me to spend a Sunday in the forest with her for a lesson in mushrooms. She and I had become friends through our mutual employment at the embassy, and I had grown very fond of her.

With our baskets over our arms, we slowly walked the forest floor as Raiija explained it all to me. "Mushrooms," she said, "grow in the shade and come in a variety of species. They have different names, and are either delicacies or poisonous."

After several hours, our baskets were full of mushrooms and we returned home to clean and prepare them for dinner. Preparation was the second part of my lesson on mushrooms. Cleaning them, frying them in butter with herbs, serving them with certain dishes. Raiija talked as we worked.

The strong flavored, wild mushrooms did not appeal to me. Like the Scottish kipper and the wild herring paste, I wanted to spit out the wild mushrooms.

Fish, of course, is a big part of the diet in Finland. An annual herring festival is held along the main harbor in September. Herring—the good luck fish—is sold raw, pickled, roasted, and fried. There is herring bread, herring jelly, herring cakes, and canned herring. The fishermen on the docks, spotting the foreigner, good naturedly coax us into trying their specialty. Some dishes are tasty, others are repugnant—such as the herring paste—and I wait until I can get discretely behind a tree to spit it out.

But local cuisine is not something I would often pass up, always fresh and deliciously prepared. Many dishes are uniquely Finnish, such as the small rice cakes. The little cakes are made with seasoned rice or mashed potatoes. After baking, a dash of butter and perhaps a few sliced cucumbers on top give them a nice crunch.

Moose, reindeer, and wild boar are commonly on the menu, tasty and nicely prepared by the Finnish chef.

While Helsinki's main harbor is the place for herring festivals and farmer's markets, it is also the place for Helsinki's women to gather in pleasant weather and sell their knitwear. They sit on chairs by the harbor, enjoying the sun, knitting and visiting. On small tables, their lovely colorful knitwear is displayed for sale—socks, hats and sweaters.

The beautiful high quality knitwear by Finnish women comes from centuries of honing the craft. Especially unique to Helsinki are the charming and unusual styles and colors of the knit hats. The Scandinavian knits are worn everywhere in Finland.

Since the days when the Russians occupied Helsinki, Russian influence is still seen. At the foot of the hill by our embassy, the large, somber Russian Embassy is surrounded by a high black iron fence. Guards stand on duty. It has a sinister appearance.

Nearby, a Russian restaurant is a hangout for the Russian diplomats who often congregate there for favorite dishes from their homeland. On occasion, I would have my dinner there. I liked to give a little flirt to Sergio, the jolly old proprietor, or just eat and listen to the Russian conversations around me.

Russian dancers were our guests during the Christmas season, hired by our embassy to perform their centuries-old hankie folk dance in our Ambassador's Residence.

The Russian dancers were dressed in their traditional costumes of red and black, and the dance took place in the Ambassador's living room. My colleagues and I warmed ourselves near the fireplace as we watched the performance. The dancers held handkerchiefs and, as they stomped their feet and danced on one foot and then another, they twisted and swirled their handkerchiefs. It was an impressive folk dance to medieval Russian music.

An elegant table of white linen had been set with poinsettia, candles, and platters of Finnish cakes and cookies. Traditional local Christmas food, and cultural performances of our host country or nearby countries, were often a part of our festivities at embassies throughout the world.

A country fair was to be held at a seaside fishing village. It was the kind of wholesome activity the Finns enjoy, and Raiija and I decided to go. Games and races took place, such as the two-legs-in-a-bag race. An old man was hand weaving baskets and had only two baskets left—certainly meant for Raiija and me.

Around noon, people stood in a line with bowls and received a large scoop of puuro, a hot porridge topped with butter. It is a popular Finnish dish any time of the day, which I felt should be served only at breakfast!

My favorite town was Porvoo, the second oldest town in Finland. Built in the 13th century, Porvoo is an hour's drive from Helsinki through green pastures, grazing cows with bells tied around their necks, farmhouses and woods, and here and there a flock of white sheep.

Porvoo saddles up against the water of a canal and is filled with old wooden houses, including the summer home of Finland's greatest composer, Jean Sibelius. His music—although sometimes dark and almost somber—portrays well the Finnish nature. It is said that his wife and five daughters were compelled to a strict silence when he was at work composing his music.

At the main harbor of Helsinki, The Viking awaits its short daily trip to Tallinn. Tallinn in Estonia lies just below Helsinki and is one of the newly independent Baltic States. Tallinn is one of those lovely European cities badly neglected from years of occupation by the Russians.

As I walked through the streets and alleys of this medieval city, I noted the solemn faces of the local people. They avoided eye contact and simply looked straight ahead as we passed. It was the "safe" public demeanor of the Estonians which they had acquired during their years of occupation.

More often than not, it was the giant Scandinavian cruise ship, the Silia Line, which I boarded. The Silia sails for Stockholm, Sweden daily, departing Helsinki at 6:00 p.m. and arriving in Stockholm at

8:00 a.m. the following morning. The Silia is also moored at Helsinki's main harbor, a 10-minute walk from the embassy, providing an easy weekend retreat in Stockholm.

As the Silia enters Sweden in the early morning, it passes for several hours through the lovely Swedish archipelago, also known as the fjords. Enjoy the beautiful views from the windows in the ship's dining room as you breakfast in its famous smorgasbord. Fill your plate with fresh shrimp and salmon, sliced meats, sausages, cheeses, fruit, juices, sweet breads and creams, egg dishes, coffee. Go back for seconds!

Nils Holgerson says the city of Stockholm floats on water—but I say it only seems that way. Stockholm is located on Lake Malar's estuary into the Baltic Sea and the Swedish fjords. The lovely old city seems surrounded by the glassy water, so maybe Nils had the right idea.

Old Town Stockholm's Swedish history is still seen in Skeppsbron's facade of merchant homes, some dating from the 1600's and the days of King Charles XI. The Stockholm Royal Palace, also in the Old Town, is the largest in the world. It has 608 rooms and is still occupied by a Head of State, but portions are open for the public to visit.

About a week or so before Christmas, Raiija and I made the jaunt to Stockholm together, sharing a cabin on the Silia. Santa Claus himself had greeted the guests as we boarded, having come all the way from his home in Lapland, located in the North Pole!

Reminiscent of pajama parties from my teenage years, Raiija and I sat on our beds in the cabin eating, talking, and laughing until well past midnight. In one respect, women from all over are very much alike—we all love to talk!

Life in Helsinki was hardly all fun. Work at the embassy actually left little time or energy to spare.

At the end of a particularly busy day, a young junior officer with an attitude took offense that his work had to wait its turn. It was not urgent and there were other projects ahead of his. He retaliated by placing unusual work requests on my desk daily and marking them with urgent deadlines. He was condescending and disrespectful.

My supervisor told me in private that the junior officer was thought to be a "Golden Boy of the future Foreign Service." Because of this, and his younger age, I was asked to overlook his behavior.

But I was much too busy and worn out to be very tolerant of Golden Boy, who already had one formal complaint filed against him. While I did not go to that length, I did speak up and sought resolution further up the ladder.

How do office conflicts get resolved?

To my understanding, the ideal way to resolve a conflict is to approach the other person in an attempt at an amicable resolution. If that fails, the next step is to bring the matter to the manager—who often did little but advise that "we all have to learn to get along."

The Personnel Office may listen, but had no real solutions. Frankly, I had the impression that they were reluctant to be involved.

Embassy people are afraid. They are afraid of jeopardizing their annual Employee Evaluation Report. The EER is written by one person—one's immediate supervisor, a.k.a. the rating officer—which gives that person enormous power over the rated employee. While a short blurb is added to the EER by the supervisor one rank higher, that blurb is often influenced by the rating officer.

Many government agencies require that an individual write a reciprocal evaluation on the supervisor (rating officer). State Department people largely feel this would be a far more favorable method.

Equal Employment Opportunity (EEO) officers are designated at each embassy to, among other things, mediate conflicts. On two occasions, I met with an EEO and found the results much as with the Personnel Office—reluctance to get involved. In the Helsinki incident, the EEO was the only close friend Golden Boy had at the embassy and, while she profusely tried to assure me that such a friendship would not influence her, she did nothing to help.

The ultimate, last ditch option, is to file a formal complaint with the Grievance Board at the State Department. While I did not doubt that board's claims to an impartial investigation, I had observed how bureaucratic words can deceive. I was skeptical that this board would not also be deceived. But I did consider this option seriously in a later situation because of the graveness involved. Ultimately, I dismissed the option because, by then, I was too burned out to put myself through the process.

Conflict and rivalry among Office Management Specialists were also common. Unlike officers, who work in relatively quiet and private offices, the Office Management Specialist typically works in open areas with many personalities and frequent distractions. This alone—psychologists agree—promotes pressure and strain in any environment. A heavy workload makes it worse.

The method most Office Management Specialists seemed to agree on was to look the other way when someone in the office is abusive. "Wear invisible blinders and ignore it," they said.

I thought back to my various colleagues who practiced the invisible blinders technique. "Joyce" nipped at the wine bottle, kept hidden in her supply cabinet. Indeed, I had sometimes wondered about her red nose! When I walked in on her one day—bottle in hand behind the door—she admitted to me that this enabled her to cope with her supervisor, an ill tempered ambassador given to demands and yelling.

Another—highly talented—colleague who practiced the blinders technique lost control one morning as she slammed her heavy safe drawers and screamed at the top of her lungs, "This is what stress will do to you!" With that, she picked up her purse and walked out!

There was the incident of a predecessor who was in the hospital—undergoing treatment for excessive fatigue—when I arrived at a certain post to replace her.

Many OMS's missed work due to migraine headaches, or other ailments. When they took sick leave, their work was added to that of another! And the merry-go-round continues.

With the appointment in later years of Colin Powell as Secretary of State, great improvements took place in the State Department. Word had it that Powell literally saved the State Department from its budget and other woes. But the difficulties many of us experienced "over there in the embassies" went unnoticed.

In time, I learned to manage my own woes as they came up, in the only ways I knew how. I was also becoming more vocally intolerant of tedious bureaucratic b.s. and volatile egotistic demands.

22
Vienna and the Hungarian

On August 7, 1998, I was checking into my hotel room in Vienna just as the U.S. Embassies in Kenya and Tanzania were being bombed by terrorists. It is a great shock when the embassies are attacked, and in these two incidents hundreds of Americans and foreign nationals were killed or maimed.

An American friend was working at the embassy in Kenya at the time. She had just arrived for work that morning, she later told me, and was in an elevator when the first bomb exploded. More deafening explosions followed.

People were screaming, and she could hear sirens in the distance interspersed with repeated explosions. It seemed an eternity, but after only minutes the explosions ceased. In her traumatized state of mind, she began to perfunctorily help people who were buried under debris and fallen ceilings. Stepping around dead bodies, my friend could hear the cries of people trapped or maimed.

Throughout the world, embassies became acutely reminded once again of how such terror could strike anywhere, anytime.

CNN reported the unfolding events and I watched each day from my hotel room. I was in Vienna for several weeks of treatment and recuperation stemming from fatigue and burnout. My doctor had diagnosed it as Chronic Fatigue Syndrome.

Initially upon my arrival in Vienna, I could do little but sleep. My hotel had an almost deserted restaurant on the balcony, and in the evenings I dined there and enjoyed the evening air and rooftop views of Vienna. Nobody bothered me. I ate quietly and pondered the lights of this city where the likes of Mozart, Beethoven and Straus once lived.

Just below the hotel restaurant at the end of the short street, the famous open air stairway known as The Strudelhofstiege Stairway stood, with a small lion's head fountain. Its name comes from the now demolished home of the Imperial Court painter, Peter Strudel, an important master of baroque.

Vienna was experiencing an unusual heat wave which was to last for almost a week. Few buildings are air conditioned and during the day the air could be stifling, cooling somewhat in the evenings. But despite the heat, and with days of sleep and good food, I began to feel stronger and interested in seeing Vienna's artwork and treasures. Being a lazy tourist is also healing.

Just outside the hotel entrance was a tram stop. The tram encircled Ring Road, passing through the city and along beautiful buildings, monuments, and parks.

Shortly after I arrived in Vienna, I met Karl Gaabor. I felt I had known him before, that I knew him very well even though I did not.

Karl was a Hungarian doctor, living and working in Vienna. He was tall and had playful, soulful eyes, and his heavy Hungarian accent gave him a distinctively foreign aura.

Whatever that very special energy is between two people, it was there with us. With him, there were no slow beginnings and no unhappy endings.

We enjoyed the evening classics. There was certainly no shortage of Mozart and Straus concerts in Vienna. Since the evenings were still warm, fans were propped in the corners of the large concert rooms, and the French windows and doors were thrown wide open in the hope of a breeze.

We sat on one occasion in a most ornate concert hall from the 19th century. Its high ceilings were richly carved with flowers and cupids. The floor was covered in red carpet, and the windows with heavy satin drapes. Great portraits of musical maestros hung on the walls, along with brass candelabras which sent candlelight and shadows flickering across the room. Guests sat along the sides of the room, and the performances took place in the center.

The Musikvereinsgebaude, home of the Vienna Philharmonic Orchestra, and the music center of Vienna, carried me back in time to another era. Enveloped in the rapture of such exquisite music, my boggled mind began to relax and let go of deadlines and conflicts and rigid workplaces.

The compositions of Johann Strauss were featured at the Wiener Salonorchester der Volksoper. Those beautiful waltzes—where else would they touch your soul so deeply but in Vienna itself? As the music filled the room, women in silk gowns of pastels and men in dark tuxedos began to dance—so gracefully—to "The Emperor's Waltz," "Where the Lemons Bloom," and "Tales of the Vienna Woods."

The Vienna Woods—I had to see it, and took a train ride there one day. I sailed on the Danube River on another day. I walked for hours on end, as well, through the streets of Vienna, drinking in the lovely sights.

Schonbrunn Palace is not to be missed, so I did not miss it! The ochre colored palace with its magnificent gardens has a long history going back to before 1569 when it was a mill.

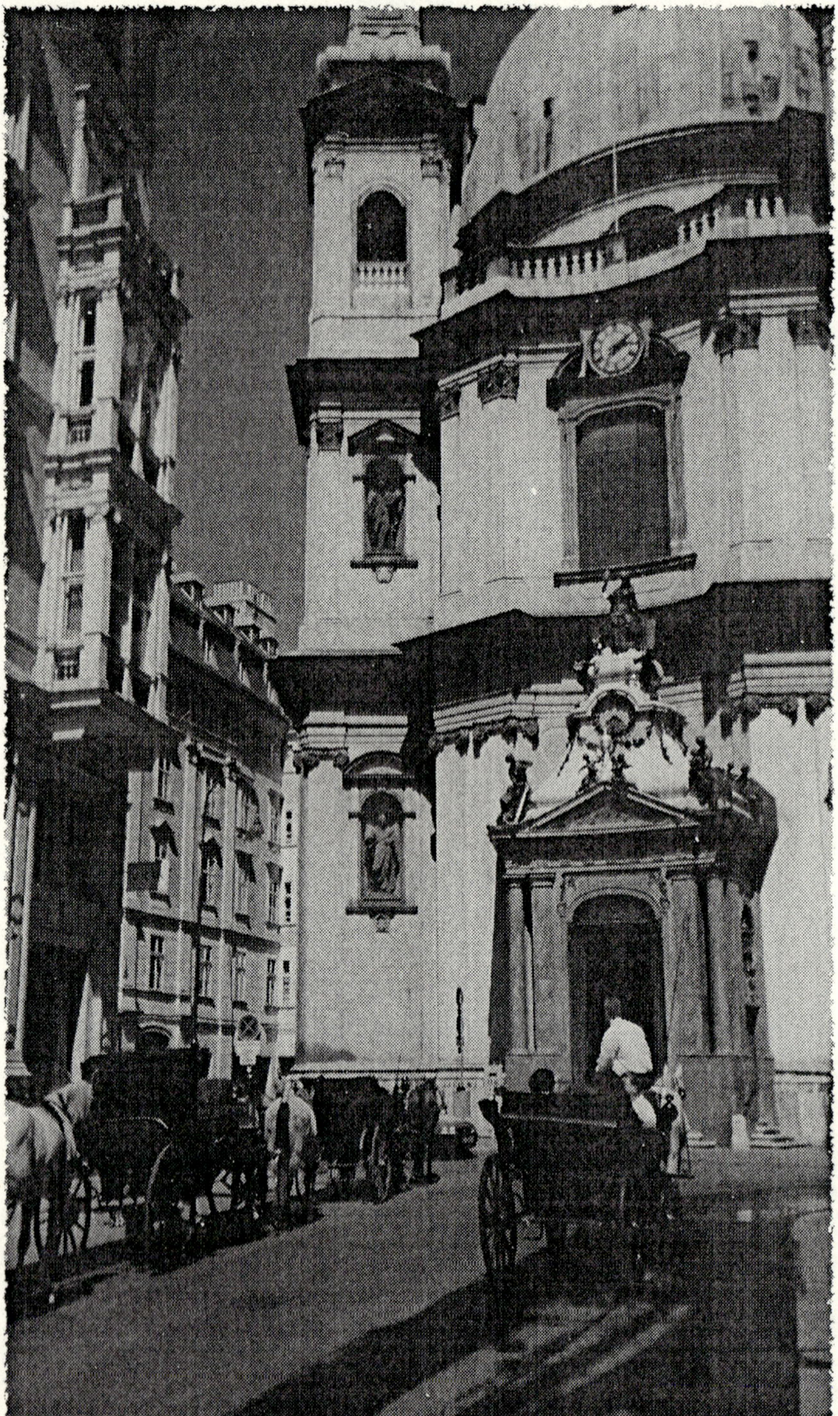

For a long time, Schonbrunn Palace was the center of Imperial family life. It was here where 6-year old Mozart performed for the Empress Marie-Antoinette, and afterwards jumped on her lap, kissed her and asked, "Do you want to marry me? Yes or No?"

Griechenbeisl—don't you love all these funny names—is an alehouse where in 1679, the time of the Great Plague, the folk singer Augustin wrote his famous song, "O du lieber Augustin . . . Augustin . . . Augustin." In later years, the Griechenbeisl became a popular watering hole for artists and political figures like Wagner, Strauss, and Brahms.

We talked, Karl Gaabor and I, about many things. We discussed, too, our work and lifestyles.

"What do you want to do?" he asked me.

"I want to be myself, to reclaim my own identity, to paint, to write, to be free. I am tired. I do not like trying always to be what another thinks I should be, told how to work, how to think, how to behave. So many conformances smother me."

Karl's interest in me is so sincere that I find it easy to open my heart to him. He shared with me parts of his own struggles and dreams. His arms felt safe and cozy, and I held his strong hand and thoughtfully studied his piano fingers as I listened to him.

He gave me food for thought. "You are passionate, free spirited . . . struggling in a rigid atmosphere," he said. "The embassy . . . contrary to your nature . . . you are ill suited under the oppressive thumb of another . . . natural creativity becomes stale and stifled and gradually dies . . . and, you do not suffer fools gladly!"

But that's where he was wrong. I do not suffer them at all!

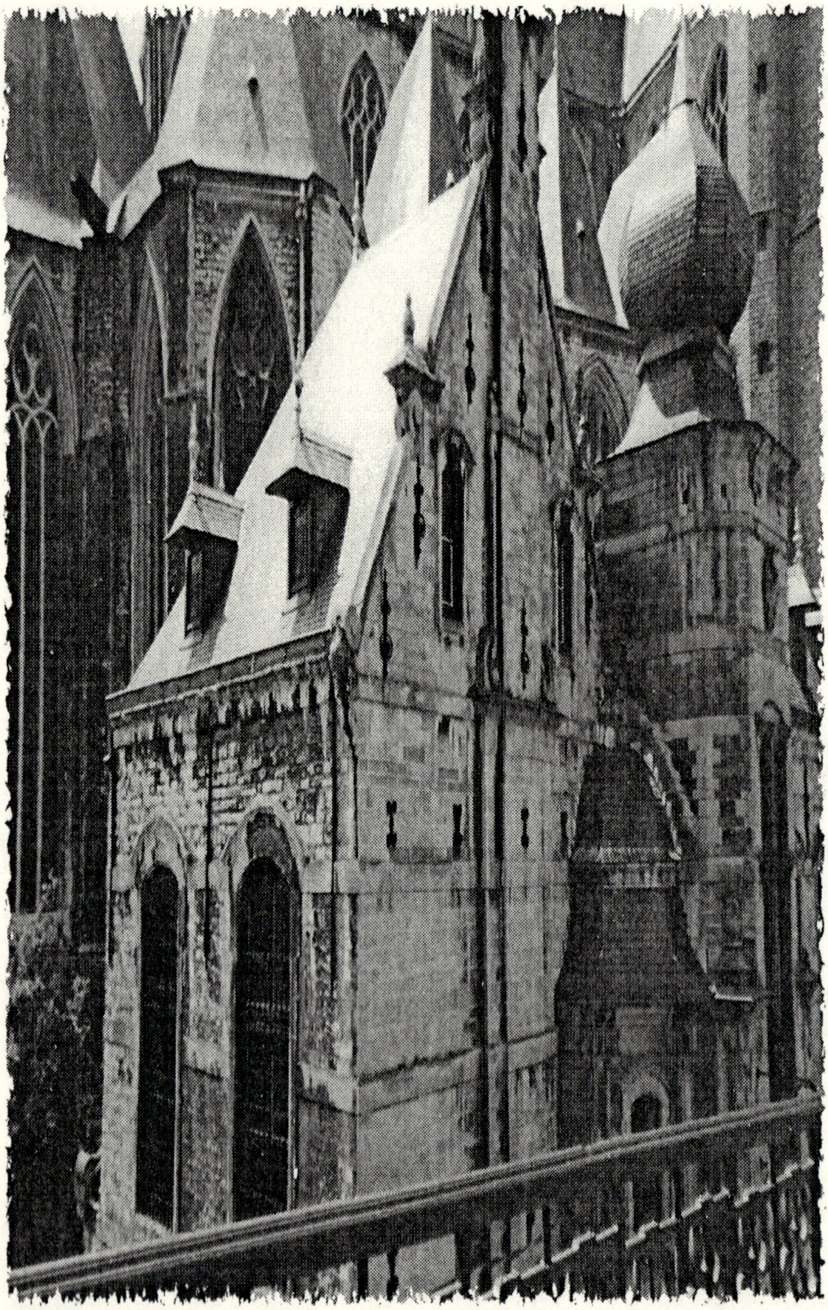

23
A Dream in Belgium

"Amy, Amy, it is okay," I said, as I tried to drag her away by her leash. "It is okay! The statue will not hurt us! It doesn't even have arms!"

We were in the Parc de Bruxelles. In the 11th century, it was a poultry yard, and today it is Brussel's largest park. At the far end is the Royal Palace of Belgium. Abundant trees offer shady shelter from the summer sun, where one can sit on benches and enjoy the gardens or watch the people walk by.

There are huge beautiful fountains here and there with splashing water, and the park is filled with towering nude statues. On their heads are stone garlands, and they look down on us with their unseeing eyes.

When Amy first saw the big stone people, she knew at once we were in danger! Looking up at a very tall Greek Goddess, she stood unflinching on all fours. She growled and barked in her most dreadful voice, but the stone statue stood its ground.

Amy never forgets. Each time we visit Parc de Bruxelles, I hurry her past the statues. But she sees them, and eyes them closely with suspicion and mistrust, snarling and growling under her breath.

Brussels, Belgium is a dynamic small city with enormous old world charm, home of the European Union, NATO, and a large diplomatic community. It is an international waterhole for regular gatherings of dignitaries and world leaders.

My new work assignment in Brussels is with the U.S. Mission to the European Union (USEU) on Av Regent. The European Union was, in 1999, comprised of 29 independent countries whose purposes include the general enhancement of greater Europe.

Upon arrival in Brussels, I was given a temporary apartment. The gigantic apartment was on the sixth floor of a tall building within walking distance to the embassy and USEU.

The floor plans of those old European apartments are sedate and appallingly outdated, but spacious, and with some redeeming features. The exceedingly long hallway, for example, was a useful means of exercise for Amy. I often tossed a ball from one end to the other, and she had great fun retrieving it.

While the living room faced the busy Av Regent and traffic noise was heard day and night, the far rear bedroom was separated by the long hallway. That end was quiet. Its French windows opened onto lovely views of Belgian courtyards, rooftops and chimneys, and at night I could sit on my bed and look out at the lovely scene.

Along with the excitement of a new assignment was the arduous task of making the transition into a new country, job, and home. This was never as true as in Brussels because USEU was preparing for a major office move.

Our new building on Av Regent was adjacent to the America Embassy. It had been under renovation for many months. When the moving days arrived, we all had our work cut out for us.

Since the offices contain classified material, contractors and movers, who have no security clearance, had to work under the eye of a security-cleared American. This made the entire move more challenging for everyone.

It rained every day during the move. The damp air was cold and penetrating as the movers loaded furniture, safes and boxes from the old building into the vans in the street. For two days, some of us stood on the cement street in the rain to guard the vans with their classified contents. We developed colds, and our legs and feet ached from the cement.

The newly renovated office building was fresh and cheerful. Unpacking and getting settled was the finale of the move, with contractors in and out daily, connecting telephone wires, hooking up computer systems, and attending to other details.

The new manager of USEU'S Economic Office—I will call her "Ms. A."—gathered us together in the conference room shortly after her arrival. She was a smartly dressed, ambitious woman rumored to have her eye on an ambassadorship. I was to be her assistant. During this first gathering, our group of about twelve adults listened politely as the new manager explained the calibre of behavior expected of us, given that this particular office was - she slowly emphasized so that we all understood—the very largest embassy economic office in the entire world.

Ms. A. seemed oblivious to how her incessant demands throughout the day infringed on getting my work done. "Run this off, make copies, do this, do that, and take this upstairs—it will only take a minute. Bring me that, do this, why isn't this working, what happened here, do this right away. Help so-and-so with that, but do this first. Come here, bring me that file, dash upstairs with this, do that on your way. It will only take a minute, so do it now."

Later—"Why isn't this done? It would only have taken a minute!"

The office move coincided with my personal move from the temporary apartment to a permanent one. For months, my days were filled with unpacking and getting settled at home and at work. But once done, I fell in love with the small town and the apartment I had chosen to live in.

Boitfort was located just outside of Brussels and was delightful. The lovely four bedroom split-level dwelling was more room than I needed, but it was available, comfortable, and a pleasant haven from the long days at USEU. Big picture windows looked out onto weeping willows and evergreens and a small lake of wildlife.

Our apartment building was shared with two other tenants above us. Christoph and Agnetta, and their dog Robin Hood, lived on the top floor, and were from Sweden. Both middle aged professionals, they spoke excellent English, and we became friends quickly.

A young Japanese couple from Tokyo occupied the second floor. They were the quietest people I have ever known, moving through the building like shadows. Since the Japanese are taught from early childhood to be quiet and considerate of others, they make wonderful neighbors!

Boitfort lies along the fringes of Foret de Soignes, a very large forest. It is a small town of timeless charm, of trees, lakes, small shops and restaurants. In the center's streets, a highly popular farmers market takes place each Sunday morning. People journey from miles around to attend the farmers market, making it a morning's festive outing.

I often pulled my shopping cart behind me and leisurely made my way to the farmers market on Sundays. Along the way, I passed my neighbors' houses, so typical of Belgium with their pitched roofs and stepped facades. Rose gardens and picket fences were on my one side, the small lake on my other.

Boitfort's many walking paths and natural beauty make it a wonderful place for walkers and their dogs. Amy and I enjoyed our companionable time together in the forest or around the small lake just outside our front door.

I gave names to the birds and geese living by the lake. Bob, the crane, was a slender shy fellow. He often sat on the edge of the lake by himself, and would fly away if we came too close.

Henrietta is the large white goose. She ran the place, strutting and squawking at the others. But when a certain old gentleman came into the park for his daily walk, Henrietta was transformed into lovesick mush. Not graceful, she wobbled awkwardly and frantically to meet him, squawking loudly with delight.

Together they sat—the old man on the bench and Henrietta at his feet—as he fed her little pieces of bread and stroked her head. When he got up to leave, she waddled closely alongside him before reluctantly returning to the lake—and her old bossy self.

When the lake freezes over in the winter, a hungry fox often came in from the forest to search for food. Sometimes the geese were not quick enough, and fell prey to the fox. It was a sad occasion if a neighbor found that one of the geese had been attacked, since we all loved them.

So when Amy and I would go out for a final wee in a winter's evening, I looked around cautiously. Once I saw it—across the lake in the moonlight—the unmistakable shadow of a fox with its long bushy tail. It was circling the lake and heading our way—fast!

Grabbing Amy, I hurried back inside the building just as the quick moving fox reached the front glass door. It stopped and looked at us—we looked at each other—and from behind the safety of the glass door, Amy confronted the fox with her scariest growl. The fox disappeared.

I hugged Amy and thanked her, explaining that her growl had frightened the fox away. She licked my hand, let out one final snarl at the door, and then we walked up the stairs together for our evening treats.

I found I was content to go little further than the charming old town of Boitfort. It is a place where time has stood still, where tourist commercialism has not touched, where neighbors say hello and life takes on a slower pace.

In Boitfort, I began to put my roots down. I met the veterinarian—a most charming doctor with an abundance of jolly laughs for his patients. Soon I had chosen a hairdresser, my favorite bakery and butcher shops, and quite by accident I found Carolyn!

Carolyn and her partner own a therapeutic beauty salon across from the lovely park in the center of Boitfort. For one hour and a half, Carolyn will pamper her client with a heavenly facial and pedicure, filling the air with luscious scents of creams from the barks of Korean trees. Her small immaculate working room is cozy with soft music, and her healing touch is nothing short of magic.

Surprisingly, what Carolyn charged for such a pampering was considerably less than similar treatments in the U.S. Whoever says that European facials are outrageously expensive has not met Carolyn!

During my first Christmas season in Belgium, I decided to design a special romantic bedroom for myself. Choosing a room with the loveliest, completely private view—of trees and gardens in the distance—I put my passion for interior design to work. An Austrian crystal chandelier hung over my bed, a few plants, and candles on the windowsill. It became the most charming bedroom I have ever had.

A bedroom is one's haven. It should be the one room in our home where privacy, comfort and beauty reign supreme. No clutter, no television, no work. Just delicious quiet, a few chosen books to read oneself to sleep, and—of course!—a little doggie to snuggle with! George Clooney would do as well.

Needless to say, the entire country of Belgium is a delight at Christmas. As in Germany, Belgium has its Christmas markets. The major one was held at the Grand Place, a large medieval Square lined with lovely ornate architecture. The Grand Place is an utter breathtaker, and at Christmas it is especially beautiful.

Here in the Place, an immense tree is lit with lights and adorned with ornaments. The stalls are filled with crafts to purchase and good things to eat. Lace shops and restaurants line the Place, and at night everything gently glows with small lights.

I put up a tree at home and strung it with lights. Not having a family with me did not keep me from enjoying the season and making my home festive.

But shortly before Christmas, I purchased fresh figs from the farmers' market and became very ill. Christmas was spent in bed with a miserable bout of food poisoning. Ah well, Santa, you let me down that year.

Just outside of Brussels is Ghent, a spectacular medieval city, and nearby Brugge and Antwerp are both wonderful places to visit. Belgium's strategic location affords travel throughout Europe itself. Paris, for example, and London are both only three hours away by train.

Each city has something unique. In Brugge, spend a few minutes in one of the lace making shops. Belgium lace making goes back hundreds of years and is among the most beautiful lace in the world. In some of the shops, one can watch the process of spindle lace, very delicate lace indeed. Deft fingers become a blur as they swiftly move dozens of small spindles wound with thread.

Belgium's world renowned tapestry is found throughout the country, but is a specialty in Brussels and Brugge. Of course, who hasn't heard of Belgium chocolate and waffles? On a side street off the Grand Place, keep your eye peeled for that tiny shop resembling an ice cream parlor. It specializes in mouthwatering waffles—light and fluffy, with a fresh mound of whipped cream. Don't tell me you're not interested!

Many interesting cities and villages were not far from home, yet they were often not easily accessible. A visit to Brugge, for example, meant waiting for a bus in Boitfort to the metro system, then to the train station in Brussels, then an hour by train to Brugge. Three hours may have passed in traveling only one way.

And so—more and more—a lazy day in my "home town" of Boitfort held greater appeal. No muss, no fuss.

It was early evening, and I had left my office and boarded a train home, as usual. Getting off the train, I walked the balance of my journey home through a lovely stretch of woods along a lake, as always, for my fill of fresh air.

Once again, I had endured the brunt of another day of criticism, outbursts, and insults by the well-dressed manager. I was hurt, I was tired, I was angry, and I was fed up.

My mind churned with the craziness of the day's events as I walked through the park. Do I have "stupid" stamped on my forehead? There is no Feeling Good about one's career under such unhealthy working conditions! And temper tantrums yet, because she couldn't find something she herself had lost!

As I continued walking, my exasperating thoughts mounted. A can in my path received a swift kick from my boot, sending it flying into a bush.

I am so sick of the Prima Donas and Golden Boys of the Foreign Service, I thought, that I could puke!

Suddenly, my throat began to tighten, and then close altogether! I struggled, frantic for air! On a nearby bench, I sat down and forced myself to relax, to calm my thoughts, to loosen my throat muscles and breathe again. Such an attack had not happened to me before—I was completely stunned.

Focusing my churning thoughts on the quiet and beauty of the surroundings, I began to relax, and slowly regained my breath. A handful of geese quietly swam by my bench on the lake, and I held my gaze on them. Pulling my woolen scarf warmly around my neck and shoulders, I sat on that bench for a long time. Little by little, my thoughts turned to the bigger picture of my life.

Everything pales against good health. I had overlooked this important fact in my efforts to protect my career.

Working in dysfunctional embassy offices for many years, I had become fairly brainwashed, almost believing that office abuse simply "goes with the territory." Yelling, scolding, and backstabbing are to be expected—just a normal part of the job. Hoping to hang in there until retirement, I had avoided looking at the damaging effects of such stress.

How wrong I was.

The Foreign Service itself had been good to me, and I had given it my best. But now? For me, it is finished. New decisions were forming in my mind.

Continuing my walk home, I quickened my step at the thought of Amy who was waiting to welcome me with her little kisses. The wild birds by the lake under my apartment had already turned in for the night, and were huddled together in the grass.

"Goodnight, Henrietta! Goodnight, Bob! Aye, an 'tis a lovely evening! Sweet dreams, darlings!"

In my own dream that night, the message was clear.

Walking down Av Regent in Brussels with my back turned away from USEU, I held a large ring of heavy jailer keys in my hand. Each key represented a price I had been paying for a career I had loved and appreciated in many important ways.

There were the good keys and there were the bad keys. As I walked, the key ring became heavier. There was no help in carrying them.

With a sudden whooosh of surrender, I tossed the weighty ring of keys high, high up into the air. As they fell to the ground behind me, I continued walking and did not look back.

Then, with mounting joyful elation, I began to skip, to whistle, and to dance! Yes! Yes!

Within days of my dream, I submitted my resignation. Three months should be sufficient time to wind down the job and lifestyle as it stood, but government red tape can be daunting. The immense amount of termination paperwork was only part of the process. I was also obliged to relinquish my government leased apartment, and return to the United States.

But I make these decisions now, and my plans were to remain in Belgium—without diplomatic immunity or government backing—for an extended personal sabbatical. Giving up my lovely apartment, however, could not be avoided. This was painful for me until a wise friend pointed out that my attachment to the apartment was only another key on my jailer ring.

Little by little, it all got done. Finally, a moving company arrived to pack my household goods, most of which would be placed in a storage facility in Antwerp.

I was on my own.

A few bad apples do not have to spoil the cart—

Deep in my heart is a soft spot of respect and appreciation for the State Department's Foreign Service.

Overall, my association with this good institution has been special and rewarding.

It is important to know when something in our life has run its course. I saw this clearly the evening I sat in the park trying to regain my breath. A healthy body and sound mind became my number one priority that evening, right where it should have been all along.

To those bent on power and glory, I say, "Go for it. But please don't step on me or others along the way."

I have other roads to travel, other paths to explore. Still, I will remember the Foreign Service with fondness.

24
The Horrid Little House

I had underestimated my great innate need for beauty and comfort in my feathered nest.

Amy and I needed a place to live during the sabbatical. Nothing fancy, just a home base between travels, to unwind, to "reflect" on my life. A small house in the center of Boitfort with a "for rent" sign in the window seemed like the answer. In my haste, and being pressed to get everything done on time, I had impulsively agreed to rent the house. I placed my signature in wet ink on the bottom line.

In retrospect, it was not the smartest thing I've ever done.

Living in Belgium as a private citizen, I no longer had the protective umbrella of the U.S. Government. While I had not really overlooked this, adjusting to it was not entirely painless. Like all American expatriates, I had grown dependent on the many things handled for us by the U.S. Government.

I began the arduous task of handling my life alone in a foreign country—rental agreement, utilities, maintenance and house repairs, language barriers, city hall permits, and you name it. Also, the accumulated stress from earlier days was stuffed deep inside me. I would not allow myself to release it until many, many months later.

In the meantime, I was managing fairly well in Belgium on my own—and learning a good deal in the process.

An unwelcome spirit in "the house" was felt immediately. Within the dark rooms and dank air, there was no mistaking the drastic difference from the lovely place I had just left! But it was affordable, and now that I have no income I must be mindful of the pennies.

Spending some time in parts of Europe which I either had not yet seen, or wanted to return to, was my main reason for remaining in Belgium. And so, my sabbatical began. I located a "sitter" for Amy, and took off for a journey with my good friends, Pat and her husband Samir.

With others, we headed for Switzerland, Venice, Florence, and beautiful Tuscany, rich with yellow fields of "rape." In Villa Garzoni by the gardens at Collodi . . . we walked on the red earth of Siena . . . and stepped back into earlier centuries of Italy's San Gimignano—what wonderful Italian cities these are! What rich history and art treasures, and I feel so lucky to have seen it.

I had searched for George Clooney and his house on Lake Como, but did not see him. Darn.

Albert Schweitzer's birthplace is in Alsace. Don't ask me to remember the name of the town. We had seen so many villages and towns that they soon swam in my head! I remember only the large stone bust of Albert Schweitzer, and the many pelicans and storks sitting in their nests on the rooftops of his town.

So the old folks were right after all—the storks do come down the chimneys to deliver babies! I had always thought it was only their way to avoid explaining the birds and bees.

My friends and I had fun. We laughed, we talked, we walked, we spent money, we ate too much.

Following the journey with my friends, I returned alone to Amsterdam, lovely Flemish Ghent and Antwerp—famous for diamonds. I visited picturesque Brugge where I bought chocolate and lace. Who can afford diamonds?

A dark storm moved across England while I was there—reportedly the worst storm in over a hundred years. Flooding caused disruption to the trains returning to Belgium, and I was stranded in England for many days.

I was staying in Heathstead, a "suburb" of London, at a small boarding house. My room was pleasant, with large French doors opening to a private garden. Since the nasty weather kept me inside, I spent many long days curled up on the divan with books. Just where is Clooney when I need him?

The severe weather finally subsided and I returned to Boitfort. I was all traveled out. My wild oats were sown.

I decided to stay put . . . to "reflect on my life" for awhile . . . to sleep in and take leisure walks with Amy . . . to be a lady of leisure on my European sabbatical!

It rained every day in Boitfort, without mercy. The cold damp air and grey skies of winter were depressing, and much walking was difficult with all the mud. For months, there was no sun at all. I began to realize that, as a private American citizen on a European sabbatical, I was not really having much fun!

But it was the horrid little house which was to be my undoing, and send me home to the U.S. Over 400 years ago, the house was a stable for horses owned by the King of Belgium who enjoyed horseback riding and hunting in the nearby forest. The stable was, over the centuries, gradually converted into the house it is today.

Privacy was nil as curious people walking by on the side street peered through the windows of my house. Fumes from cars driving up and down the side street filled the house and, while I prefer fresh air and daylight, I found myself closing the windows and the curtains.

Amy was terrified of the steep rickety stairway, and refused to climb it. I had to carry her. Each floor had only one very tiny room, and invariably I would be on the ground floor and need something from the top floor. I was up and down the wobbly stairs constantly.

The bedroom was located on the top floor, with a pitched beamed roof which leaks when it rains. The floor was often wet and, without fail, I banged my head every morning on the low hanging wooden beams when I arose from bed.

The potbellied stove on the second floor smoked so badly it could not be used. Soot from the stove had accumulated over the years, and mingled with the unhealthy stench of mold inside the walls.

My sabbatical was spent—not reflecting or relaxing—but haggling with contractors, struggling with language barriers, tending to house repairs, and wishing the rain would go away.

When I told the landlady about the strange noises I often heard in the night, she confessed that her boyfriend had been murdered in the bedroom just before I moved in! She suspected the house to be haunted. "Why didn't you tell me before I moved in?" "It might have scared you away," she said. "Yes, you have a point, it might have."

Acquiring a non-diplomatic living permit from the city hall in Boitfort was of itself enough to cause some people to give up. Despite downright admirable attempts on my part, I never did receive my permit.

But in the end, it was Laundry Day which tipped the scales.

The convenience of a washer and dryer in the home was something I missed most. But hard situations call for hard solutions, and I designed a laundry strategy.

Laundry had to be done at least three times a week since I could only carry a small amount at a time to the public Laundromat. Therefore, I will divide the laundry thus: On day one, I will do sheets and towels; on day two, dark clothing; and on day three, whites and lingerie.

A typical laundry day began by climbing to the bedroom at the top floor where I pulled together my bag of laundry. Kicking the bag down the two flights of stairs, I then slung it over my back and walked across town to the tram stop. Originally, I had tried using my grocery cart, but could not pull it up the steep steps of the tram.

After a ten-minute tram ride to the public Laundromat, I spent 3 hours with the Belgian housewives. On my first visit, operating the machines—which had instructions in French—was highly confusing, but someone kindly demonstrated for me. Soon the Belgian housewives and I were on friendly terms. Laundromat comrades, we were, chatting and laughing as we did our washing and folding.

My clothes both washed and dried, I packed them into my bag, slung the bag over my back, and climbed up a steep hill to catch a tram going in the opposite direction. Finally back home, the bag was pulled up the two flights of stairs to the bedroom. The job was done, and the day spent.

On a particularly cold November laundry day, sharp winds blew and drizzling rain had sidewalks slick with mud. I left the Laundromat with my bag of clean whites and lingerie, and began the upward trek to the tram. Suddenly I slipped on the mud, and the laundry bag fell from my grip!

A sharp stab of pain in my ankle kept me from standing up. I lay on the sidewalk and watched helplessly as the wind blew my underwear all over the street!

A nightgown went sailing through the air and caught itself on a man walking downhill. Blinded by the gown, he struggled a moment to free himself. As he did, a gust of wind swirled the gown upward where it stuck in a tree branch.

Underpants blew aimlessly here and there, and I watched in horror as a car ran over my bra! My good one!

Someone helped me to my feet, and I hobbled to a nearby bench. My ankle was sprained, and retrieving my laundry now seemed hopeless. The bag itself was nowhere to be seen. I sat on the bench and watched as underpants flapped from someone's windshield, and pajama bottoms waved from the shingle of a shop like a flag in the wind.

That's it, I thought. I've had it! I surrender! I give up!

My sabbatical had seemed like a good idea at the time. But I was tired of the rain and mud, of laundry, of repairmen who don't speak English. I broke my lease. I am going home.

A few weeks later, Amy and I were on a plane bound for the U.S. But fate had one final trick up its sleeve. As we approached Amsterdam, where we would change planes, the pilot announced that we would be "entering a severe storm." He told us to keep our seatbelts on.

It was the mother of all storms. The rain beat against the windows and the wind shook the massive plane with a violence which made other storms feel like gentle breezes! I was terrified. With white knuckles, I clutched my armrests tightly for a very long time.

Finally, we approached the airport in Amsterdam. The severe storm continued, and several planes were lined up in the air circling the city and waiting to land. We were forced to do the same. I continued to clutch my armrest, mumbling little prayers with my eyes squeezed shut.

Twenty four hours later, the long, long journey home came to an end as our small domestic plane moved over the vast mountain range of Arizona, splashed with pastels of pinks and violets from the bright sunshine.

One last time, I listened to the voice over the loudspeaker. "This is your captain speaking. We will be landing shortly at Sky Harbor Airport in Phoenix. The weather is sunny and a pleasant 70 degrees Fahrenheit. Thank you for choosing American Airlines, and have a happy life."

> *"Mid pleasures and palaces though we may roam,*
> *be it ever so humble, there's no place like home."*
>
> —John Howard Payne

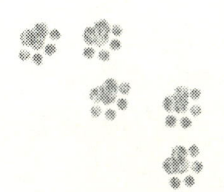

About the Author

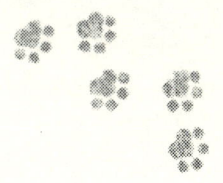

Jeanne Jie Ahn

lives in Phoenix, Arizona

with Amy and Wolf,

where she writes and paints.

This is her first book.

Printed in the United States
49895LVS00003B/238-249